IN THE AMERICAN JUNGLE

[1925 - 1936]

In the American Jungle

[1925-1936]

WALDO FRANK

Photographic Decorations by William H. Field

Essay Index Reprint Series

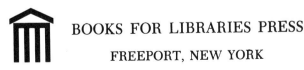

BOOKS FOR LIBRARIES PRESS

FREEPORT, NEW YORK

First Published 1937
Reprinted 1968

LIBRARY OF CONGRESS CATALOG CARD NUMBER:

68-20301

PRINTED IN THE UNITED STATES OF AMERICA

to my friend Adolph S. Oko

FOREWORD

For the general idea and design of this book, I am indebted to my friend, Harold Clurman, the director of the Group Theater. During several years, he urged me to publish a collection of my papers similar to "SALVOS" which united certain of my short critical writings from 1915 to 1924. I was always too busy—and the notion of a miscellany does not appeal to me. At last, at his request, I handed him from my files what I could find of my articles and papers published in the past twelve years. I was amazed to find how much it was. Several months later, he returned to me a selection, reduced by two thirds. He pointed out that what he had put in order was not a miscellany but *a book* with a beginning, a middle and a conclusion: a book even with a "plot"!

The materials that compose this "collective portrait" of an era which spans the Boom, the Depression, and (perhaps) the beginning, in Spain, of the new World War that may end the world we have all lived in, appeared originally in the following periodicals (of New York, unless otherwise noted):

The Adelphi (London), *The Dial, Europe* (Paris), *Harper's, The Menorah Journal, La Nación* (Buenos Aires), *The New Masses, The New Republic, The New Yorker, Occidente* (Rome), *El Repertorio Americano* (San José, Costa Rica), *Scribner's, Soviet Russia Today, Sur* (Buenos Aires), *Virginia Quarterly Review, The Guardian* (Philadelphia).

Many other magazines reprinted or translated some of this material, but since I have no full list of these I have not named them.

W. F.

New York, December, 1936

CONTENTS

ix

THREE: BOOKS

FOUR: SOME PRACTICAL CONCLUSIONS FOR THE SURVIVAL OF MAN

"... *in a dying world, creation is revolution.*"

"Our America," 1919

"*The American jungle is rich in denatured elements of a transplanted world: it consists largely in those deposits, cultural, political, economic, which justify our calling 'the new world' the Grave of Europe.*"

"The Re-Discovery of America," 1929

ONE: BOOM YEAR SKETCHES

1. I DISCOVER THE NEW WORLD

a.

The most important room at home was the library. Our house was the usual four-story brownstone segment in the unbroken wall of an upper West Side block. There were plenty of windows. Those to the north looked out upon the street where grocery wagons rattled by day and by night the gas lamps dimly slumbered. Those to the south gave a broad view of another wall of houses which at dark became fantastic with lighted windows holding many secrets and black silhouettes mysteriously alive behind drawn blinds. And beyond the houses was the glow of the great city. The library had but a single window; it was too little for so large and low a room. Even by day the library was dark and, since the window opened on a strip of yard choked by an ugly ailanthus, I never looked through that window. When I was in this room New York did not come in; New York stayed distant and silent. The real world became this world of books; and almost all the books had come from Europe.

Among the pictures on the walls were those of two Americans: Washington and Lincoln. But they had little to do with the America outside the window. They spoke to me less eloquently than the novelists and poets of England, than the thinkers of Germany, than the Athenians and Romans all living on the shelves. This library in my father's house in the city of New York was a sanctuary of Europe. It glowed with a secluded quiet and with a life of its own. And here my childhood lived with an intensity and depth of feeling that not school, not the streets could give me.

My father nearly every year went to Europe. We would go down to the ship often, on the eve of his sailing, board

3

the great vessel, and dine with the captain in his cabin. I was in Europe then: everything, from the food we ate to the words we heard, was strange to America. Father sailed away, and mother bundled us children into a train. We got at last into a shimmer of meadows and of young green trees. But even in the mountains Europe was not far distant. Letters would presently arrive with foreign stamps. They were long letters: page upon page of personal description in which my father narrated his adventures in Hamburg, in London, in Paris. His trips were short—business trips. When he came back he brought Europe still more vividly along; in the air of his clothes, in the scent of his label-plastered luggage. And then mother was always there: and that made more of Europe. Mother was an artist. She sang every day. Beethoven, Wagner, Brahms, Schubert, Schumann, Wolf—these were the voices that came with us even to the mountains.

My room in the city home was on the top floor. I was the youngest, a tragic fate since it meant my going earliest to bed. It was not easy, this clambering up from the lighted drawing room filled with the cheer of guests, through the shadowed house. But the fourth floor was mine, and already I was a confirmed breaker of laws. I knew that my father would presently sit down at the organ or the piano to accompany my mother. I would then take a blanket from my bed, wrap myself snugly, and seat myself on the stair. My mother's singing came clearly through the house. School was a dim fable beside the reality of those songs; even the strong words on the library shelves were weak by contrast. That lovely, breathing voice with its perfect modulation and its subtle colors brought the lands across the sea miraculously near as I sat in guilt—and in ecstasy—upon the stair.

So when I went to Europe (several times before I was old enough for college) I found lands familiar to the library of my father and to my mother's music: familiar also through the American poets, Longfellow, Lowell, Holmes. Cooper's redskins and sea rovers were more remote to me than the cockneys of Dickens, the Parisians of Balzac. As to Poe, whose wistful little house my father showed me in a Fordham waste of goats and cans, his land seemed a wraithlike world in no way kin to the rectangular New York that was, for me, most of America.

Of course, this European "nature" of my boyhood was wholly and merely conscious surface. My hours of school, my mates of the street, the values and activities of parent and relative, under all, the food I ate and the air I breathed—flesh of my flesh, bone of my bone—were American. But these depths were voiceless, and I did not know them. Even the family traditions: the adventures of my father's father in New York during the Civil War, the tales of my mother's mother about the Yankee army that burned her Alabama home and stole her heirlooms, and about her running the blockade in a tiny rowboat in Mobile bay (with mother a child in arms and the constant fear that if she cried the Yankee ships would find them) failed somehow to come as close as the great tales I read in Homer or in Tolstoi: tales of Europe. America was in me, of course; but too close for my roving mind to know it.

b.

In my fifteenth year I had a great adventure. I picked up a history of American literature which spoke, coldly and slightingly enough, of an unknown poet, of whose curious style there was appended an example called "O Pioneers!"

I procured a green-bound volume, "Leaves of Grass"; it had a title page in archaic type and the portrait of an ancient bearded sage, all grey, who signed himself Walt Whitman. I read, studied, annotated, as I might have done with the Bible if I had been reared religiously. Whitman stirred deep voices in my soul; he inspired me. I believe in those early days I understood him well enough. But one so obvious fact escaped me, since I was not ready for it: the fact that this man was an American, that his experience was related to my own and that this was why I loved him! I thought he was as remote—and holy—as a Hebrew prophet!

That spring there was the annual oratory contest at the high school. The usual bright lads rose before an auditorium of a thousand people and bespoke "The Spirit of '76," "The Blessings of Democracy," and so forth. And then a strange thing happened. A short, black-haired boy stood upon the rostrum and for half an hour harangued the audience about the merits of an unknown, dead poet called Walt Whitman. He must have been eloquent as well as amusing, for the judges gave him the gold medal for his effort. But the whole affair remained somehow outside his experience as an American. These teachers who had rewarded him for praising Whitman kept on quoting Longfellow. Whitman's value seemed well symbolized by the useless medal of gold which the boy's mother put away and which he never saw again. Whitman was an outsider, a myth—almost an outcast.

But Europe came ever closer. I was done with school and too young for college. So I was sent abroad. I discovered myself at sixteen, at seventeen, to be of an age which on the Continent was deemed the age of a man! I consorted with students from every land of Europe: Russians, Spaniards, Serbians, Jews from Egypt, burly football players from Great Britain. They were not "pretty" fellows. They knew life—women—books. We sat about at night, drinking our tea with rum; and the air was less thick with tobacco smoke than with the thunder of exciting talk. Revolution, art, morality, death: all the old dwellers of the books which I had met in my father's library took on flesh, grew warm, grew urgent. And here at last, so many miles from his Manhattan, Whitman became alive; Poe found recognition. "America?" said my European friends. "It is the place that gave us Poe and Whitman."

I had engaged my room at Harvard. But I wanted to go to Heidelberg, I wanted, like my friends, to make the rounds of the great universities of Germany, England, Paris. I wanted to persevere in this world of midnight tea and rum with its dizzy flights into art and metaphysics. Europe beckoned me on, like a dark, mellow woman in whom the Mother eternally old and the Lover wondrously young were merged. And my father would not have stood against my will. He was an imperious, passionate man, whose prime passion was respect for the personality of others. A tyrant in matters of deportment, he hated all interference in adventures of the spirit. He had watched me, perhaps amused, perhaps with a hidden pang, go about at the age of twelve with my undigested load of Ibsen and Zola and Tolstoi. He had observed me, bored with school, become a truant, frequent the vaudeville shows or barricade myself from furious teachers in the office of our high school paper. Now, when the formal letters came from Heidelberg, telling the young American that he knew enough to be admitted, my father would not have said no, whatever his conviction. But my older brother was less philosophical. He came to Europe; and in a hotel room high above the Seine we had what for me was a decisive battle.

"You are not going to Heidelberg," said my brother. "You are going to be an American, by gum! And what's more, you are not going to Harvard. You're queer enough as it is. You're going to be not only an American, but as *human* an American as I can make you. I'm going to send you to a place that will smooth out your angles and your crotchets. Yale for you." . . . And to Yale I went.

I suppose I had been ill-prepared for the "dear old Campus." My classmates were engrossed in football, not in ideas; in Greek-letter fraternities, not in secret revolutionary orders. They got drunk on beer and sang sentimental songs, whereas my friends in Europe had sipped their liquor soberly for the most part, and got drunk on Nietzsche. Good, groping, earnest fellows, my chums at Yale seemed children to me. I went through college a rather cantankerous rebel. To amuse myself I wrote dramatic criticism for a local paper, losing no occasion to bewray America's woeful "lack of culture"; I played Bach; I wrote a book on the Literature of Modern France; and always my eyes continued to turn east, across the Atlantic Ocean.

Active journalism in New York was a leap from a nursery to a sort of jungle. The academic cloisters had struck me as anemic imitations of the full-blooded youthfulness which I had seen in Europe. I liked sport well enough; but was there not as well an athleticism in literature and in philosophy? Now came New York once again: a New York of murders, robberies, politics, and visiting celebrities who spent the interviewer's hour telling him pleasant things about America which were not so.

This New York seemed wholly body. While the slums reeked with poverty and vice, while the high spirit of youth was trampled out by the thresh of mechanical progress, the City seemed aware only of problems of traffic, of taxation, of money. A vast town, New York; but since it was concerned only with the mechanics of sheer physical growth, it struck me as a baby—a sort of Brobdingnagian baby. If a man proposed municipal ownership of public utilities, or cheap gas, he was treated like a monster. If a woman was suspected of infidelity, it seemed right to drag her to a divorce court; and the important thing—the only important thing—seemed to be to ascertain the fact; the deep hidden significances of her character, of her unhappiness, of the subtle treatment of her husband—all these elements of truth were ignored. I could not accept this gross, this infantile America, which was all the America I knew. Being a child myself, I made the same old gross mistake: I imagined that my Paradise existed "over there," across the sea. I packed a bag at last and went to live in Paris.

c.

When I arrived it was nightfall. I left my bags at a hotel and wandered up the Boul' Mich'—the gaudy thoroughfare of the Latin Quarter. I saw no face that I knew in the thronged terraces of the cafés which made two fertile banks from the Gardens of the Luxembourg down to the Seine. But I felt happy and I felt at home. I began to write. I found myself in a world where writing—the sheer creative act—was considered a sacrament and a service: not because of what it brought, not for what it did—for itself. It was in the air—this rhythm of creation. Life was looked on as a lovely, mysterious adventure, and its true priests were they who sang of it, who pictured it, who revealed its beauty. I made friends. Here, among these swarms of enthusiasts who spent their days arguing about a picture or a poet, I found men after my own heart. And I found a woman, a true daughter of this world who took me in and made me part of it. And then, after a brief year, just as I was beginning truly to be at home, I packed my bags and I went back to New York!

What had happened? I was having a good time and a successful one. Living was cheap there. It was extremely easy for a journalist like myself to send articles and stories to the United States, convert the few dollars into many francs, and live like a young lord in this perpetual holiday town where poverty was no disgrace, where there was as much honor in contributing to certain magazines as in being elected to the Senate! Did not wealthy ladies of Paris find the same thrill in climbing five musty flights of stairs to the garret of an ob-

scure American author that our own ladies found in dining
with celebrities from Paris? Was there indeed not a whole
world here fashioned for the artist and ruled by his desire?
Paris itself, vast and modern, had the leisurely freedom of an
aristocratic village. Here was a huge city in which there were
happy people, in which there were trees and gardens, in
which there was room for all moods, all liberties—even for
a bit of license.

I had more than I had ever had, and yet I gave it up quite
simply because I did not want it, and I could not stand it. In
several of the cafés of Paris there gathered artists from
America. Many of them had not been home in years; most
of them came from small places in the interior and had had
no contact with Europe until they had come over. They
spoke seldom of our country. But when they did, they
sneered, they jeered, they swore they were done with the
barbaric land that had given them birth. I could not argue
with them; so much of what they said was simply fact. Yet
it was in the company of these Americans that I began to
feel most sharply my need of coming back. If what they said
was true, all the more urgent was the return of men like
themselves who claimed to be conveyers of the truth, creators of beauty—men who could endow America with what
they accused America of lacking.

But I went little with these expatriates. My knowledge
of the language, my love and, bit by bit, my work gained me
an entrance into the true world of France, which before the
War was the home of so much of Europe. I was happy here,
but I was not *needed*. I was being nourished by what other
men, through centuries and ages, had created. I was a para-
site. At least, so it seemed to me. I do not believe that I
thought further in those youthful days. Certainly, I thought
scarcely at all of what I was going to find when I returned.
I knew simply that I was going home. I left the best friends

that I had ever had, the most congenial home, I left my love
(she never understood). I took a boat. I rented a room in
Washington Place. I stared at the dirty wall—and wondered
what madness had driven me. No matter. I was where I
belonged!

d.

The year was 1913 and I was twenty-three. I was alone
and miserable as I had never been. In Paris they had not
understood why I had left them. But in America no one even
knew that I was here. I had outgrown my old friends. I was
done with newspapers. Everything that a young man most
needs—companionship, ideas, love—was beyond the ocean.
Here? I lay on my iron cot and stared at the blank walls; I
heard the elevated trains pound past and the arrogant motors
shuffle and the crowds press, press in their weary quest for
money—in their vast indifference to all which made *my*
world. I was unable to eat, unable to sleep—unable to work.
At times, in my weakness, I thought of what I had left behind in Paris. But always I knew that I was not going back—
never going back until I had proven to my friends abroad,
both the Europeans and the Americans, that I was right in
leaving.

In 1914 America was not what the young artist or writer
found ten years later. There were no magazines hospitable to
virgin efforts, there were no Little Theatres, no liberal weeklies. The land seemed a hostile waste, consumed by the fires
of possession. Whatever "literature and art" there was had
to be imported from Europe in order to find a market.
But did not this fact prove that such as I were needed? The
very fact that life was hard here, that life did not seem to
want me, that America was quite resigned to letting me
starve—did not this prove that I was *needed*, and that I had
come home?

So I set to work upon the pleasant task of making myself wanted in a world that seemed to be getting along extremely well without me. I soon learned that it was getting on so well, chiefly on the surface. I had a vision then, in those dark days, which gave me light and strength, and which has never left me.

I saw our land as a fumbling giant child, idealistically hungry as was no other land in all the West, but helpless to express its hunger. Our forefathers had come here brimful of religious energy: Puritans from England, Catholics from Spain, Jews from Germany and Russia. And here were material things that must be done: a continent to clear, bridges to build, a nation to house. Our fathers had learned to perform these substantial chores; they had performed them so miraculously well because of the spiritual force which drove them. But now that they longed to express their deeper dreams, their subtler ideals, they did not know how. So that, for want of better, they poured all their poetry and most of their religion into the business at hand: made it express their idealism which they could not express otherwise at all!

We spent so much time making money because the poets had not yet come to teach us to make better things. We were so proud of our machines because the builders of more significant beauty had not yet come among us. We were such busybodies about the personal habits of our neighbors—keeping them from an innocent drink or even from a cigarette—because the teacher had not yet appeared to show us better ways of ennobling our souls. And finally, we marched about in white sheets, passed restrictive laws against immigration, grew intolerant of the chaos of creeds and races in our midst, because we were not yet strong enough, mature enough, to conceive of a unity of inclusion rather than of exclusion.

Now I was ready to see America. I had intellectually or in the flesh been "round the world." I had known personally the men of modern Europe, studied the masters of ancient Greece, Israel, and India. I discovered America last—which was the right way to discover it, since America is to be the last word, the summing up of all the yesterdays which have poured their blood upon the American shores.

I went west. Under the noisy, dirty, braggart mood of Chicago I felt a childlike spirit—I found childlike men. I found a fertile and sweet world pushing up in this town which Sandburg called the Hog-butcher of the world—pushing up under the coal and the grime like springtime grass beneath the muck of winter.

I helped to edit a country paper in the heart of Kansas. I spoke to the farmers, wrote for them, lived with them. And though I had done the same thing with the intellectuals of Paris, I found here a warmth of response which I had not found abroad. Here in this crude corngrower hungering to "git America and his dream together," and in his overworked wife scheming to give her girls the "culture" she had never had, was a seed of the spirit which needed only nurture and the sun to flower. And I had talks in the kitchens of solitary farms that moved me in a way mysteriously deep and gave me strength.

I lived with coal miners. I found them hungry for light, possessed of an infallible instinct for the tragic beauty of the world. They, too, were spiritual seed long underground and ready to push up. And when a fellow who had mined since he was twelve and who had never seen his dad by light of day piloted me through a leaky shaft with a care that was loving and paternal, I realized what I had won by giving up salutes of another sort in Paris.

I went south—to the country which my mother had left as a baby. I spent months in lodgings in that slumberous aristocrat of cities, Richmond. Here, too, were esthetes, weavers of silly images of distant Paradise. I did not see them. I saw a people, stricken still under the curse of a past and under the load of an intricate present: a people hungering for light, for expression—a people hungering and, hence, a people growing. I came to know the Negroes in the cypress swamps of Alabama and Mississippi. I lived with them, I spoke to them in their churches and their schools. In these dark breasts was a flame. I realized the wondrous wealth of spirit and of dream which America possesses in her Negroes.

And I saw the Indians of the Southwest pueblos. In their classic ceremonial dances, in their deeply unselfish religion of nature, in the dignity and restraint of their lives and culture, I recognized an American past—and an American example. Here was a spiritual splendor which America had created. Like all our past it was waning. Would we create it anew in our own culture?

e.

Finally, after the War, I went again to Europe. I had begun to put my vision of America into books. Many intellectuals had sneered. A large group of them had even come together under the leadership of one of the Americans who spend their time in Paris and had published a fat book to prove that America was hopeless, an altogether unlivable place. Much of the response which my books had won had come, not from the intellectuals, but from those very byways of our country—the farms of the West, the cities of the North, the fields of the South—where I had wandered and where I had been nourished. And some of the response had come from Europe. My books had been translated. And now that I was again in Paris the writers of that great city called me to them and told me with warm hospitality that this new America of which I wrote was what *they* needed. For, they said, the spiritual power of Europe was declining. Europe's noon was past. Europe, which had created and nurtured us, now needed nurture! If America was indeed to be a land to distil new spiritual values out of our modern chaos it would be the savior of the Old World!

Some of the writers of France and England had been here, and were pessimistic. "Do not believe him," they said. "He and his sort are only importations from Europe—they represent a transplanted dream of the Old World. They cannot thrive in America. They will be crushed out. Their light is a twilight, not a dawn. The future of America is steel, more steel; is gold, more gold; is the triumph of a sordid, ignorant Herd. There is no hope."

But at these men I smiled. They had seen what I saw as a boy: they had been repelled by the crude, the ignorant surface. . . .

A few days before I left for home I was sitting in a library infinitely richer than the one in my father's house. It was the library of the master, Anatole France. There he sat in his red skullcap by the open fire. About him in manuscript, in illuminated volume, in precious bibelot, ranged wide treasures of European culture, and in him lived the essence of that culture—the exquisite distillation of the thought of a hundred ages.

"Make no mistake," he smiled at me, "Europe is a tale that has been told. Our long twilight is before us. But I believe in your American dream. And I will tell you why. It is not because of your books. It is because of the pictures I have seen, in common magazines, of your girls and your women. You have said a great deal about Puritanism, about materialism in America. Those glorious girls belie all that. How could an ugly world produce such women? How could such women produce an ugly world?" . . .

1925

2. A SAVAGE ISLE

a.

I've been away from home for almost a year. In France, in Germany, in Lithuania and Poland, in Egypt and Palestine and Tunis, I've talked with eager men about my own fabulous country. Everywhere people knew about America. They told me all about it. I learned a lot.

I'm a peaceful fellow, not given to argument. And I'm impressionable, delighted to agree with what is told me. This I find particularly easy when what I hear is pleasant; when I am taken, for instance, in my capacity of American, for a citizen of Eldorado or of Ophir. So gradually, as the months of my absence grew, I found myself accepting what I heard, in Europe, Africa and Asia, about my native land.

By the time I took ship from Boulogne, this—more or less —is the portrait of America which the industrialist of Essen, the rabbi of Posen, the Vilna medical professor, the Tunisian judge, the merchant of Damascus, the Parisian dentist, the nationalist of Egypt, had impressed upon me:

America . . . meaning above all New York . . . is the most modern, the most civilized, the most genteel, the most efficient, the most expeditious, the most comfortable spot on earth. In America, there are no low or humble classes. In America, everywhere, the families dwell on the twentieth floors of palaces equipped with electric ice and radiant heat; and when they descend to the street it is to roll away in private autos. In America, everybody has a hand in the state; everybody has a heart for public welfare; everybody reads; everybody considers everybody's rights to peace and comfort. In America, the rich lavish their money upon scientific progress for its own sake; and of course, in America, everyone is rich.

. . . In America, the women are beautiful, free and pure. They are comrades to men. The American man is as pure as his mother. Vice is not tolerated, drink is unknown.

. . . It is true that this American folk is overconcerned with material well-being. But at least it has uplifted material well-being to the rank of an art. The American people have perhaps too great a care for money. But, at least, they spend it with splendor, and get for what they spend their heart's desire. For here are gleaming cities, marvelously fed with sun and air; here are farmlands ribboned with smooth roads and labored by miraculous machines.

. . . In America, to sum up, are men and women elegant, cheerful, leisured, powerful, serene. The rest of the backward world is jealous of America, of course. The world, in places, quite sincerely thinks that there are spiritual values which shining America may have missed. But America is the apogee of material refinement. Beside American towns, Paris must seem an unkempt village, Warsaw a dumpheap. . . .

b.

Finally my boat put into the great American harbor. I came up on deck, my eyes shiningly ready to enjoy the America of the talkers of Europe, Africa and Asia.

I saw no scintillant city rising like an army of arrows toward the Sun, its father. What I saw was a conglomerate of buildings, formless with haphazard shapes, a phalanx of skyscrapers as formidable from the distance as an old comb lacking half its teeth. A sprawling and grimy town above the noble Hudson. And the famous buildings, if they were at all the symbol of power, made me think of a baby giant, in weak control of his muscles, who had heaped this tilting mess of blocks upon the floor of his playroom.

The river-front streets had a brash rottenness that hurt, after the mellow rottenness of Fez. The houses were cheap and dirty. They revealed no imagination: a dull obsession seemed the architect of these innumerable banks of brick. A folk had dumped these houses where they stood, with its mind elsewhere or totally absent, with its heart cold or altogether lacking. As the taxi shunted me along, going slower than a rickshaw in Pekin (a taxi dirtier than any in Madrid, and driven by a man who needed but a soiled burnoose and a turban to brother him with the sword-eater in the Tangier Sacco), I thought of the improvised squalor in certain modern sections of Egyptian towns and of the far sweeter and swifter rhythm of the Saharan camel. And as the traffic crawled under the marshaling terror of the cop, I remembered the ease and speed with which one flies through the intricate network of Paris. Fifth Avenue has a splendor; Park Avenue (when at last I reached it) flaunted the elegance of a Brobdingnagian refrigerator, electrically cooled. But I'd gone through an hour of back yard and alley to get there. . . .

I went uptown. I discovered empty lots throughout the heart of the city, and unpaved stretches of street where my car bumped precisely as I had been bumped on the winter-logged roads of Poland. Indeed, more and more, this iridescent city of men's dreams—in its disorder, in its dirt, in its noise, in its lack of form and style—brought to my mind the towns I had seen in Eastern Europe: towns where for ten unceasing years armies, rebellions, insurrections, pogroms, have spewed their havoc.

I dismounted at last from my taxi, and began to look into the faces of this most pampered, ultracivilized and genteel people. Since they are having a good time, enjoying the "top of the world," why are they so gloomy about it? Since they are at ease in their Zion of physical comfort, why are they so uncomfortable, so nervous, so harassed? Since they have been polished off by all the polishing machines of the Modernist Machine Age, why do their brutal faces make me quake? I am no dauntless Galahad. But I have roamed the water front of Antwerp, searched the night kasbah of Algiers, tramped the lightless wastes of London's Wapping, tempted the traps of Cádiz and of Jaffa. I have never seen faces more sullen, more dehumanized, than these of New Yorkers. I forgot all about my conversations with the informed gentlemen of Europe, Africa and Asia. I recalled certain statistics and knew that I was in a town where thieving is a soft profession and where holdups and assassinations hugely outnumber the totals in populous European countries.

Also, I was forced to remember that alcohol intoxicates. In my first ten hours I saw more drunkenness in my native village than I had observed in as many months in Spain.

c.

At last I was safely in bed in a room the price of which for the night was a little over the cost of a week's rental of a furnished farm in France. There came to my blasted ears, beneath the zephyrous purr of a million motors emitting carbon gas and of a thousand radios drenching the air with the still more noxious fumes of ballyhoo, fragments of flattering talks about my native land in Paris, Berlin, Warsaw, Jerusalem and Cairo.

"Comfort" . . . I heard: "speed . . . efficiency" . . . "mechanical perfection" . . . "civilization too easy, too happy, too refined." . . . On the fields of France they had once builded great Gothic myths; and Egypt has her Sphinx; and Palestine wove the legends of Jehovah. Now, the sons of these mythmakers croon fables of an America where houses sing with gladness, and men move noiselessly and swift from pleasure to pleasure.

Please do not mistake me. I have no grouch; I am not pessimistic. I live in the land of my birth through choice; I deem myself fortunate in being a New Yorker. But the notion that our country is at an apex of perfection is the most inept falsehood. We are barbarians in a savage jungle, we are at the sultriest beginning.

That, precisely, is the fun of living here. Everything, however primitive and basic, still must be accomplished: the present generation of Americans are more profoundly pioneers than Daniel Boone, more original adventurers than Columbus. The myth consists of supposing that we are, to date, more than a lot of babies rising from the womb of Europe.

Of course, the European and African and Asiatic supporters of this myth have been helped by ourselves. They have got their "information" and their "facts" from the News. That modern Wonder, compact of cable, print, radio, and motion picture—has it not "linked the whole world close together," making each man know all about his brothers? And could I expect the American myth to fail to carry in Morocco, when it succeeds right here?

Grab your paper and plunge into the subway. The steel corridors have an infernal beauty and the subway stinks. The noise deafens you and you are jammed for forty minutes between strap-hanging troglodytes all reading the same paper. That paper shrieks an incessant alternation of Lust and Death, fulfilling the portrait of a savage jungle. No matter. On the editorial page you will be sweetly informed that your land is the Pinnacle of Progress, your town the culmination of man's seeking ages. And you, too, will be convinced of the American—the modern—myth.

d.

I know a way out, if you want one. Let the conduits of "information" and "news" be placed in the hands of philosophers and men of science. For instance, give the dailies to the metaphysicians; the weeklies to the psychologists, the radio

and movies to experts in social science. And let it be stipulated that no edition and no story be released, until the *entire Board agree upon the truth.* This would at once diminish the output of press, radio and cinema to precisely what that output was in the year 1200 B.C., and thereby enhance our accurate knowledge of the world—and of America—to what that knowledge was in those more illumined days.

1928

3. A MOB AND A MACHINE

I went up to the opening ball game at the Polo Grounds. A number of thousands of others went along with me. I suppose it may safely be surmised that all of us were there to have a good time. However varied our definitions of what a good time is, all of us, at least, must have had the idea that a good time was to be had at a ball game.

What happened to us, up there, strikes me as pathetic. I am not referring to the particular brand of ball played that afternoon by the Giants or the Braves. It was typical baseball, more or less: and it was the typical scene.

Here was the great stadium filled with the black human mass. The field is enormous; the stands must be huge to compass the field. The majority of us were pretty remote from the inner diamond where most of the game takes place. On the periphery of it all were we—we, the great human throng— spread parabola-wise around the field. And in one corner of that field was the tight, shut diamond: and was the machine of players going through its motions.

It would be hard to exaggerate the abyss that separates a ball game at the Polo Grounds from the vast crowds that watch it. We all know the picture of the hungry lad peering at the man in Childs who flips the wheat cakes on the grid inside the window. It seems to me that that boy is less remote from his cakes than we were from our ball game.

Just think of those titanic stands of steel. If they are not wholly filled, their emptiness makes a menacing unlit presence all about, chilling the spectacle of the game. And if they are packed, they form a human mob so great it is unwieldy. No normal ball game can stir it more than ten seconds out of every hour.

We and the teams, moreover, had so little in common! Good baseball, such as is habitually played by the Major Leagues, is a smooth-running, impersonal affair. As little is left to the discretion of the players on the field as it is possible to leave them. They are tools, or rather parts of a mechanism run by a "mastermind" who sits on the bench. Batsman and fielder mechanically carry out motions whose plan and purpose are established for them. Even in the ultimate personal element that remains—the hitting of the ball, the fielding of the ball—the good player is a specialist, a coldly trained performer whose ways are very far removed from the ways of the urban, sedentary throng. The beauty of baseball, indeed, is precisely in its mechanical perfection. It is related to the beauty of a machine, rather than of art.

Far, far away is the crowd. It is not close in any sense, as is the theatre crowd, for instance, close to the actors on the stage. A theatre is a shut, packed unity: crowd and performers are physically knit. And what the physical proximity of audience and stage does not effect, the emotions expressed on the stage supply. Humor, pathos, passion, dancing, music—these are all symbols enacted by the players and immediately current in the life of every man and woman watching. But the ball game is a machine: by and large, it remains as separate from the mob as might a brilliantly intricate dynamo set out upon the field.

Sitting there, that day, I understood why Babe Ruth—

ignoble, fat fellow that he is—deserves his vogue. I understood that a man like the Babe is indeed greater than the National Game. It is such as he who enable the wistful mob to have some sort of contact with the game. For baseball is only clockwork; but the Babe is a boy—moody, clever, human. He "gets across." One crowd sees the game: another crowd follows it on the scoreboard of Times Square; America reads of it in Kalamazoo and Junktown. All, with a difference only of degree, are separate from this highly organized, privately owned, secretly controlled affair of baseball.

Here comes a player, with whom the crowd can identify itself. Babe Ruth catapulting the pill into the grandstand is a symbol. There have been subtler batsmen, but all of them, Lajoie, Wagner, Sisler, Cobb, aimed for the base hit which stays *inside* the field. The Babe's home run is an effort on the part of the machine to *connect* with the crowd. When the ball reaches the bleachers, contact is established. The game and the watchers of the game for that instant have the ball in common. Babe Ruth is the demagogue of baseball.

Not only is Babe Ruth greater than the game: such little episodes as the periodic scandals, so deplored by moral managers and punctilious pressmen, are little less than godsends. If they did not crop up from time to time, Judge Landis would do well to invent them. They, too, introduce into the machinery of baseball certain negotiable passions: public responses to bribery, temptation, nobility and vice, come to reinforce the old worn response of partisanship—a response difficult to sustain when players are swapped from town to town like cattle. Anything that makes us feel—even if what we feel is only anger—helps the game.

What a hungry, wistful crowd we are, seated in our ascetic seats! The game itself rarely holds us. Most of us, where we are placed, cannot spot a ball from a strike, until we see it posted. We cannot tell Bancroft from Marriott at the bat, without looking up the number and consulting our score card. And save for a few tense moments, the game is as static down there as a dead motor on a winter morning.

No wonder we are driven to help ourselves to entertainment!

We call every player by his first name. That helps. It makes him less remote, away down there.

We shout advice to him. Praise. Vituperation. We josh him, we cuss him out. That helps. It makes us, in some wise, participants, after all, in our great National Sport.

When a ball comes our way, we make the most of it. We shout at a long fly, even if it is caught. We pray for a home run in our particular direction.

But even when the game runs on, smooth and cold and remote, we can make use of it. It permits us to act like children—or like madmen. That helps, by golly! Where else can we scream ourselves hoarse—about nothing? Where else can we make all the strange, uncivilized noises of which the human throat is capable? We hoot, shout, boo, scream, whistle. We get excited—without consequences. We get profane, abusive, grandiose—without danger of having to pay. Downtown, excitement about much is bad business. Here, corybantic ecstasy about nothing is good form. To hell with the ball game, after all. We can enact lyrical dramas of rage, disgust, beatitude—flinging our jewels of gesture to the empty air, even if the game be a machine and a sell.

And after an hour and a half of this, we can pack ourselves like grains of sand into a stifled elevated train, and read in the headlines of the paper we have just bought what a significant national event we have just witnessed. . . .

It is quite true that the old-fashioned humble game was better sport. The bleachers hugged the field. The players were visible: we could see the sweat on them and the look in their eyes. They made more errors, but even in that were they not closer to us? Well, like everything else in our America, the Game's got bigger—and that means better. Even sport had to be specialized. It used to be an enjoyable means of moving our own bodies. Not any more. Now there's a machine that does the moving, while our forty thousand bodies sit packed and rancid in the grandstands. You gotta expect to pay for the privilege of belonging to the most progressive country on earth.

1925

4. MURDER AS BAD ART

Nearly every day you see the statistics in the papers. "Half as many homicides in Erie in an hour, as in England in an era." "As many assassinations in St. Louis in a second, as in Yucatán in a year." "More murders in Manhattan in a month, than in Schleswig-Holstein in a century." From which it is to be inferred that private slaughter is an American activity.

When, moreover, you observe the high consideration accorded to our slayers—a consideration expressed in most cases by letting them alone (and this, in a democracy where such a privilege is almost unheard of!) or—in the few authenticated instances of capture—by hero worship and adulation, it becomes further clear that we regard the murderer somewhat as Spaniards the matador, as Frenchmen the poet, as Germans the philosopher, as Jews the prophet.

Murder is an American expression, a folk art. It contains some virtue so close to our desire that we have protected it jealously from the class distinctions which begin to encroach on our once so purely democratic life. The American murderer can win a front page, be he millionaire or beggar. The same sob sisters will write him up—gilded clubman or lowly loafer. There is no hierarchy here but Merit; no limit to glory save the intensest competition. Murder, in short, is an American art. My quarrel with it is that it is bad art; and that America's growing devotion to it threatens our cultural progress.

Consider, first, the psychology of murder. Murder is above all a solution. We take an elementary case. *A* hates *B*—hates the sight and presence of *B*. So *A* kills *B*. *A* no longer sees what he hates to see. *He has succeeded:* he has found a solution. This is the instinctive murder. We will complicate it with a higher impulse. *A* wants *B's* purse. *B*, alive, would prefer not to give his purse to *A*. So *A* shoots *B* or slits *B's* throat. *B* no longer objects to giving *A* his purse. *A*, once again, has succeeded. He has found a solution. This is the emotional murder—what the Europeans know as the *crime passionnel:* since the commercial desire, the will to earn, is the dominant American emotion. We go still higher in the category. *A* wants *B's* girl, or *B's* social status as Beer Baron. *B*, active and alive, is too handsome and too clever. *A* spoils *B's* beauty by bashing in his face, and overcomes *B's* intellectual superiority by bashing out his brains. *A*, now unimpeded, wins Girl and Fortune. He has succeeded again: found a solution again. This is the intellectual murder: since Shakespeare and Milton severally tell us that love of woman and love of fame are the last infirmities of the noble mind.

Having thus placed murder under the Microscope provided by a scientific age, we have detected in it a constant germ: what might be called the *success bacillus*—the will to a quick solution. Now it must be understood why murder is so advanced and wide a practice in the United States. We are believers in success: we are clamorers for a solution: we are no brookers of delay. Take our three hypothetic situations between *A* and *B*; and consider how in a less successful milieu than our own they might be blunderingly met. *A*

French *A* hates a French *B:* he grins and bears it—or he fights, perhaps vainly, to overcome his hatred—or he avoids *B*—or possibly he comes close to his foe and, by studying him well, strains to turn hate to love. These are arduous endeavors, for which there is no *guarantee* of success. None of them *gets results*, like arsenic or a bullet.

A London *A* covets the purse of a London *B*. Unless he is as atypical as genius, *A* will not dream of murder. He will pick *B*'s pocket, or gamble with him, or slip by stealth into his room at night—or even do without! Again, it is clear that success is less assured. The solution is in doubt: the result is far below 100 per cent certain.

And now, finally, *A* belonging to any of the effete societies of Europe has a rival in *B* for a girl and for social fortune. He will probably try to get at the girl (an uncertain method where a moment's success "carries no insurance") or he may try to outstrip *B* by study and application. The processes are long, difficult, full of hazard. The American way of assassination is sure-fire.

But the American method gets so quickly and nakedly at the result, by destroying what stands in the way: *which is Life itself*. And not alone the life of *B:* what *A* avoids—trial, struggle, doubt—is just that content of experience which enriches living and is the stuff of art. The American system is very competent, and very sterile. It is related neither to life nor to art: but rather to the machine.

Let us consider our other American arts. We shall then see at once how general is this love of a *quick* solution; and how systematically we eliminate from life those elements which might hinder a solution. Quite recently we were mad over the Crossword Puzzle. The puzzle was soluble: it made success easy: and it contained nothing—neither sense nor content—except the incentive toward success. Even if one did happen to fail, despite the aid of dictionaries and of neighbors, in finding the "3-letter word meaning the adult of kitten," next morning's paper put an end to the agony. Similarly, there is the Movie and the Popular Story. They must contain a mechanism leading in simple and directest terms to Success and a solution. They must dispense with any forms of "life" that might impede solution. We can see now how harmoniously murder fits in with the other common ways of American Law and Order.

So much for our recognizable arts. If we turn to our public life--to our "serious" side—we encounter the same habit. We have social problems: and we solve them. Folks get drunk on alcohol? Easy: abolish alcohol. Roundhead foreigners cluttered up our landscape? Easy: abolish immigration. Dour dramas corrupted Sweet Sixteen? Easy: censor the drama. Crazy communists upset bedtime story mood of bourgeois gentlemen? Easy: jail 'em and let the Supreme Court of the United States outlaw their nonsense. These are all problems they still have in blundering, backward Europe. By gosh, we've solved them.

And we're constructive, too: not merely defensive. Having money means having a good time. We've learned that. So we are abolishing every value, and throwing in contempt each occupation, which does not aim at money: either in the earning of it or in the display of it, once it has been earned. And finally, success is success. Having discovered this, there is nothing left but to murder all moods and impulses which would deny this crucial American proposition.

You have the idea. We jolt off more folk in New Jersey in a week than they do in France in a generation, because murder is so consonant with the American Idea. Of course, murder's the low form of our art: a folk art. (We have our pickpockets, too.) But you can't get away from it. The murderer is a go-getter. The murderer has a problem, and he solves it. The murderer sees what he wants, and he takes it.

The murderer believes in quick action: he is a maker of suc-cess: he is a man with results. ("Success" magazines and popular platform artists please copy.)

And all this makes for bad art because—as Goethe put it—"art is long." The short cut gets you "there." But what if the "short cut" cuts out life itself? You've had nothing on the way. And when you are once "there," what can you do but start again—on another short cut—for the next place? This is the joker in our competence. We do away with the means: and behold! The Means are everything and the End is noth-ing. It's like the modern Sunday afternoon. We used to go nowhere in particular, on foot: and see the country. Now we motor a hundred miles to X. And X is nothing. And we've gone so fast, and swallowed so much carbon monoxide gas, that the way was nothing either. So we speed on to Y and to Z, ad infinitum, ad nauseam.

To solve the problems of life is very simple. All you need do is to eliminate—to murder—life. That gets rid of the prob-lems: and that explains 99/100 of what men call civilization. For life is all Problem, and the brave dwelling therein: and the solution is death. A good life is the art of avoiding quick solutions. And murder—this so popular American practice, this so simple mechanical means toward a solution—is a good symbol of the bad art of America.

1925

5. THE BATTLE OF A CENTURY AND A HALF

PHILADELPHIA (JULY 4, 1776—SEPT. 23, 1926)

The rain was the hero of the evening. The gentle falling rain. It appeared second on the scene, pattering down so mod-estly just after Tunney had climbed up, and preceding the

Champion Dempsey. It was not greeted quite so cordially by the crowd as were Gene and Jack. But ere long it made itself felt. At the end, it held undisputed sway.

The rain was the hero of that memorable hour in which the Mauler of Manassa lost his crown to the Sweet Marine—for a variety of reasons. To begin with, everybody saw the rain; and don't you dream for an instant that every one of those good 130,000 American patriots who had come so far—at such expense and trouble—just to celebrate their country's Sesquicentennial birthday, *saw* the Fight. Did the seats lack visibility? Not a bit of it. A marvel of architectural finesse is the great stadium. But even Mr. Rickard could not stretch the structure of men's sight nor mold to a more plastic shape the sort of scrap he had staged. The seeing was carefully graded, as everything should be in an orderly Republic.

For $27.50 (up) you *saw* the Fight, and the stripe on Jack's trunks; you saw the exquisite process whereby Dempsey was softened, slowed, mauled, unshaped by the obdurate indifference of Tunney. The sum of $16.50 gave you two men—one square head and one oblong—manifestly clad in purple and blue trunks; face and condition a blank, but bodies spinning visibly enough, and hopping and hugging and lunging, boring and jabbing in a ten-round dance. Fairly balanced, they were, under the heavy crown of the loud-speakers. No one went down, no one went through the ropes. Tunney was steadfast and Dempsey was wild. So $16.50 got a mere guess at the decision of the Fight you had come so laboriously to behold. At $10.00, what you saw was a couple of bright bugs with swift antennae, making love or something in true insect fashion—and getting nowhere, so that you could notice. And at $3.30, you beheld, all about a far flame, a spot, a sky of moveless, pivotless heads, a sky rolling with human thunder. And that was worth the money.

But when the rain came, the gentle falling rain, it played

no favorites. It did not pour buckets on Mayor Walker's crown, and drip a mere drop on Paddy. And how the rain was needed! Don't you believe it put a damper on that mob. Individual men and women may have been disgruntled— although they didn't show it. But the crowd itself, and the spirit of the show, *called for* the rain.

In the mists which tided to the crowd from the high shell walls, see a symbol of tedium, and you've got the idea. A solid, stolid thing was the mob, massing from the ringside. When the lights that stared from brackets all around went out, the crowd seemed dead. Myriad heads rose from the flanks of the thing like carven facets—like knobs—like artificed protuberances on a woody substance. You felt that a plane, if it were big enough, could run over the vast surface, and smooth it, and smooth off the heads. You felt there'd be a lot of sawdust, and that's all. You were unjust, however. For when the lights screamed back, shedding their green-blue ice on the hot crowd, you saw that each of these myriad individual knobs had a face: mostly a man's, perhaps a woman's, face. The expression was dull, not too lifelike; and almost never varied. But if you doubted the monumental genius of the painter of all those phizes, you couldn't help admiring the assiduity for going to such trouble.

Then the Fight, to make the stadium come alive. Shouts, cheers, murmurs, ran at first through the inert thing: trickled, jabbed at it, harried—and failed to fuse it together. Many sparks and no flame. The spirit of the evening was not a spirit of fire. Sogginess, wetness—spirit of the rain was what Philadelphia summoned from its weary streets to meet the wearied visitors from afar. And that's why, when the rain did fall, it was right. You can't blame Mr. Rickard. How could he know? How could he know, for instance, that this stadium, unlike other circuses, sprawls too horizontal from the ring, is too fluid in its forms to be galvanized into a furious hard passion? A fight scene should be more vertical, more funnel-shaped. Then your scrappers have a chance, with their lean frail arms, to weave a spell to pull the human lump together—fire it, make it the mad, single-howling creature which loomed above Dempsey and Firpo in New York. . . . And how could Mr. Rickard foresee that his two prize babies, this time, would keep their feet so well?

If the prize fight is to outlive its present mastodonic bulk, and not—like other dinosauri—collapse from sheer flatulent vastness, the pugs' arms will have to grow stronger so that there is more flooring, or their legs will have to grow feebler, so that there is more flopping. In a huge stadium, you can see a man go down flat—and that is always worth a week's salary and ten hours' sweating in trains. But boxing, boring, sparring, dancing, spinning—but a bloody nose and Jack's shut eye—what'n'ell do such fine points get you, when you cannot *see* them? The fat ball park developed the fat Babe Ruth. Slugging makes contact with the huge modern mob, where all the place-hitting of Nap Lajoie would be lost. The fisticuff equivalent of a fast-bounding ball in the bleachers is a couple of giants tumbling each other, as in the Dempsey-Firpo fracas. There was none of that in Philadelphia.

The crowds were childish about it; and you cannot blame them. They wanted action: thudding, sudden action. Without it, they were bored. How far they had come! what hours they had voyaged, leaving wife and children! what hours' hard earnings expended! what sweat exuded! what shoe leather worn away, in order to be in Philly! Was it to see two boxers, bobbing in a white-roped ring? Once they were there, they couldn't wait to get home. A knockout in round one would have delighted them. Immediate action—what the French in another context call *la jouissance immédiate*—that was the infantile temper of the crowd. They howled down the announcer, when he wasted time on adjectives. They were nonpartisan. They were for Tunney when his blow landed; they were for Jack when the thud of *his* glove came over the acred heads. They were for anybody who'd bring it all crashing to a decisive thrill. Poor public! Hadn't they paid two million dollars for *something?* I suppose that is why Mr. Rickard, whose influence with the weather is well known, brought down the rain.

Which leads me to our Showman. The show was, of course, the packed stadium. Or, if you prefer, the show was the show itself. The Fight was the pretext for bringing the show together. To this end, Jack and Gene fought for championship. To this end, one hundred and fifty years ago, our fathers fought for independence. So that Philadelphia might have her celebration and dawdle through it meagerly for many months on such nurture as the Pageant of Freedom (loss $700,000)—and recoup it all in the sudden financial glory of a scrap fight, which a hundred-odd thousand paid for, and which the radio stay-at-homes alone followed clearly. But if the Show was the show itself—who saw it?

Not the newspapermen, not the frontiermen in the wide, cheapest spaces. All of them erroneously had their eyes on the ringside. The chief appreciator of this thing of beauty was the chief creator of it: Mr. Tex Rickard himself.

From 8:00 to 9:30 P.M. I followed this enraptured artist as he moved from entrance to entrance of his golden dump. I was happy to catch the esthetic gleam in his eye, and to hear him murmur:

"Gee! Only look at 'em all! See that silver blimp tipping the stadium askew as if we were on a boat in a storm. See that Penn State Building yonder, like a city in the air. See the heavens rolling, rumbling near. All so fluid, all so fairy-like—above the solid substances of my crowd! One hundred thirty thousand . . . solid . . . solid . . . *paid for!* By Michael Angelo," cried our leading modeler of mobs, "it's worth earning half a million dollars to make a thing as beautiful as this." . . .

And so, to make that beauty perfect, he summoned down the rain. It worked on the crowd like water on a thirsty plant. It eased them—brought them together. It gave them something more immediate and urgent than that distant dance in the ring. Water, drooling from one bosom to another, joined them. The little raindrop, bounding from head to head, made brothers as it bounded. We knew that our forefathers, fighting for freedom, had fought to make a Nation, after all.

Men and women removed their hats and swathed their heads in handkerchiefs that gleamed in the gloom like turbans. The stadium turned Oriental; the fight fans became worshipers at some rite. Now, the remoteness of the bout was good—since a rite before an altar should be occult. Now, the cavortings and borings of two men on a light-blazed box seemed fitting. And it was well that a little man in an incongruous dinner coat should make noiseless speech under a diadem of arcs and amplifiers; and that his voice should loom, by some sudden miracle, into each shadow of the conch-shaped pile. And, finally, it was right that at the very end, at least a hundred thousand of the worshipers (who had, they thought, come to *see* a fight) should stand quiet until the Metal Voice belched forth the news to them of *who had won.*

Slowly, sweetly they plashed away through the mud and the motors, toward their distant homes. Through the waterlogged rhetoric of a National Fair which needed a prize fight to put it on the map. And the heavens wept gently.

But when we reached the Penn Station at Broad Street, all my hopes for mankind were reborn. With a greater drive than Dempsey's, with more stamina than Tunney's, silent mobs of men stormed with drenched bodies through the gates

—to the New York trains. And then I knew that my brothers, after all, were capable of enthusiastic action when some high purpose urged them.

1926

6. ENNOBLING OUR CRIMINALS

So it has come to this. They're advertising for the crook and the yegg. The first practical sign of the uplift was in the modest little placards which blossomed out some time ago in the "L" stations: they reminded prospective robbers of ticket offices that, *if they were caught,* they'd get from six to seven years. The suggestion, of course, was: not to be caught, and doubtless some few courageous men were thereby inspired to do better work. But now there are to be flamboyant posters—every bit as good as the old ones which urged us to Buy Liberty Bonds, to Save Sugar, to Save the World from the Kaiser. . . . These new works of democratic art speak out to all whom they concern: "You CAN'T win. Ships Don't Sail Beyond the Arm of the Law." Or, "You CAN'T win. You Have to Get All the Breaks. One Little Slip Means Sing Sing."

It is fair to assume that these exhortations are not addressed to the little girl who works all day in a milliner's shop; nor even to the plumber riding home from his pipes. There must be a criminal class, large and plebeian enough to use the streetcars, to whom these advertisements are devoted and whom they are aimed to improve. This is highly significant as perhaps the final proof that we are a democracy. I feel, however, that much good material is neglected by not putting the posters also in the taxis.

At last the criminal class is to be exalted. Today, of course, it is small pumpkins to hold up a bank clerk or sandbag an aged millionaire as he saunters from his club. Mediocre men —men of conservative instincts and cool passions—have degraded the ranks of crime. All this is now to be changed. The crook is to be challenged! The yegg is to be dared! "You CAN'T WIN" shout the ads. This will, of course, discourage the weak members. It will fire and inspire the strong ones. It will weed out the cautious crooks. It will raise the moral and spiritual standard of the whole fraternity of pillagers, marauders, brigands, thugs and pirates who grace our peaceful land, and serve to circulate moneys and emotions.

Dick Turpin, Robin Hood, the great corsairs, had no encouragement like this. They worked against a spirit of states and peoples which in every way encouraged "virtue." When one thinks of the drawbacks of those days one wonders that picaroons, spielers and strong-arm men survived at all! It merely goes to show the indestructibility of genius. Men were discouraged from peculation by thoughts of God, and by the subtle suggestion of the priests that it was *harder* to go straight! Moses had thundered: "Thou shalt not"—with the assumption that, of course, *thou couldst*. Jesus of Nazareth went even further. He made it clear that it was almost impossible to be good. For ages, the aristocracies and the churches kept up their propaganda, discouraging crime on the ground that crime was easy, forgivable and mean.

We have changed all that. "You can't win my swag!" challenges the banker, knowing well that this is the very tune to inspire the daring crook against him. Indeed, the best of this new scene of our Democratic Drama is the altruism of the leaders.

They have suffered, after all, very little from holdups. Crime has been endemic, but sporadic. The land buccaneering art needed uplift and stimulation. It needed the standards and the token of popular support which advertising—that university of democracy—alone would give it. Enough vivid posters encouraging superior youth to bust safes or board bullion-carrying motors—through the method of challenge and of a call to adventure, and we can look forward to the day when all banks will be broken, all rich ladies stripped of their jewels, and all motors in the hands of thieves, save, of course, those taxis which are already run by licensed yegg-men.

Our ruling class disproves the cynicism of the materialist philosopher. Are they not now inspiring a criminal class, with educational posters, to despoil them?

But perhaps there's a way out of this dilemma, after all.

Everyone knows that about fifty years ago our pioneers and pork-barrel experts instituted the campaign which has resulted in the present flood, throughout the land, of novelists and poets. Advertising methods in those days were more intimate, because the science had not been standardized. Yet the process was essentially the same as that now begun for the benefit of our criminal classes. Instead of shouting in posters, it was whispered about: "Write Poetry—and Starve." "Creators—You Can't Win. The Possessive Arm of the Law Will Get You, Even in Paris."

The result, of course, was Greenwich Village, and our ten thousand Little Theatres. In the bright lexicon of youth, there's no word of challenge like CAN'T. But the crowning stroke of this maneuver for supplying our land with a sufficiency of poets, was the system of awards and prizes which has since sprung up.

The creators, of course, were first *challenged* into existence by the possessors. Then, those who were wise enough to make their imagination and their art work *for* the possessors, were paid sumptuously in coin.

Similarly, bank robbers and holdup men must first be inspired to know the dignity of their calling. These posters will help to draw the right class of energetic youth. All that remains, then, will be to announce positive rewards for those criminals who make good.

1925

7. READING THE SPORTS

Oh, how glad I am that spring is coming and that baseball's here! For once again, I can get something from the papers. I am what America would unanimously call a highbrow. Put me down as that, since the Majority Rules. It is because I am a highbrow, spending my days and nights in philosophic contemplation, that I rely on the sports in our dailies. During these last months, life has been bitterly empty. At its best, pro football is a vague business, and tennis is the sort of game you must see in order to believe. I have suffered frightfully for lack of news. But now I am myself again. The sun shines promisingly in my window. Mayor Walker has thrown out the first ball and at last I can spend my pennies evening after evening, for Baseball Finals: certain at last of having *news* to read.

It is, if you insist on explanations, because I am a highbrow spending my days and nights in philosophic contemplation that I require the sports. You don't see? Well: let's examine the matter like two highbrows together.

I prop my morning paper carefully (so as not to spill it) against the water tumbler, with its edge held down by the plate which holds my grapefruit. Right column spread: Briand and the League of Nations. Do I read it? No. Why do I not read it? Because I am not concerned in International Affairs? Wrong again. It is because I am concerned in International Affairs, and know something *about* International Affairs, and know a good deal about papers—that I skip this column. For I am aware, whatever the true crux of the

crisis, that I'll not find it printed. Vague conjectures, superficial facts, details, a perfect avoidance of everything causal
—of all that *counts* in this particular matter—this is what my
faithful paper spreads before me, on International Affairs.
Next door, an article about the Police and Bootlegging and
the Crime Wave in our city. I am exceeding interested in
all crime news, and in the liquor market. That is why I skip
the column. If I desire to be sure what really happened, I
must wait till I can drop in on the boys who know one thing
and who write another. . . . Left column: the big story
about Congress. It also fails to qualify. Nothing but the hot
air is in the print. The real plots, plans, motives, are as far
from this open page as are the committee rooms and dining
rooms of Washington from the visitors' gallery at the Capitol.

I turn the page. I fare no better. Discovery of ruins in
Yucatán, Egypt, the Gobi Desert. I know the "desk" has
sedulously deformed the trickle of "quick" news which the
telegraph has shot across the sea. . . . Divorce? I'll get none
of the violet rays of subtle human truth in this odious, scarlet, lyingly "whole" report. Taxi smashup? Perhaps the
names at least are right (though even they may be misspelled,
unless they're famous). Music? I happen to know too much
about music to marvel convincedly at Marion Talley's voice.

Ah, but here is the book page! I may glance at the ads.
They tell me at least, with a modicum of truth, that Mr.
Mencken's new novel is out; and that the Hexameter Epic
to which Mr. Broun has devoted so many years of silence
is to be published in the fall. But will these lengthy and
pontifical disquisitions about the current output give me
either *facts* or credible *opinion?* Alas! I fear not. There is
more honesty and candor here than in the sections devoted to
politics and crime. But not more competence. Real information about books and art requires an informer with back-

ground and perspective, and fairly permanent esthetic stand-ards.

And I crave facts! I'm a highbrow: I want to *know* at least of SOMETHING that's happened in the world, since yesterday. So I turn to the sports page.

I am told that Babe Ruth fanned three times, and I believe it! I am told that Vance pitched as good a game as that famous one of Walter Johnson's, five years ago in Detroit. I'll stake my dollars, it's true! Here is the statement that the Giants blew in the seventh and the Pirates hammered five earned runs. I know it! I know the runs were earned! (What a relief it is, to know anything at all in our chaotic world—when even the atom has crumbled!)

I am pretty certain that these boys in the Majors are really Major Leaguers, and deserve to be there, by the best of base-ball standards. I believe these baseball critics. I am willing to accept, without the tedium of a personal inquiry, that the fellows who are playing in Paterson or Oshkosh are not as good as their brothers in Big Time. But I am quite as sure that the real Major Leaguers in politics, law, business, litera-ture, education, are usually ignored by the papers; whereas every morning there's a new crop of tenth-rate Minors in the five-column spreads.

McGraw would stand for no Mayor Hylan in his line-up. It wouldn't pay *him*, as it paid Tammany. No sentimental blurb can hide the fact if Ruth has batted .170 for a week. No lack of a blurb can blur the fielding and batting splendor of George Sisler. There's plenty of stuff about the past, that we believe in; plenty of hopes for the future. But today—what can we believe today? In the sports I get rare satisfac-tion, for I can say: "It's in the papers, and I do believe it."

You've got to have *some* certainties at breakfast. You've got to have *some* English written in a style living, appropriate, honest. There's plenty of fiction: forty pages, daily, in our average-sized journals. Forty pages of cake. That's all very well. But, being a plain highbrow, I need a little of the bread of fact. Thank the Lord for baseball.

1926

8. THE NEW CONQUISTADORES

So I went to Florida for a rest. . . .

Of course, I left all my money there in real estate ventures, and had to return by boat. This is a cheaper way than Pullman, and I soothed my pride by arguing that it would round out my experience. In Miami, Sarasota, St. Augustine and Jacksonville, I had encountered nothing but millionaires. There must be a nether side, an "other half of the world," even in Florida. More modest revelers in sunshine surely must go south by winter and doubtless I would find these coming north by boat.

I was mistaken. The steamer was crowded. Every cabin and berth were occupied by men and women who, according to admissions obliquely and nonchalantly let fall in talk, were larded with money. Everyone had tried to get a *de luxe* stateroom, alas! and had failed. Everyone, moreover, was traveling by boat because of a tender love of the sea. There was not much wind; but a good portion of our company were sick. Nor do I recall any gazing at the ocean, save on one or two instances when porpoises were sighted. Perhaps there was more sea to the voyage than the pampered landowners had bargained for. It is true that from beginning to end the boat was utterly surrounded.

And besides, there was too much of an intellectual, cultural, public-spirited nature to discuss on board for any childish pleasure in salt water. These were men and women on a holiday. Yet, everybody knows that the athletic mind finds rest, not in lazing, but in a simple change of the topic of cerebration. These men and women had gone South ostensibly in quest of sunshine, alligators, golf and bathing. Their alert minds had soon discovered that Florida today was the very apex of American progress, the cynosure of all live American eyes, the ideal of every purse possessed of the creative impulse to increase and multiply. What more inevitable than that, returning to their estates in Kalamazoo, Newark and the Bronx, they should discuss and discuss?

We were foregathered in the smoking room.

"They are sure doing wonders down there in Florida." A heavy Elk spoke with gleaming eyes. His chest was deep and so was his voice. It was strange how two-dimensional those eyes seemed.

As the four others of us round the table nodded and sipped our near beer and chewed at our cigars, I became aware of a strange presence overhead. The smoking room was fitted out after the fashion of an old English inn. In the ceiling were open rafters clouded in smoke. And here, straight above us, through the darkling mist, I saw another group of men gathered like us about an oaken table.

At first, I thought that there must be a mirror in the beams, catching our group through the haze; for these men above were placed like us. But as my vision cleared I saw that they were different, after all. They were clad in steel coats of mail; swords swanked angularly at their sides; they wore flaring boots; armored gauntlets were drawn off, and freed the harsh-haired fists of conquistadores clasping silver goblets filled with ruby wine.

My neighbor answered—a weasel fellow, all grey, whose nose seemed in a perpetual tremor of scenting and searching:

"Why, Jacksonville's population alone has doubled in ten years!"

—Tell the Padre that we have made another hundred converts, came from the smoke-veiled rafters.

"They got 268 manufacturing plants that can turn out $50,000,000 worth of goods a year."

—Our first stone building at San Agustin is a school for the Indians.

"You know that filling-in of marsh water front at Sarasota cost the Ringling Brothers about $10,000. They sold it at $13,500 the acre."

—The new Cathedral was built by Christian natives. We have sent the deed of the property as a gift to the University of Salamanca.

"Miami has a transient population of 90,000. That's what pays . . . the transients."

And over my head the echo:*—We are being urged to marry with the Indian if need be, and to settle. Are these men not the hidalgos of a great land? Has not Don Francisco called them brothers of the Spaniard?*

"Fifteen thousand hotels in Florida." The Elk eyes glowed.

—A Mission in the Everglades at last! was the refrain.

"The whole thing is stupendous," came the shrill voice from the grey man at my side. "It's the greatest land rush in the history of the U. S. A."

"Which means, in the history of the world," said a surgeon who operated in lots on the side. He was a man burly and sinuous. There was in him something of the otter and a good deal of the boar. "Why, compared to this, the great movements of history—the gold rush into California, the dash to the Klondike, the opening of the Middle West and the Northwest with Harriman and Hill, were puny."

He was an eloquent as well as learnèd speaker. And as each glorious instance rolled from his soft mouth, there came an echo mysteriously transformed by the smoky rafters. . . .

—Movements of history . . . passage of the children of Israel across the Red Sea . . . the quest of the Holy Grail . . . Crusades . . . Columbus. . . .

"But it ain't business only!" I protested.

"You bet not," said the Elk. " 'Come to Florida and see the nation at play.' " He quoted the great line without hesitation.

I saw our nation at play. Motoring . . . movies . . . lot jugglings . . . motoring . . . walnut chocolate fudge sundaes and bad booze . . . motoring . . . boosting, boasting . . . motoring. . . .

Overhead clinked silver goblets. The conquistadores were humming a "malagueña." From the mist about them came a glow as of mellow vineyards yielding sunny wines, and of women dancing. Below, hard lips told of sport.

Said our Elk: "I dropped in on the Yankees at St. Petersburg. Those boys clear a fortune even out of training."

The tale of sport from overhead was different. Honor and love were counters; the players risked life and joyously won death.

"Not alone a nation at play," exclaimed the surgeon. "Florida is a frontier with all the culture of the capitals. Here is a whole state being opened up, with the best accommodations! For modern improvements, New York's got nothing on it."

"And they ain't forgot religion," added the grey man with the tremulous nose. "They just put up a church in De Land, cost $300,000. You bet I bought all the lots I could in a town like that. Where they spend money on a church, they're going to stick. A swell church means business."

—Our Mission was builded by volunteers from the old Settlements elsewhere. They were not paid, of course; but we had to shoot many infidel natives who did not understand

why we wanted to build so fair a church in a land that was not ours. Yes, many were killed and some were tortured. There is no room for infidels. We let the gold go home for the greater glory of our Gracious Queen.

"Well," cried I, emptying my mug of legal beer, "Florida is certainly a hum-dinging first-class show of American progress."

"It's enough to make you proud," said the Elk.

"—and rich," smiled the sly surgeon.

"Why, in Jacksonville every guy in town's got to wear a big button—and if he don't, you just bet he gets into trouble. It's yellow and on it is printed in red [those are old Spain's colors, you know]: WE ARE BELIEVERS IN JACKSONVILLE."

—We are believers in God, came clearly from the rafters.

1925

9. TWO FACES

In the literary office of a certain magazine there is a vast table piled with books. "Mostly junk," the editor will explain. My hand feathers the outskirts and picks a volume with title: "Calvin Coolidge. His First Biography." I am not permitted to speak of it here. Nor shall I linger wistfully over the so symbolic circumstance that a book about a living President should be a thing void of ideas, vile in composition, rancid, and false in spirit. Within its covers, I found the portraits of two faces: one of the President and one of the President's mother. Thereby hangs my tale.

She was beautiful. She looks out at you in a black dress of satin, sterncuffed in white, high-collared, with a cameo at the throat. The hands lie demure in the lap. The hair is drawn tight and sideways to the ears. She looks out at you, not so much from the frontispiece of a book as from New England.

She is impressive. The sharp small chin is firm. The mouth is pursed, its prim lips faintly flexed into a downward frown. The nose is straight. It has delicacy; its nostrils seem to quiver not from emotion, but from restraint of emotion. Under the plastered hair is a forehead high and ample: a square forehead which is the feminine form of the stern unsubtlety of pioneers. It holds a mind serene through exclusions, correct through lack of doubts. The eyebrows are straight as a whiplash. Above them the flesh puckers like a girl's, ere the forehead's rigor claims it. But the eyes are deep-set as in some dark seclusion.

They glower. Their gaze is reproof. And their sight is a shadow. Pain lurks in them, muted and proud, and constant. There speaks a virtue assumed, a mastery willed: almost a habitude of judgment. The eyes dominate all. Under the girlish brows with their faint fleshliness, above the exquisite nose, within the contour both fragile and brittle which the folded hands whitely enhance, these eyes are paramount. Tenderness turns hard; frailty assigns itself master; weakness wills itself mighty. The result is a transformation. This face, so gracious in its elements, gives for its final word inhospitality and shutness. The result, in more personal terms, is Calvin Coolidge.

His face is the response to his mother's. She was the obscure farmer's wife in the Connecticut River Valley. There, as with countless other women, her loveliness had its begrudging bloom. Winters long as a siege, summers of swift fever, the inclement lordship of Puritan ideals, made her astringent. Weather attuned to will hardened this flesh and drew the spirit down to the sure rigor of material affairs. Virtue became a saying of Nay and an economic cunning. Poetry took property for symbol. And so at last, on a certain

Fourth of July, this daughter of New England gave birth to Calvin Coolidge. Not she alone. A whole decadent Puritan tradition gave birth to him; fathered his spirit; molded his memorable face.

The little man waxed great. And as he grew, his face became the caricature of his mother's fairness. It is a caricature horrible in its significance, superb in its logic.

Chin, mouth, nose, brow, eyes of Calvin Coolidge are children of the splendors strangled in his mother. Her face already is this twilight, is a recession of splendors. Her features speak but greyly an ancestral greatness. Moral power, will, devotion, chastity, singleness of vision, bore this woman. But the essence of their means to life made the mind intense to the exclusion of content; made the beauty neurotic; made the virtue shut. Made, inevitably, their own culminant death whose Person now presides the American lands.

The chin of Calvin Coolidge has grown pointed, out of all proportion: it is a shallow, contentless thrusting. The lips have almost disappeared. The mouth is a crease of shrewd, complacent purpose. The fold of resolution beneath his mother's nose becomes a dugout of meanness. The nose itself is bulbous, perhaps with too much half-baked nutriment: it is a proboscis of forwardness unchallenged along the path which the canny eyes select from all the paths of the world. The forehead is blown into a windy conch, unruffled and unfilled save with the echoes of dead covenants. It crowns the face like a seashell; and the face itself becomes, beneath it, a pucker of soft parts like some naked creature peering forth for food. The head, indeed, is the Rhetoric of absence. The face is the expression of an immaculate instinct for sure and mean details.

Again, as with his mother, the man's eyes give the key. They have lost the tragedy of hers. They have flattened, hardened, and come out to the surface. They do not, from a secret depth, glower upon a hostile world: but have pressed, with a twist and a leer, to Victory. They twinkle. They have the lasciviousness of cold possession. They are the logical eyes of the battener on nullities: the eyes of the democratic politician.

So, as Calvin Coolidge, professional legislator, might declare: The Nays have it. Here is a face at last, ultimate and stripped to the model of a will like a machine. A face where no dream lingers beyond the dreams approved by a smug world: a face which no thought troubles that has no answer in the current coinage: a face that knows not passion, unless it be charted and chartered in the Statutes. The mother's frown is gone with the conflict it expressed. Here, in lieu, is a smirk. All the realms of spiritual risk which her men, good pioneers, to such good purpose barred, have here stayed out, indeed. A race's turning of its ideal power into the body of Success becomes this face and body, stripped to cunning, instinct with the spirit of acquisition. The symbol becomes a man; the man becomes a symbol. He crawls up the greased ladder of public honors. He becomes a leader and an idol, in whom the mob can worship its own meanness. . . .

1926

10. THE DRUG ON THE MARKET

It is prevalent and poisonous. And the land is proud of it. Its manufacture is a huge industry; its sale is a popular art. Billions of dollars are spent in making it: millions more go to the appurtenances of its use: and billions are paid in wages to men and women who devote their lives, openly, to its production, distribution, upkeep. The states all license it, turning a tithe of the wealth spent for it by our people to their own coffers. Great magazines and newspapers grow

fatter with its advertisements. Some papers, indeed, are entirely given to its commercial and esthetic aspects. And no publication, however ethical in editing its columns, however adverse to such drugs as coffee or tobacco, refuses to display its blandishments for money.

All America lives under its influence, and does not suspect that it is enslaved by a drug. "Shows" are planned yearly in great towns to propagate its sales and sing its praises. Special sections of the dailies detail its progress. Schools teach the beginner how to enjoy it. And everywhere ordinances and officials tune the whole life of the land to the needs and habits of those who use it.

It comes in varieties of kind which display distinct differences in expenditure of money. And these gradations have a truly hierarchic value. In a democracy where castes are vague, where money-power has few manifest badges of dress or standard of living; where, indeed, millionaire and clerk go to the same movie, read the same books, travel the same roads, and where intellectual distinctions must be very carefully concealed, the conspicuous uses of this drug have become a standard of social status. The lowest classes aspire, first of all, to earn the means of *visibly* possessing it. When they have risen so far, they may be said to have a foot on the first rung of the Ladder of Success. Thence, they are urged, instructed, exhorted, by advertisement, editorial, numberless methods of herd pressure, to progress upward. It is neither uncommon nor unworthy to mortgage a farm or keep it bare of such luxuries as furniture and books, in order to purchase a more showy form of the drug: one whose effects are swifter and whose price is higher.

Like all drugs, this one has estimable virtues. Its effect is great on the motility of man, when used in moderation. It is a synthetic product. It is not found in a state of nature, but must be concocted; although, of course, from natural ingredients both mineral and vegetable. I do not know how man first came to put it together. Probably his love of new combinations led him. I doubt whether the incentive to increase our mobility on earth was there at the beginning. (The thing, by the way, was invented in Europe; and in Europe, largely still, it is controlled within the limits of good use.) But America soon transformed it from a delicate ornament to the mastering instrument it is today. It increases man's power to move things, and to move himself. It increases his power to see things. It opens up to him stretches of the world he might elsewise never reach: communities of action and intercourse with other men whom he might elsewise not come near enough to work with.

This virtue of the drug is a positive contribution. It makes it not unworthy to be placed in man's esteem beside other concoctions long known and loved. Alcoholic drinks, for instance, with their heat-making, cheer-making, fat-making, nerve-relaxing power: tobacco, which is a subtle sedative to mind and stimulant to nerve: coffee and tea which cheat fatigue: opium, morphine, cocaine, ether, by means of which men and women are helped across the crises of the body without the drain of too great suffering.

The drug's most typical and most desired effect is the sense of *self-motion*. The user feels that he is "on the go." The faith that he is covering ground or getting somewhere (although that "somewhere" be of no intrinsic value) is, of course, the type of morbid rationalization common to all addicts of all poisons. The sensation of flight is the main matter. The drug is a means of physical escape. It becomes a symbol of psychological escape.

Now, "progress" is an American superstition whose chief feature is movement. To progress, you've got to move on: you've got to be perpetually passing from what *is* to what will never, never be—since as soon as *that* is, it also must be passed. This superstitious tic is potently flattered by the effects of our drug. From being a means of motion and escape, it has grown into a symbol of progress. It began by cajoling our nerves. It ends by cajoling our ideals.

Of course, this subtle transition from use to abuse is generic of all vices. Far too soon, the ill annuls the good which tempted us into the path leading to addiction. But with older narcotics, men have had time to learn the dangers hidden in delight. They have elaborated mental and moral mechanisms to protect them. It is deemed a "social vice" in Europe to drink too much liquor. Men almost everywhere have become "afraid" to employ opiates without the doctor's sanction. Sometimes this instinct of defense hardens into law. America, for instance, as befits a timid land, was armored by Constitutional Amendment against the ravages of a mug of beer, against the blight of a little glass of wine. (This may not be known to the reader, who can verify it by consulting any lawyer.) The instinct of self-protection is naturally strong in the small and the weak. This makes it all the more amazing that America has developed no defense, and no awareness of the need of defense, against the holocaustic uses of this drug on our market.

The reason is, that we have not yet had it long enough. The lapse from use to abuse has been too subtle and too short. And the reason is, also, that there has been confusion between the sensory effects of the drug and what Americans consider their ideals. The notion, for instance, of bare movement as value—is this, indeed, a human value or is it the delusion of a drug fiend? or the idea of utilitarian progress whereby all present life is successively sacrificed to a never-reached tomorrow? or the standard of measuring worth which makes man neglect himself and give his love only to the accumulation of dead external objects? It might well be argued that such "values" as these are the results of a drug habit, rather than the spiritual traits of a Great Republic.

The key to the popular appeal of this narcotic is, then, an induced sense of flight—idealized into the delusion of "progress." The addict becomes nervous and restless. He hungers to "progress" with his drug to help him move; and also he aims to heighten the outward splendor of the drug itself, so that the world may judge his "progress" in the world by it. Battening on change, he dares not stop. He must go on moving. And since even motion can become a constant almost as steady as rest, he must be forever changing his pace of motion. His life must be accented motion—ever irregularly accented. And change, from being a means, becomes an end.

Now follow other results. Swift movement, increasing the extension of our sight, enfeebles the intensity and quality of what we see. With the delusion of seeing more, we see less: with the delusion of unfolding more miles of the world, the span of living shrinks. The drug is foe to meditation, to solitude, to careful and loving observance. It frees the addict from resorting to himself in the crises of dullness: he need not explore the devious trails of his soul, when so many, wider, asphalted roads are beyond him. But meditation and leisurely observance are the traits whereby life becomes real.

In lieu of them, we have the bare experience of passing. Moments are not dwelt in; they are overcome. The "present" of life, no longer a treasure to be mined, is a barrier to be vaulted. But moments and places are real to us only in so far as we put ourselves *within* them. Now with this drug the converse happens: we take ourselves *away* from moments and from places. Moments and places grow void. Life becomes a succession of zeros.

Within each soul there is a kindred process. The drug

is a substitute for thought and for emotion. So hallucinatory is its sensuous effect of "progress" that the addict literally *moves out* of his troubles. Are troubles not matter for thinking and for feeling? And do not thought and feeling require some rest—or at least some constant, unconscious motion—in order to be enjoyed? This drug of ours, spelling flight, flight from the hour and the place upon us, brings flight as well from the problems of life that fill the place and the hour. . . . Remains only motion . . . only the emotion of motion.

The drug's use is a short cut: and nothing is more dangerous and sterile. A short cut through time, through place, through life—leads to death! Life is swift, and the value of life is the value of every moment. A machine, an act, a drug which makes us leap this moment is murderous. Alas! here, too, there has been confusion between the effects of a narcotic and what we consider our ideals. For we are proud of the short cuts with which we clutter and sterilize our world. Newspapers, telephones, radios, are imperious short cuts, demanding that we devote an ever-increased portion of our days to details and surfaces of men and matters we might well ignore. The use of this drug eliminates the ground between the "beginning" and the "end." But both "beginning" and "end" of anything are abstractions, darkness, death. The *between* is life. So the use of the drug lessens life.

It has another, curious effect upon the user: a subtle one, hard to grasp—but not without importance. It lifts the user from the embrace of living things, setting him, half insulate, in a machine. To walk the earth, to sail the sea, to ride a horse or plod behind one in a buggy—to drink the heady brews of grain or vine—these are all ways of touching life. But to box oneself into a thing of iron, and race through the verdurous world as fast as ever one may, is to get almost out of life, even without the common aid of accidents. It is to exile oneself from the sensuous growing earth which is our ultimate food.

Now, to move is to overcome resistance. And to overcome resistance *too well* is to avoid life's loveliness which dawns on men only when they are forced to pause. The perfect, unconscious mechanism of an animal knows neither thought nor beauty. The child begins to think and to enjoy, only when life stops him. This drug of ours induces a child's heaven—or an animal's. It makes things too easy: seeing the world, seeing folks, seeing your girl, too easy. And man can stand the adversity which bores him, far better than a lubricated ease. To see an endless series of places is to value none of them. To see too many folks is to see too little of oneself. For the value of things lies, in great extent, in the amount of ourselves we must put forth to get them. Take love-making, for example. Resistance and time are so necessary for its right consummation that even the brutes know it. Make the tryst between the boy and the girl too facile and too swift—eliminate the hazards of invading little brothers in family drawing rooms—and the couple will very soon prefer the delights of a hard-won brown bottle to the delights of each other.

So the vicious circle rounds. And the drug whose use was to bring increased power and joy turns its addict impotent and sad. This specific concoction has done much to make of us a gloomy people. Or, perhaps, it was the other way. Being a lugubrious lot, we have fallen victims to a drug which turns us even worse: making us roll along on lines of motion far less fancifully pleasant than the devious ones induced by alcohol.

Unfortunately the drug's ill results have not yet made us sick of it. We are merely demanding more of the same. Swifter mobility to kill time and trouble; more elaborate and expensive emptinesses to fill empty holidays. In the

American town, the effect is sadly visible. The streets are cluttered with the wheeled instruments in which the drug is used. And the air is fouled with its miasmic fumes. And the poor folk who took to it in order to be free, in order to know flight from trouble, find themselves grooved into traffic lines, manacled by traffic laws, crawling like slaves under the haughty signals of the cop.

Verily, the hour calls for some great solver of problems to save the nation. I think at once of Mr. Henry Ford. He has been so successful in solving our transportation problems. He has earned so much wealth in that beneficent task. And he has shown himself so eager to go on serving his people— if possible, in bigger, better ways! Has he no scheme for curbing the evil uses of this Thing which causes our noble countrymen to roll along the landside in a complacent stupor?

1927

TWO: PORTRAITS

I. MEN

II. AMERICAN TRAITS

III. IDEAS

I. MEN

1. RANDOLPH BOURNE

A girl friend of his mother snatched him away from the wise arms, to hug and coddle him; let him slip and dropped him from the balcony where they were standing. This is the origin of the sad mutilations with which Randolph Bourne went through life. The tale has the true depth of a legend. The affection of a young woman, clumsy with unskilled love; the desire to share, to help, perhaps—and as aftermath, the lifetime of agony and visible disgrace. This is the sort of irony that Randolph relished, and bore with him through the world. Beholding him, one felt that his deformity somehow was not the profane traditional one: it was rather the stigmata of some miscarried loveliness.

He was very deformed. Not alone was he dwarfed and hunchbacked: his face was twisted, he had a tortured ear, his color was sallow and his breathing was audible and hard. He walked in a cape that hid him. He took a chair for the first time in your presence, let fall the black shroud about him, and revealed a form so mangled that you despaired ever to find sufficient ease for the sort of conversation his immediately brilliant mind demanded.

But the magic of Randolph Bourne was not separate from his poor body, and at once you knew this. This is why, in writing of his splendid spirit, it is meet to dwell upon his misery. Within half an hour, your discomfort was gone—so miraculously gone that your mind was prone to look about for it. But whenever, in the future, awareness did return of the grotesque shape in which this spirit was imprisoned and was doomed to walk, it was intellectual altogether: the mind needed to stir the senses with the thought of it, while the senses moved in full ease within his presence.

It was Randolph's eyes and hands that brought about the wonder. The hands were exquisite, gentle, quiet. They seemed made for such clear profundities as the playing of Bach: they bespoke his style—the caress of his ruthless understanding. And they flowered from his body with the inevitable irony of all his being. The eyes were penetrant, studious. There was a reticence in them, after the adventure, not before it. You knew from them that Randolph Bourne was wise, and that he had withdrawn some subtle spirit of himself forever from gross contacts: that he had learned to see and to experience without the ill-focused turmoil of too close contacts. So surely consonant were his hands and eyes with what he said, that the body became a sort of Christian *Lest Ye Forget*—a sign to thrust you back into the humiliating coil of life, from the high freedom of his discourse.

All of him had this counterpoint. His spirituality was shrewd; his warmth was ironical and measured; his gaiety was leashed; above all, his direct caustic wit was barbed with a general indulgence. The body had forced on him this complex economy of emotion. And there ensued from it a splendor of free energy for every challenge of liberty, for every accolade of the creative life. This little man, indeed, so celled in a crushed body that even breath was hard, became a rounded athlete of the spirit, as none, perhaps, of us who have survived him. The loss of Randolph Bourne is a shadow that lengthens. . . .

1925

2. CHARLES CHAPLIN

a.

Chaplin's eyes are a blue so darkly shadowed that they are almost purple. They are sad eyes; from them pity and bitterness look out upon the world. They are veiled: while the man moves forward with irresistible charm, his eyes hold back in a solitude fiercely forbidding. No one who sees the eyes of Chaplin can feel like laughing. They are the one part of the man which does not show in his pictures.

For fifteen years these eyes have looked out on Hollywood. Much nonsense has been written about this suburb of Los Angeles, which is itself a suburb of the country. America reviles it as an indecent stranger somehow lodged in its midst, or romanticizes it into a scene from the "Arabian Nights." But, of course, Hollywood is no worse a place than any provincial city of our land; nor better. Hollywood's producers are typical money men; its directors are typical professional men; its actresses and actors are typical girls and boys. Its army of mechanics, craftsmen, engineers, are the usual American sort: grime them up a bit, lower their wages, and they would fit in to your town garage. Hollywood's swarm of aspirants buzzing about the lots are typical floating seed of the American jungle: the wastrel seed that finds no soil to root in, whether it rots near home or blows away. Only in one respect is Hollywood unusual: its girls are really as fair as all girls would like to be.

Hollywood is the perfect mirror of banal American success. Ordinary souls dream extraordinary dreams—in the way of ordinary souls. And in Hollywood the dreams come true. Here is uncounted money, here is glamour, here is the exact mechanical production of that ideal to which success means a show. And Chaplin, with those frightening eyes of his, which almost no one ever sees, looks out upon this world, his home since he was twenty-four. There is another world which he looks in upon: the grey, grinding London of his childhood. He loves the London slums; for these slums were his and they are in his heart. But on his mother's side the blood of Chaplin is half gypsy. Through her, whom he brought from England to live near him on the Coast, yet another world lives in him: a world of meadows and irresponsible laughter.

In the city of success he carries with him the taste of the London slums. But even there he was not at home: even for that sad past which formed his body and his mind he has a grim, ironical refusal—since there, too, the gypsy in him was a stranger.

This counterpoint of sympathy and denial is our first clew to the man. The drawing room of his house is packed with bibelots, pictures, bric-a-brac, sent him by the admiring splendor of the world. Here are tributes from Chinese mandarins and from the royalty of Europe. And here, too, on the wall, hang a few colored lithographs of Whitechapel and Wapping. Chaplin loves to take these from the wall. They depict streets that are like some cold inferno, in which the people stir slowly like souls stripped of all save the capacity to suffer. Watch his eyes as he looks at this picture of his childhood world. They are at once too soft and too hard. The emotions of understanding and of refusal are separate in them. In this room I once sat with Chaplin while the Comte de Chasseloup exhibited to us what are perhaps the most terrible photographs in the world: close-ups in progressive detail of tortures and executions which he had collected in China. We looked on the deliberate process of men being carved alive—as a butcher quarters a calf. We saw faces black with the horror of their pain, and then white with the relief of death. And in Chaplin there was the same counterpoint of feeling. His eyes took in the tremendous pity of these portrayals of man's way with man. Suddenly his eyes hardened; he jumped up, and his mouth was cruel. "There's humanity for you! By God, they deserve it. Give it to them! That's man. Cut 'em up. Torture 'em! The bastards!" . . . The pity he had felt was intolerable to him. He summoned hardness to wipe it out: to save himself from this danger of being overwhelmed. Chaplin does not wish to give himself to any emotion, to any situation, to any life. Life draws him too terribly for that. Whatever he feels must immediately arouse its opposite; so that Chaplin may remain untouched—immaculate and impervious in himself.

With this same reserve he moves through Hollywood. He is no recluse. His secret apartness is far subtler than that. He frequents the Coconut Grove at the Ambassador, where the slightly decayed youth of the Coast ferments in dance. He sits for hours in the smoke of his friend Henry Bergman's restaurant on the crowded boulevard. He goes to parties—to those of his friend Marion Davies at her Beach House, to those of William Randolph Hearst at his ranch. And wherever he goes he is the life of the crowd. He acts, he mimics, he plays, he insists on amusing and on being seen. But always there is the same immediate wavering away from the life about him and from the effect he produces. He does not give himself nor does he really take. Above all, he does not aggressively refuse any advance or emotion. He is noncommittal.

Intactness—this is the principle that best explains the balance of opposites in feeling, conduct, thought, which he sets up. He is like an atom that must journey alone through the world. The atom moves an intricate course, swerving here and there, myriadly attracted, myriadly repelled, seeming to give, seeming to respond—always remaining free and alone. A direct refusal of the world about him would mean a definite relation with it. This is not Chaplin's game. If the world draws him, he responds—passive. His course has been swerved, but he is uncommitted. He resolves every force with its opposite. Emotionally this means that he frustrates in himself every impulse of utter giving or of utter taking. He remains unpossessed and ultimately unpossessing. But this deep frustration is the key to his profound success. Do not pity him for it. He is no pitiable creature.

With sure instinct Chaplin has guided his personal life through channels where he would be always alone. He loves the world he lives in, and despises it. He does not want to change it: no man is farther from the fervor of the prophet, and yet few men have done so much to show it up as ridiculous and worthless. He does not want another world. He uses this one, just as it is, in order to ensure his aloneness. But, were he really alone, he would meet in the silence of himself some acceptance which would prove his unity with the world. So he courts the world, and dwells in it, in order to frustrate such a possible self-encounter.

There was a time when Chaplin seemed to me a kind of fallen angel: an angel cursed by God with all human feelings and with the inability to fulfill them: cursed with the gift of evoking laughter and love and with no power to take laughter and love to himself. But this was a sentimental error. The inordinate tenderness of the man, his gentility and grace, are checked by his native rejection of the self-bestowal to which such qualities must lead. Hardness and ruthless egoism are as primal in him as the generous emotions. He refuses to be lost in any synthesis of love. He must remain the atom of himself. And in his perfect poise *between* the forces of the world— the poise of opposites—this is what he remains. And this is what he wants.

What he wants, Chaplin has infinite resources for getting. The shrewd technique of his art is but a phase of the same art in his life. This is the man who, when he was first approached with an invitation to enter pictures—untried and unknown—jacked up the initial offer of seventy-five dollars a week to twelve times that figure. "I saw they were anxious," he explained to me. "When I said to them, 'I think I'll study philosophy; I don't care for acting,' I saw them go white. That's how I knew what I was worth." And this is the man who, three years later, when Mary Pickford, Fairbanks, Griffith, Hart and himself were in danger of being shamefully exploited by the business end of the game, gathered them all together into "United Artists" and preserved a fair portion of the treasure to the men and women who were doing the work. Chaplin is endowed with consummate powers for connecting with the world. "I'd make a great banker," he once told me. He is intelligent, so intelligent that he intuitively grasps the abtruse currents of modern thought, esthetic, political, even philosophic. He is sensitive, so exquisitely that the gamut of human joy and pain plays endless responses within him. And he is passionate and earthy, a lover of good food and of women and of racy words. All these gifts naturally conspire to make him one with the world. Yet there is in him this dominant need to be one only with himself, to submit to no marriage, to let himself be lost in no union, to which his mind and sense impel him. What, in this diathesis, can he do? He can keep on moving. He can make his life a constant journey through the inconstancy of impressions which, if he dwelt with them, would bind him. He can make of his life an *escape*.

b.

The life, then, of this first master of the motion picture, is motion. His art is the treasured essence of his life. The theme of the Chaplin picture is Chaplin himself, in relation (opposition) to the world. He journeys through it, immeasurably roused, solicited, moved—yet aloof, yet intactly alone. The form of the Chaplin film is his own body, set off by the world: his body made into a mask behind which the man, all intact, goes slyly and painfully on his impervious journey. And the plot of the Chaplin film is merely some sequence of episodes in this constant opposition of himself journeying through life and never fused within it.

Of course, it is not as easy as it sounds. Precisely because his work is the incarnation of his life mood, of his life journey, its birth is a delicate issue. In the beginning there is the atomic Chaplin, cast in some role that will motivate his passage through the required number of reels. But that passage— as pawnbroker's assistant, circus fool, convict pilgrim, fireman, seeker of gold, tramp, janitor, country bumpkin, etc.— that passage must be blocked out with events. Each foot of the film is an event, an encounter between Chaplin and the world. Since the art is to be the essence of his life, it, too, like his life, must be completely *fleshed;* and must breathe! From each encounter, either with another person or with some inanimate object like a brickbat, there must rise visible and palpable the personality of the entire journey. So each event of the film must be a work of art in itself. And there must be sequence, breathing, flowing, mounting. Each event must rise into the next until the mass of events becomes a plastic music where each episode is a note. The whole tale is a motion of events to represent the journey of the man— his escape, intact, through the myriad mass of life.

The mood of the tale, being intimately Chaplin's own, is carried within him. What he must wait for is the precise scale of episodes that will form the mood. Even when the events have come to him (the particular stunts of the film), they must be weighed and measured. Where do they fit in? Do they fit in at all?

This period of gestation is painful and long. Chaplin lies

abed an entire morning. He broods, measuring the tentative "body" of his tale by the inner sense of what he wants. This sense is infallible, but it is inarticulate save as the completed picture will be its articulation. Chaplin does not know, he has no words for saying, the exact timbre and gamut of physical actions that will express this particular body of his life journey. The picture will be his knowing. . . . Meantime, several miles away, his studio awaits him. It is a charming lot, several acres in size. Here lives Kono, the remarkable Japanese factotum who manages Chaplin's personal journey through life, who serves as a kind of intelligent oil against the inevitable frictions of the inevitable encounters with stranger and friend. Here wait his general staff: Alf Reeves (who has been with him since music-hall days), Harry Crocker, Carl Robinson, Henry Bergman, Henry Clive, Roland Totheroh—possibly the director Harry d'Arrast, who once worked with him in Crocker's present place and who remains his chum. All these men are distinguishably sweet, sensitized, intelligent, aloof in the crass Hollywood world. (That world is full of workers who carry on after they have left him, bearing the stamp he gave them—Menjou is a celebrated instance.)

The staff all feel the tension of their chief. The strain, indeed, is so great that there are men in the "industry" who could not stand it. At last, possibly around noon, Chaplin arrives. The instant has come when he is ready. He has dropped into his clothes, stepped into the limousine which waits all morning at the door, with the engine throbbing. He is hatless, tieless, and his vest is open. But the clothes are the most dapper product of the London tailor. He wears them, at work, like a gypsy. Even in this detail there is the meeting of the Chaplin opposites. Gypsy and exquisitely groomed young gentleman delete each other: leaving, as ever, merely Chaplin.

He joins his crowd in the little bungalow on the lot, where lunch is served and where he has his dressing rooms. Tentative moments of the film are brought up, altered, discarded, readjusted. Chaplin paces, his face hard, his mouth half open, his eyes far off in himself. Infinitesimal details are studied, rehearsed, discussed; gags, postures, meanings, properties, business. Walking up and down, the little man holds in his head the film's inexorable rhythm, the inner logic of its growth. As the ideas fly back and forth, in words and mimicry, Chaplin brings them to the measure in himself: rejects or accepts.

There may be months of this. Nothing seems to be going. The corps of workers champ and chafe. Chaplin moves with his preoccupation through his habitual life: parties, dinners, wanderings about town, swift flights with friends, long hours alone. At last certain scenes, having withstood the critical pause, seem certain. Carpenters and plasterers get busy. Sets rise on the lot. Chaplin wanders about among the hammers, alone or with his group: judging, silent, suddenly exasperated, lost in a new angle of vision—giving sharp orders that destroy the work of weeks. A shot that cost a long journey to location (and $50,000) will be ruthlessly scrapped. Later a scene will be repeated a literal hundred times; and, if the fifty-ninth time was right, each detail of it will be so clear in Chaplin's eye that he will reproduce it for the camera. Finally, a thousand feet of photography will be collapsed into a yard so pregnant with the essence of the event that it will move, intact like the man himself, through all the world.

This perfect consciousness of Chaplin as craftsman would, of course, be less conspicuous in any other place. (In Paris, for instance, where men work with words and with pigment as Chaplin does with human masses, his métier is understood as merely the highest form of a common practice.) But Hollywood is a usual American town—not a capital of artists. And the studios of Hollywood confine their precision and consciousness to problems of mechanics and finance. They are monuments of esthetic vagueness, intellectual nullity, artistic hit-or-miss. The usual story, to begin with, is an externalized contraption put together by the combined shrewdness of half a dozen wholesalers parading as writers, scenarists, directors and producers. The actors have no accurate technique. The directors have no conscious control. In such a combination the chance artist is helpless and lost. When a scene is "pretty good," it is shot. And the result is the kind of flat approximation that feeds the dreams of the millions. But by the time Chaplin gets ready to rehearse a scene its precise place in the architectonic of his tale has been measured, even as the theme itself has been measured in his life. And as he rehearses, he knows what happens. I mean that he knows the interplay of muscle, mass, space, and their focal value as the camera lens will catch it. He is no expert in photography. In his especial choreography he is supreme.

All organic life has a commanding, individual rhythm: the beat of a heart, the slant of a mind, the indecipherable stir of cells must go with that rhythm. Such an organic rhythm besets the consciousness of Chaplin, incarnating his subjective mood into a story. At the beginning, he knows the rhythm only. He has to grope for the episodes to flesh it. But when he finds his episodes he knows what he wants. And at the moment of shooting a scene he knows how to recall what he wants. And he can do this because, from the twist of a leg to the flicker of an eye, he knows how everything is done.

c.

All this, however, has not explained what it is that Chaplin is doing. His work may be the incarnation of his personal escape from those trammels of life to which his sensitivity and capacity for love expose him; his way of escape may be shrewd with all the shrewdness of his cockney-gypsy genius; and the esthetic expression of that journey of his soul may be done with consummate craft. Yet the inward value of the entire adventure is not yet clear.

We can best approach the significance of Chaplin's art by considering another constant presence (besides himself) in his meditations on the story, in his conferences with Crocker and d'Arrast, in his rehearsals, in his final prunings, acceptances and rejections. That other presence he always alludes to by a simple name. He calls it "they." "They" is the public. "They" collaborates unceasingly with Chaplin. "They" has the final veto over even Chaplin himself.

Of course, a similar "they" seems to preside over all the lots of filmland. But in the usual studio there are a number of men pawing over the platitudes of the human race in the deliberate effort to concoct from them a pattern which the public will pay for. Chaplin, too, is a child of the theatre. And there is no theatre without a "box" in front. But in the studio of Chaplin there is, most really of all, a man of the people—a cockney, a gypsy, a music-hall fellow—who looks into the eyes of the world as into a mirror, in order to see *himself* more objectively and sharply. So it is that, coming to Chaplin's public, we return to the man. By means of this reflection we can see at last, in clarity, how he manages his escape and what it is which, behind the mask of "funny-legs," goes its immortal journey into the heart of the world.

Chaplin looks upon the world of today. He sees failure: poverty, agony, disease, chaos, fear, pitiful passion, pitiful love. He sees success: deceit, garishness, tinsel, boast, disillusion. He sees his own past in London—his mother in the drab uniform of the poorhouse. He sees his own victorious present. He sees and feels too much. He is afraid of being lost in this world. There is a kernel of him that is neither this success nor this failure: a core in the man that can dance its own life if only it may remain alone. That is why he must escape; why he must look on all the invading world as an enemy and must hate it. Chaplin is a hard and princely fellow: his brow is strong, and his jaw and his mouth. But the modeling about his temples is girlishly tender, and the deepest spirit in his eyes is a retreating terror. He is afraid for that core in him of grace and loveliness and youthful dance. To protect it, he will fight—he will employ all his skill, all his hardness.

Now consider Chaplin's public, which is the modern world. In each breast live grace and loveliness and wistful dream. But in the common man that personal treasure of each heart cannot remain intact. Family, business, law and war invade it. All civilization becomes a foe, trampling on this secret heart, dispersing its dream, bruising and breaking its love.

Chaplin, who has striven to keep it whole for himself, has made his fight for the world. Here, in his films, the grace and beauty of the human "atom" are visible once more. Behind the mask of Chaplin—behind the swinging cane, the ambling, painful feet, the tight drawn coat, the cocky derby hat—marches the common loveliness of man—marches and journeys as it must through a hated modern world—dissociate from social forms, shabby, despised, pitiful, poor; yet miraculously intact and miraculously triumphant.

Rousseau, I suppose, perfected this tragicomedy of the modern world, with its dualistic conflict between beauty and civilization, between love and man's habitual life. Marvelously gifted, he gave to the world its rationale for the impulse to creep back into a mythic childhood, to worship the self at the expense of the towering forms about it. As Mr. Lardner might say: "Jean Jacques started something." Charles Chaplin has finished it. (Even the cut of his comic coat recalls the romantic century—the age of Alfred de Musset.) The cult of loveliness at war with the sobrieties of life could beget no greater art than this journey of Chaplin carrying beauty untouched through an atmosphere of heavy institutions, of brickbats and policemen. French intellectual, London clerk, Chinese coolie, Mexican peon, Park Avenue child, in the common distress of their submission to a world too full of money to leave room for singing and for dancing, can gaze together at this secret triumph which Chaplin has enacted for them. His song explodes their oppressive world. His primitive refusal to "grow up" in the "respectable way" becomes the modern spirit of revolution.[1]

d.

In the old days Charles Chaplin worked not less meticulously, but a good deal faster. His theme has always been the exact transcription of the mood of his life. But when his life was simpler, the bridge to his work was more immediate. It was easier for the man to remain impervious, intact, virginally himself. The instinctive operation of his will had found no invasion too bruising or too tiring for him to repel. But he has had to pay the toll of his way; and that toll has grown great. It is hard to sustain one's solitude when one is so full of eagerness as Chaplin; and when, precisely because the world loved his aloneness, the world has done everything to destroy it. His recent struggles, not so much against the clamor of the public as against his own human need for that peace and love which can be gained only by some union with another, have made him conscious of himself. Consciousness and weariness have stood between him and his journey—slowing him and

---

[1] Arturo Mom, the Argentinian writer, tells us that Lenin once said: "Chaplin is the only man in the world I want to meet." It is a story readily believed. Chaplin's art expresses the germinal seed of the revolt—tender and ruthless, romantic and realistic—which Lenin's technique attempted to fulfill. Chaplin and Lenin—they are probably the two most potential spirits of our age. Bring them together—pure individualist and pure collectivist—into a single force, and you have a vision of tomorrow.

slowing his work, which is the expression of that journey. His hair has turned grey, and his beautiful face is lined.

"The Circus" marks the crisis. The terrible year [1] that separated its first-made scenes from the last brought a new somberness into his art. The picture on which he is at work at present is the most meditative, the most complex, the darkest story he has ever imagined. A progress like that which distinguishes the end of "Don Quixote" from its rollicking outset is manifest in his work. Chaplin is still alone; still intact. But the fight he has had to wage in order to remain so has worn him. It is the natural destiny of so passionate a man to lose himself. Thus far Chaplin has refused this death. It would mean, indeed, the death of his old gay art. It might mean the birth of a new tragic artist.

Meantime the circumstances of his career in Hollywood have conspired to perfect his solitude. Here was an artist whose theme was an essential motion: the pantomimic medium of the motion picture was there to express him. But now the motion-picture industry of Hollywood decides to talk. Chaplin, whose excellence made him solitary enough, finds himself almost literally alone.

A little more entirely than he may have dreamed, he is having his way. He is alone in his great house, alone with his few friends, who love him but who cannot really reach him. He is alone among his professional comrades, who, unlike him, have abandoned the silent picture. Chaplin has reached a goal. A goal is an end. An end can be also a beginning.

1929.

[1] The year of his trouble with his second wife, the truth about which has not been told.

3. D. H. LAWRENCE

Lawrence lived his entire life in a transition. Hence his painful and irascible temper: hence also his illuminations, exquisite and unbearable as direct contact with a nerve.

One world he had left: the world of plural "facts." He was no dupe of the parade of detailed separatenesses that clutter mortal eye. He knew that this world of things, this matter-of-fact and practical world of commonplace, was false; for he had left it for a truer. But that other world he never quite attained: the world of unity and wholeness, whereof all things are momentary foci. He was close enough to this world to be pulling away from the other: but he was not of it sufficiently to accept the world of "things" in the transfigured sense that makes things real. He was close enough to the true to win from it vision and power to illumine the "things" he fought; close enough to create a vision of them as an artist. Yet he was not of the true world of organic oneness so deeply as to incorporate himself within it and thereby to be at peace with the many.

He was always striving to organize himself in wholeness: and always failing, and always furious and exacerbated by his failures. These failures are his life, and are his books. The characters of his stories are never wholly persons in the sense of either world: the passion of the writer of his books is never wholly either illumination of his characters as organic bodies or life within the characters themselves.

Lawrence was exiled from the moderate pace of things that enact their part in the Whole unconsciously. This blessed naturalization he had left forever. He could never share the peace of the clod which knows not its share in the Life it enacts. Nor could he accept the clod, from within the realm of the conscious Life itself. The ecstasy of knowing himself part of the Whole was never quite natural for him; he never assimilated it into the processes of living. To possess that ecstasy, he had to deny the lineaments of life: he had to seek extraordinary moments. The true ecstasy of knowing the many common things of the world as the common features of life's oneness was never his.

He was imprisoned in transition. And he frantically strove to incorporate himself entirely in the world of truth by lopping off his attachments to the separatistic world that dragged him. Thus his denial of "mind," of tenderness and pity, of the feminine as contradistinguished from the female. These were qualities that seemed to hold him back near the world of "many-ness" which he hated as false. He was neither strong enough nor clear enough to know that it was his failure to fuse these qualities into wholeness, rather than the intrinsic qualities themselves, that thwarted him and kept him divided.

1930

4. HERBERT CROLY

Most men are set and long past growing before they are forty. This is true of the conspicuous and successful, no less than of the common. They have contrived, from their first impacts with the world, some attitude, trick or gesture; it works; they stick to it until they are repetitive as machines. Herbert Croly was a growing man until he was stricken; and the rate of his growth kept on accelerating with the years. This rare capacity, which toward the end transfigured him, was his true genius.

If we analyze the nature of his growth, we come close to the man, and understand what made him so sound and beautiful a being. And the first trait upon which we come is his humility. Herbert Croly was authentically humble. Not humble with the inverted pride of a Franciscan or of a character of Dostoevski's—because of raging lusts intolerable to himself which he had to flay into their opposite lest they drive him mad. Herbert Croly's humility came from a true sense of himself in the world—a sense of true proportion. In the years when I knew him, at least, he never seemed to be looking upon himself alone: always, he felt and saw and thought himself within a texture that was the world. From this proportion came sobriety and humility; and from this organic contact with life's sources, a springlike energy that kept him growing.

There was nothing, I suppose, superficially brilliant or arresting about him. He was in cool fact what Whitman romantically sang: a "divine average." By which I mean that he was a man whose pre-eminence came from the purification and exaltation of those traits that made him most like others. With the shining talents of the market place he was not lavishly gifted. The talent he had is rare in any mart: the passion for growth, the moral, intellectual powers needed for growth, and a courage in devotion to the life of growth that served him in his long fight as sudden illumination serves the romantic hero.

How differently shrewd he was from the shrewd men with whom he deliberately consorted, and whom he ruthlessly noted while, for the most part, they took scant note of him. This world of atomic egos, bursting with pride and will, and disappearing into the darkness of the mass, after their brief explosion. And Herbert Croly, beginning in the mass, groping his obscure way through a sense of brotherhood and life, into true personality, into wisdom. His first impulse was to accept. And this alone marked him off from his intellectual generation, and made his discoveries far more potential. He had a sympathy for the commonplace. His humility, deriving from his sense of proportion, made him instinctively, even intellectually, share. Here, his "averageness" ceased. For what he accepted and shared he weighed with the same quiet ruthlessness that he brought to bear upon himself. That is why, at the end, he had won a deeper vision of his world than had any of his fellows. He had begun by letting himself be part of it, refusing nothing. From within, he had scrutinized, purified—inexorably judged.

Yet, if in this spirit, temper, method, he was different from the New York in which he worked, it was because he carried on so purely an American tradition. It is true, of course, that he did not come of old American stock, both his parents having been born in Europe. But it is also true that in the making of Americans lineage is the least factor. The immigrant is potentially American: that is why he came: he is brother in spirit, if not in blood, of Roger Williams or of Franklin. Moreover, the land itself stamps the child more deeply than do his fathers. Thus, despite the European background of Herbert Croly, there was much of the Puritan about him, a great deal of the pioneer. He trekked our continent of the modern spirit "on foot," slowly and laboriously blazing his way through the American chaos. He understood creatively and creatively served it, because he had given himself to it; and this he had done because—like Emerson, like Whitman, like Thoreau, like all its deepest critics—he had faith in it.

These homespun traits, almost exactly transposed from the plane of the American forefathers, reveal the nature of his ideological growth. The man who, twenty years ago, wrote "The Promise of American Life" had been essentially one who accepted the intellectual pattern of the hour. Herbert Croly was thinking in terms, then, of government commissions with ideals of knight-errantry, of moral agencies somehow working out through legislative bodies. His way of facing the problem of the good life at that beginning would have been familiar enough to Gladstone or to Burke. But, having accepted the pattern, he applied to it a sincerity of penetration rare in any hour. His book, instead of following, became the test—and the destroyer—of its own pattern. He was feeling his way; and all of his career may similarly be termed a feeling of his way.

This trait gives the quality of his style; it lacked charm and ease because it was a process rather than a conclusion. It never flowered; it burrowed and made roots: whatever energy it evolved from its growth turned downward into deeper roots instead of blooming upward. From the standpoint of English, this is a grave defect. A written style should be a fruit, not an embryology for some future fruitage. But from the standpoint of the promise of American life, the style, like the man himself, was the very substance. His words portrayed the passage of the author slowly, circuitously through the jungle of half-decayed surmise which is the heritage of our generation. The ultimate light of what he wrote was the consequence of that passage. His words might be said to have ended with light, in contrast to most modern words which begin with glitter and end in darkness.

This book of 1910 began with a certain premise: America has the political technique and the human equipment to fulfill itself. The book studies the equipment—institutional, personal —turns back on its premise, and rejects it. The book does not conclude; it institutes. While the author writes, he grows: instead of ending, he changes. At the finale, he is free of the pattern of his hour, truly free since he has first accepted it and lived it through.

More than once, he espoused causes that seemed contradictory to the essence of the man as I later came to know him. Thus his acceptance of the War, his sponsorship of the Progressivism of Roosevelt, his apparent dedication to the Pragmatism of John Dewey. But to condemn him for this was to misjudge him by standards that did not apply. Herbert Croly was not a prophet; he was an experimental and emergent force within the body politic—the force that energizes prophecy and must precede it: he personified the gradual principle of detachment within the process of his time. He was not espousing these causes that were, indeed, denials of his essence, so much as living through them, and as growing through them. By his acceptance of the War, of the noisy and supine Progressivism of Theodore Roosevelt, of the spiritually prostrate Pragmatism of John Dewey, he was—in his own way—getting beyond them. And his humble method is, to me, the only possible promise of our nation, which, too, having accepted these false positions, with a self-knowledge and a humility like Herbert Croly's may also get beyond them.

His ultimate refusal was significant because he had lived through what he rejected. Herbert Croly went through a gamut of faiths in political reform; that is why his final doubts about the political method and his convictions on psychological and religious re-education were important. He was well versed in the instrumentalisms and technological credos of his day; that is why his recognition of the nuclear spiritual force within the person and beyond the reaches of pragmatic methods was important. He knew the principles and methodologies of modern engineering; that is why his transposition and application of them to the problem of the person were important, and why his ultimate religious interest—emergent from a practical participation in the affairs of our day—was so convincing and potential.

These later phases of his growth were clear only to those who personally knew him. He spoke of two books that he was going to write: a sequel to "The Promise of American Life" and an intimate record of his own evolution. I do not know if any part of these works was ever set down. But I feel that the quality of the man and the form of his spirit were best revealed to his friends. At night, within the shadows of his bookshelves, a release came to Herbert Croly. He was morbidly sensitive. He spoke so low that when one ate with him in a restaurant it was difficult to hear what he said. Yet to have raised his voice in a public place, one felt, would have been an outrage to the nature of this man who was, without doubt, the deepest publicist of his generation. In his own occult way, Herbert Croly had embraced the world. A kind of dogged heroism through the years had driven him to accept the crass contacts of politics and journalism. For that was the method of his philosophy: his knowing was action. But now, in the stillness of his room, his knowing became words. What he said had a luminous strength, like wine kept long. For these were words aged in the cellar of himself. The exquisite perceptions had grown strong in secret. His eyes glowed, at such times, with his words. He was relaxed. A flame burned from the hard wood of his reticence.

Like an old wine, this strength of Herbert Croly's was not aggressive. It did not come to you; you had to find the means of taking it. He had none of the prophet's and mystic's need of self-assertion or of liberation from the trammels of his time. His method was always the same humble one: to work in the substances of the day, to live his day, and slowly to go on emerging without separation from the day's humble matters.

Some men synthesize the actuality of their time. Such a one was Theodore Roosevelt, once Croly's friend. Another kind, more rare and more precious, synthesize not the day's actuality, but its promise. Such was Herbert Croly. But even within this group, he was unique. These men are likely to be at odds with their hour, and quite aloof. Their method of revelation is often the prophetic attitude which refuses all participation with the actuality which they transcend. But

Herbert Croly synthesized American promise by his acceptance of the American fact. He did not intuit his promise, he distilled it from the facts themselves. He was very far from the conventional prophet or mystic. His exquisite nerves grappled with the iron and blood of the twentieth century. What could come of this embrace of an almost feminine spirit with a body in which plunged a billion horsepower? The spirit of the man remained undriven, clear; it became the record of a slow revelation.

If we translate his career into terms of our national destiny, how does it read? America runs the gamut of political credos. America sets up its external technologies and worships in them its own infantile power. America swears by the machine, and patterns from it arts and folkways. Under highsounding slogans of pragmatism and instrumentalism, America submits to the hour—to all the miseries and tyrannies of a caste clad in the immediacy of the hour. But America will, from its experience, return unto itself; learn that there is no substitute for the strength and value that reside secretly in man, and that there is no conduit to mastery of the world other than mastery of self. America will again hear the voices of the fathers who came to create a dwelling place, not for gilded slaves of the machine, but for man—a world made new, not by mechanical proliferation, but by the growth of the spirit of man and woman.

Such was the progress of Herbert Croly, who moved through the American jungle to find himself, and in himself projected what must be the destiny of his country, if that destiny be salvation. The promise of American life has had no truer form than this life.

1930

5. SIGMUND FREUD

a.

The nineteenth century in Northern Europe was a time of Titans struggling to create worlds of their own. The medieval Catholic world had crumbled: simple or timid souls still lived in it, but for several hundred years the strongest spirits had been engaged in tearing it to pieces. This destruction was, of course, creative; was, indeed, largely the cultural work of the sixteenth and seventeenth centuries in astronomy, geography, physics, economics, mysticism and esthetics. But it was work of pioneering or analysis, rather than of synthesis. And it bequeathed to the eighteenth century, not a new world for the whole man to live in, but a miscellany of abstract, mutually discordant principles with which to begin to build it. These principles were known as laws: there were the laws of mathematics, of mechanics, of biology, of the natural and the economic man. They were all based upon the law of reason, and this was religiously believed in. The destructive centuries had not invented the faith in reason; that faith was a legacy of the Catholic world which reason, by shifting its premise, undermined. Reason, to be hypostasized, requires an unchallenged premise; in Catholic theology this premise was the revelation of the Bible; now it was to be the revelation of the human senses or of the original rightness and divinity of man. With such instruments, abstract and confused, the forerunners of the nineteenth century (Kant, Rousseau, Blake, etc.) strove to create a cosmos of their own to replace the glorious fertile world of St. Francis, Aquinas, Dante.

The period of great romantic art was ushered in; and it had many forms. In philosophy, there were Schopenhauer, Hegel, Spencer, Comte; in the novel, there were Balzac and Dostoevski; in music, there were Beethoven, Moussorgsky,

Wagner; in painting, there were Delacroix, Ingres, Cézanne; in the sciences, there were Marx and Darwin. All these men, despite immense distinctions, were of one family. They were in touch with objective reality, masters of inquiry, often discoverers in the fields from which they mined their materials. But their constructions, unlike the worlds of the great Catholic creators right down to Bach, Descartes, Racine, were the embodiments of the personal will of their creators. There is, here, no contradiction; nor were these nineteenth-century worlds less "real," because personal, or of less social use. Man is not an isolated atom. The genius who erects a world in the image of himself—if his self-search be deep and his self-mastery strong—will produce a work of universal nature. The more profound the subjective impulse, the more complete the command over objective nature in order to fulfill it. That is why the scientific realism of a Cézanne qualitatively equals that of a Darwin; why a poet like Wagner portrays the reality of Middle Europe; why an economist like Marx may write as emotionally as Isaiah; and why we find in the solipsistic verse of a Rimbaud prophecies, which science has fulfilled, of the nature and behavior of the atom.

I have needed to speak of these nineteenth-century Titans, because Sigmund Freud, whose work dates from the 1890's, is the last of their line. To understand him, we must know his family. It was a family of men moved to replace, by their own work, the broken synthesis of Catholic Europe. They were all absolutists, seeking in some genetic principle of unitary vision the pattern that God supplied in the old order. The law may have been progress and reason or (as in Dostoevski and Rimbaud) their denial; may have been will or (as in Schopenhauer) its overcoming; it may have been some genetic rule like the survival of the fittest, sexual selection, Aryan-Lutheran supremacy, class struggle, etc. Always there was implicit in the texture of these men's constructions an absolute rationalism, or the nullification of reason; a faith in the sufficiency of the senses as a report of truth, or total rejection. These worlds, risen from an abstract and absolute law, were built of materials preponderantly personal—more idiosyncratic, indeed (although the work were a book on economics), than the love lyric of any medieval poet who accepted his immersion in a common cosmic pattern.

The twentieth century will be different: its creative work will be to reconcile and integrate apparently contradictory laws by the aid of supersensory dimensions. It will be the relativistic age, in which the discoveries of the absolutists of the nineteenth century—Nietzsche and Marx, Dostoevski and Darwin, Rimbaud and Spencer—will be worked together for the making not of worlds, but of *the world*, and not less personal because socially pragmatic. To this new era, barely ushered in by men like Bergson, Whitehead, S. Alexander, André Gide, Franz Kafka, etc., Freud does not belong. But in the perspective of cultural history, he will be seen as a contemporary of Darwin, Schopenhauer, Dostoevski, Marx; and he may be known, by the fecundity of his work, as their equal.

b.

Freud began as a physician; as one seeking to heal human ills. But he found, in the dark places of the human heart, a world as personal, tragic and universal as the world of Dostoevski. The psychological system of Freud is, first of all, a great human drama. Here, in the arcana of the soul, are complex organisms: the superego, dwelling place of the fathers—conscience and tradition; the id, hinterland of the immense accumulations of instinct, habit, appetite; and between them the ego, where lives the individual will. These organisms are interacting units, from whose clash rise devious characters with strange names: cathex, complex, sex-urge, death-urge, neurosis, fixation or repression or sublimation of libido. They are all filled with the life of action; they make lyric and epic conquests of the objective world; they also interlock in secret combat or in more terrible alliance, giving forth the gamut of emotions from horror to ecstasy, and producing the many mansions of human deed from pastoral beginnings when the infant offers its prized excrement as a gift to its mother, to heights where men make philosophies and religions.

This world of Freud has complex unity. Among the welter of symptom, dream, and cultural act move the "heroes": the radical urge for life (sex and self-preservation) and the masochist-sadist hunger, born of life, for the return to death. And like all the esthetic constructions of the nineteenth-century Titans, this world has a personal savor. "The Interpretation of Dreams," Freud's pivotal work, in its revelation of a passionate individual nature may be compared with the "Confessions" of Rousseau (the father of the century), with Dostoevski's "Notes from Underground," with Volume I of "Capital," with Schopenhauer's "The World as Will and Idea," and with "Thus Spake Zarathustra." A man is speaking. He is building a system from his discoveries and observations by the use of a legitimate instrument of science. But first and last, *a man* is revealing himself. And only less intensely is this true of all Freud's books. Whether he writes of the genetic sources of Da Vinci's art (in "Leonardo da Vinci") or of a savage totem (in "Totem and Taboo") or of a slip of the tongue (in "Psychopathology of Everyday Life"), he brings himself to the construction. While with healing hand he touches the lesions of a soul, he is really carrying to these dark places a flame from his own Promethean nature.

Most men solve their inner conflicts by forgetting about them (with the magic of ready-made solutions or of drugs, sexual, mechanical, alcoholic, patriotic); some men need to create a world of their own to solve them. Marx, suffering within himself the lesion of social injustice, created a world that mankind will use as a rationale of cure for its social diseases. The humbly religious Darwin, agonized by an age of "Enlightenment" that had dissevered him from God only to marry him with chaos, forecast a biological order where the human species could begin again to find the peace of integration between its lowest and its highest parts. Freud also makes answer to a personal conflict.

He is a man who accepts the dogma of nineteenth-century science. "There is no other source of knowledge," he says, "but the intellectual manipulation of carefully verified observations, in fact, what is called research . . . and no knowledge can be obtained from revelation, intuition or inspiration." This is pure eighteenth-century rationalism. Thus armed, he goes down into the irrational depths of the soul, a chaos to be conquered. His highway is the dream; and the Freudian technique of dream interpretation by word and thought associations and by the use of symbols is one of the mightiest acts of the imagination. The domain where the dream has led him, which he calls the id, is a jungle of the lusts of human organs aprowl like wild beasts among the tropical trees and swamps of primeval habit. But Freud will not surrender to this phantasmagoric and miasmic world; he will draw forth from its flux, by means of reason, energy for the three-dimensional world of reasonable practice, and this limited world he will insist to be the one reality. It is a struggle between uneven forces, and the consequence is a psychological design (called "real") that is drenched with the passionate and heroic will of its author.

It is illuminating to compare this Freudian world with the world of Dostoevski. The novelist explores the same Amazonian jungles of the unconscious, made manifest in their most morbid extremes. He, too, has gone down, through the need of an integrating principle that shall transfigure this chaos into truth. His method is the precise opposite of Freud's. Dostoevski follows the unconscious impulse of men to its irrational source, and he accepts this source as the sole reality, finding in it his God and his values. He rejects as unreal the contradictory world of reason and all the social-moral constructs of reason. This rejected "conscious" world is dream for Dostoevski; the nineteenth-century culture built from it in Europe is false for him; and in the obscurantist ecstasy of what Freud calls the "lowest levels of the id," the Russian finds his salvation of "waking." Freud moves toward the irrational source only to reject of it what reason cannot bind; and only such energies of the unconscious as reason can draw back into a world of social conformity will he call "real." The materials of Dostoevski's art, made plastic in the great organisms of his novels, are identical with the materials of Freud's world made into the looser esthetic form of a psychological system.

Dostoevski does not succeed in his absolutist attempt to deny reality to all experience of reason: if the irrational ecstasy is man's sole waking, there is much sleep in his books, and hence their substance. The same holds with Freud. He would be the first to disclaim victory in his attempt to naturalize all the energy of the id within the domain of reason. There is much "sleep" and much darkness in his system: hence its livingness.

Time and again, Freud is led to limits where he is face to face with Dostoevski's "real"—the mystic and the occult. "It can easily be imagined," he says, "that certain practices of the mystics may succeed in upsetting the normal relations between the different regions of the mind, so that, for example, the perceptual system becomes able to grasp relations in the deeper layers of the ego and in the id which would otherwise be inaccessible to it. Whether such a procedure can put one in possession of ultimate truths [there speaks the absolutist devotee of reason] may be safely doubted. All the same, we must admit that the therapeutic efforts of psycho-analysis have chosen much the same method of approach. For their object is to strengthen the ego, to make it more independent of the super-ego, . . . to take over new portions of the id. Where id was, there ego shall be."

Freud does not admit the premise of the mystic method, which is, of course, that the cosmic lives within the individual unconscious (the id) so that the following of percepts to their source rounds man's circle to God. But Dostoevski, typical mystic in revolt against the world of reason, would not see the implication in Freud's rationalist method: if the findings of reason are universal, reason must be cosmic. This rationalist premise is also mystic, and also irrationally rounds the circle between man and God. Freud, like all the nineteenth-century rationalists, is an unconscious follower of the older, ethical Kant. Dostoevski was a conscious, and hence a more reasonable, mystic. But both groups of absolutists, in their attempt to exclude a part of man's equipment for finding truth—the one group reason, the other group organic intuition—are doomed to failure. And in Freud, no less than in Dostoevski, this awareness of limitations gives the poignant note of the Titans who are helpless to create a world against the indefeasible God who is the Whole. In all the great nineteenth-century creations, there is this discord between the will and the work. It gives to the pages of Freud a personal vibration that is not the least of their value.

c.

What of the scientific values of Freud's work? Psychoanalysis is, first of all, a therapy in the treatment of nervous and psychic disorders. Thousands of physicians, for the most part in the Central European and Anglo-Saxon countries, practice it, and seemingly with success. But therapy is the least important aspect of Freud's work. Most of the ills of personal maladjustment which the Freudian analysis may cure are symptoms of the disorder, economic, social, cultural, of the contemporary world. The right way to overcome them is to attack the disease, not its individual symbols. In this task, the light thrown by Freud on the human psyche is of great importance; the actual relief given to a few persons is immaterial. The time required by an analysis, and the expense, make the method (under our present system) available chiefly to the type of idle woman and parasitic man who are not worth saving at the price of the lengthy effort which the analyst must devote to readjusting them into a morbid world. It would really be better for the whole leisured class, who have supported so many analysts in luxury, to be converted en masse to the Catholic Church. They could all go to Lourdes, whose record of cures is vastly more varied. There is this difference, however. When a patient finds relief at a Catholic shrine, no one is the wiser: the cure has been worked in an invulnerable darkness. But when even the most useless society woman is analyzed by a Freudian, although she may not be cured, the analyst and science know something more about the human soul. Psychoanalysis as a therapy is justified, in so far as the physician is more important than the patient.

Freud, therefore, is within the tradition of his Jewish fathers, to whom Wisdom was never (as it was with the Hindus) an end to be independently attained, but the common fruit of the tree of humane living. Freud, the physician, is moved to heal the suffering of his fellows; and from this humble, socially immaterial ministration has issued a deep knowledge.

I am not qualified to judge the precise final values, as objective science, of the Freudian system. But, of course, objective science has no final values. Despite its assumption of definitive laws, the light of generations makes of the science of any epoch a mere trend or method toward knowledge. That scientific work whose path is followed farther, is good work; and here is its ultimate value. Thus the mathematical science of a Pascal or a Leibnitz is good; and in this sense, it is already clear that the Freudian technology is good. His dicta on any specific problem, such as the origin of neurosis or the setup of the psyche, may be amended. Indeed, Freud has himself refuted several of his early propositions. For instance, he used to hold that in the anxiety neurosis, the repression caused the anxiety, and his analytic experience has now taught him, as indicated in "A New Series of Introductory Lectures to Psycho-Analysis," that the anxiety comes first, and that its source is a (disguised) actual trauma. In the technique of analysis, this reversal is important. But it reveals at what deeper level than any fact or system lies the scientific value of Freud's work. Freud's vision of the soul as an organism in dynamic integration with the physical body, with the social body, and with the historic body of mankind, has given us a *method*. And by this method we have come more close than we had come before to the sources of behavior, to an anatomy of ideas and emotions. Already, the uses of the method have proliferated widely. It has shed light on the social origins of man, anthropological and cultural; and on the problems of character formation without which there can be no science of education and no science of ethics. By its fecundity, the method of Freud's psychology will perhaps prove to be as good science as the method of Darwin's biology or of the Marxian historical critique.

I have said that the least value of Freud's work is its therapy; I may amend this by saying that in therapy lie its greatest evils. Persons who go to psychoanalysis to be cured of neurosis or of a functional maladjustment, inevitably look for guiding values which anciently were given by religion. They seek *a way of life;* and the analyst is placed in the position of spiritual leader. This is not Freud's claim. He scouts all Weltanschauung beyond the scientific acceptance and ordering of the report of the senses. These rationalists are all naïve in their failure to recognize the limiting dogmatism of their creed. A measuring rod that negates what lies beyond its scope is the sternest of dogmatists. The man who disclaims any individual norm of values, and yet deals with the subtlest problems of human adjustment, implicitly accepts the values that are current and actively rejects what lies outside his measure. The patient is sick because he does not fit into the world as he finds it; the analyst who cures him helps him into this world, which means that he has set up, as the desired norm, the values of the world. If the analyst is not aware of this, his acceptance is merely the more blind and his work upon the soul of the patient the more irresponsible. This is a serious criticism to be made against psychoanalysis from the viewpoint of a world sorely in need of revolution in the domain of values. And it may well be that the maladjusted neurotic of today is closer to the norm of healthy social transformation than the neurotic whom Freudian analysis has made "fit and content" within a society of false individualism and cultural decay.

A more serious, because more philosophical, indictment is that the Freudian system (not the method) makes of mental life a region without polarity with either cosmos or individual person. The explorer Knud Rasmussen once asked an Eskimo, who lived within the ice of the Arctic Circle and whose food was the raw flesh of caribou, "What do you understand by the soul?" And Ikinilik, the savage, answered: "It is something beyond understanding, that makes me a human being." Freud, the man, would probably agree; Freud, the nineteenth century rationalist, cannot admit of this "something beyond understanding." He must draw his charts of human behavior, his maps of the mind, without allowance for this "x." But what if the "x" is needed to produce, from Freud's hypothetic id and ego, the human being? What if all Freud's analytic counters, lacking this "x," do not add up into the synthesis— the actual person? "The id," says Freud, "is the whole personality and the ego is within it." But Freud's id is a chaos of instinct and desire, timeless and spaceless, from which by definition all cosmic connection is excised. How does it manage, out of its anarchic tidings, to throw up the ego and the superego with their cultural cosmic sublimations? Where is the forming factor? Dostoevski, who finds God at the irrational and subnormal source, has a more logical explanation. Jung, the Swiss psychologist, although he lacks Freud's intellectual genius and although his work is not, like Freud's, a great esthetic body, is more logical, calling the id the "collective unconscious" and finding there the cosmic seed that can explain the human fruit. You can insert no new element, says Whitehead, in an evolving organism. It must be there at the beginning. Freud, in his rationalist refusal to allow within the id, at least hypothetically, the mystic "x" which can alone explain the flowering from the muck of the intellectual and esthetic capacities of man, meets the tragic fate of all rationalists whose ultimate syllogism proves the irrationality of the rationalist dogma.

But whatever the reader judges to be the validity of the Freudian system or the virtues of his own use of his method, he must know, as he reads the books of Sigmund Freud, that he stands within the presence of true human greatness. Freud, indeed, is one of the supreme intellectual heroes of our time: one of those men who make life more livable for us all through the fact of their existence. In his writings, we sense the heroism of his effort, armed alone by faith in reason, to conquer cosmic continents. We think of the first Spaniards, exploring with the blunderbuss and a Cross, yet giving the Americas to man. Freud, also, with a faith and weapons

equally foredoomed, has discovered a new world which, by
outliving him, will make him immortal.

1934

6. SHERWOOD ANDERSON

One must approach the stories of this storyteller in the
spirit of reverence, in the spirit of mystery—as one approaches
the child. Let the critical come after. If one begins by analyz-
ing Sherwood Anderson, one will not receive him; and all
one's analysis will go for naught. Let him lodge in us un-
grudgingly; not till then let our intellectual questionings have
play.

For his tales are a testimony; and they testify to the still
infantile revelation of Our America. What would have happened in Europe, if the naïve confessionals of convert Gaul
and Frank and Goth had been analyzed before they were
accepted? Anderson's books are a relation of the search for
fresh religious values; a groping toward an Apocalypse in our
own inchoate terms. Woe to us if we do not nurture this act
in the childlike simplicity of the man who gives it!

We shall create a Scripture in our land. And of the stuff
of Scripture are the glowing songs of "Winesburg, Ohio," "A
Story Teller's Story," the subsequent volumes. Scripture they
are not. They are not hard, clear, strong enough for that.
They are to our new Scripture that shall be, possibly, as were
the lost Songs of Miriam to the subsequent Books of Moses;
as the pre-Vedic psalms to the Rig-Veda; as the stammering
testimonies before St. Isidore of Christians from the Rhine
to the Guadalquivir, to that medieval Scripture of Abélard,
Anselm, Aquinas. They are source, a living inchoate source.
We must let them speak in us and for us, in order to grow
beyond them.

If we fail to accept them, America will turn against them. There are already signs of this revulsion—weakness turned into bravado—in the shrill gestures of young-old men like Ernest Hemingway. We shall have to spew out this false maturity; we shall have to go back and *live through* Anderson in order to grow beyond our childhood.

From the molder heap of nineteenth-century America rise flames of longing and dance a moment in the air. Then they fall back into the smoke, lost, fetidly lost. There is still too much damp muck for the divine bonfire which America shall be. We cannot yet burn. We can get ready to burn.

Such is the burden of Sherwood Anderson's books; they are a playing of wistful flames over the muck heap. There have been other flames, hardier, greater. Either they came before our modern muck heap, or they played on its edge. The flames of Thoreau, Melville, Poe, the fire of Whitman, stood clear enough away to cast light to Europe. Anderson's flame is more modest. But it is at the heart, not at the edge of the molder. It does not light Paris and London; it helps warm *us*. It helps prepare the muck heap for the great bonfire. Its value lies in its inwardness, in its humble staying.

All the tales of this storyteller are little inward-creeping tongues of fire. Anderson himself is a fragment flame flickering through America's chaos: licking, curling, dancing, smoking, fainting. He is not organic, he has no body and no eyes. He ignites nothing. He warms, he lessens the dank, he cleanses the stench of the muck heap. After, the bonfire.

When we have accepted him, we can place him; and by this means place America. Looking upon this man's nature, listening to his words, above all to the dull beat of his feet, we realize what a task this is: to make America into a holy land. Elijah and Amos wrestling with their idolaters, the Judges and Prophets swearing to force their pack of stubborn shepherds into the Word of God, had a task no harder than ours who

would make America into a luminous land. If you have doubts,
here are books to strengthen despair; if you hesitate in your
need to transcend despair, here are books to hearten you by
their songs of man's mysterious emergence.

Whence came Sherwood Anderson? and what had he?
If this be not God in his blundering step, in his blinded eye,
then God is not immanent on earth. Not intelligence, not
shrewdness, not cultural purpose, moved this man. To the
end he will be deaf, dumb, blind. The Midwest lives in his
stories but not in his knowledge of himself. He comes to
New York, a man past forty years. Can you say that he *saw*
even one skyscraper, even one person? High men, low men,
bitter men and sweet, dance in equal delirium before him. He
goes to Europe, a pilgrimage through the detritus of his own
youthful readings about Europe. So he has gone through
life: so, in a true esthetic form of faint emergence out of
chaos, he has created his tales. Creeping flames searching in
muck and drench for the dry brand, striving so wistfully hard
to catch on, to ignite!

I spoke with a sharp critic from England about "A Story
Teller's Story." He disposed of it with ease: it lacked form,
it lacked clarity of image and thought, it gave nothing of
Ohio, nothing of New York; it was vague in picturing the
associates of childhood, the transition years; it had no incisive
word on the artists encountered in the East. The European
mind could not touch the flavor of this revelation. What it
saw as muddle is search; what it saw as evasion is honest
effort.

Sherwood Anderson used to sing of the gods, the new-
old gods coming out of the corn into the streets of Chicago.
Primitive gods they were, almost phallic. Mere trunks of
power, moving; mere conveyancers of life greyly luminous
into the builded blackness of our cities. Sherwood Anderson

is such a god, himself. There must be many, ere the new Elohim grow into the new Jehovah.

1926

7. HART CRANE

I dwell in Possibility
A fairer house than Prose,
More numerous of windows
Superior of doors.

EMILY DICKINSON

a.

Agrarian America had a common culture, which was both the fruit and the carrier of what I have called elsewhere "the great tradition." [1] This tradition rose in the Mediterranean world with the will of Egypt, Israel and Greece, to re-create the individual and the group in the image of values called divine. The same will established Catholic Europe, and when it failed (producing nonetheless what came to be the national European cultures), the great tradition survived. It survived in the Europe of Renaissance, Reformation, Revolution. With the Puritans, it was formally transplanted to the North American seaboard. Roger Williams, Thomas Hooker, Jonathan Edwards; later, Jefferson, Madison, Adams, carried on the great tradition with the same tools, on the same intellectual and economic terms, that had been brought from Europe and that had failed in Europe. It was transplanted, it was not transfigured. But before the final defeat of the Puritan avatar —a defeat ensured by the disappearance of our agrarian economy—the great tradition had borne fruit in two general forms. The first was the ideological art of what Lewis Mumford calls

[1] See "The Re-discovery of America," 1928.

the Golden Day: a prophetic art of poets so diverse as Emerson, Thoreau, Poe, whose vision was one of Possibility and whose doom, since its premise was a disappearing world, was to remain suspended in the thin air of aspiration. The second was within the lives of the common people. Acceptance of the great tradition had its effect upon their character; and this humbler achievement is recorded, perhaps finally, in the poems of Robert Frost.

Frost's record ("North of Boston," 1914; "Mountain Interval," 1916) was already made when the United States entered the War; and the War brought final ruin to the American culture of "free" individuals living for the most part on farms, whose beauty Frost recorded. The tradition which had tempered the persons in Frost's poems had already, before the Civil War, sung its last high word in the old terms that were valid from Plato to Fichte. And this, too, was fitting, for the Civil War prepared the doom, which the World War completed, of the agrarian class culture. But the great tradition, unbroken from Hermes Trismegistus and Moses, does not die. In a society transfigured by new scientific and economic forces, it must be transfigured. The literature and philosophy of the past hundred years reveal many efforts at this transfiguration: in this common purpose, Nietzsche and Marx are brothers. The poetry of Whitman was still founded on the substances of the old order. The poetry of Hart Crane is a deliberate continuance of the great tradition in terms of our industrialized world.

If we bear in mind this purpose of Crane's work, we shall be better prepared to understand his methods, his content, his obscurity. We shall, of course, not seek the clear forms of a poet of Probability, like Frost. But we shall also not too widely trust Crane's kinship with the poets of the Emersonian era, whose tradition he immediately continues. They were all, like Crane, bards of possibility rather than scribes of realization. Yet they relied upon inherited forms—forms emotional, ethical, social, intellectual and religious, transplanted from Europe and not too deliquescent for their uses. Whitman's apocalypse rested on the politics of Jefferson and on the economics of the physiocrats of France. Emerson was content with the ideology of Plato and Buddha, his own world not too radically differing from theirs. Even Emily Dickinson based her explosive doubts upon the permanent premise of a sheltered private garden, to which such as she could always meditatively retire. These traditional assumptions gave to the poets of the Golden Day an accessible, communicable form; for we, too, have been nurtured on the words of that old order. But in Crane, none of the ideal landmarks, none of the formal securities, survive; therefore his language problem —the poet's need to find words at once to create and to communicate his vision—is acute. Crane, who began to write while Frost was perfecting his record, lived, instinctively at first, then with poignant awareness, in a world whose inherited outlines of person, class, creed, value—still clear, however weak, in Emerson's Boston, Whitman's New York, Poe's Richmond —had dissolved. His vision was the timeless One of all the seers, and it binds him to the great tradition; but because of the time that fleshed him and that he needed to substance his vision, he could not employ conventional concretions. In his lack of valid terms to express his relationship with life, Crane was a true culture-child; more completely than either Dickinson or Blake, he was a child of modern man.

b.

Harold Hart Crane was born in Garrettsville, Ohio, July 21, 1899. His parents, Clarence Arthur Crane and Grace Hart, were of the pioneer stock that trekked in covered wagons from New England to the Western Reserve. But his grandparents, on both sides, had already shifted from the farm to

small-town business, and Clarence Crane, who had inherited
his father's general store in Garrettsville, became a wealthy
candy manufacturer in Cleveland. Here the poet, an only
child, lived from his tenth year. At thirteen, he was composing verse; at sixteen, in the words of Gorham Munson, "he
was writing on a level that Amy Lowell never rose from."
In the winter of 1916, he went with his mother, who was
separated from her husband, to the Isle of Pines, south of
Cuba, where his grandfather Hart had a fruit ranch; and this
journey, which gave him his first experience of the sea, was
cardinal in his growth. The following year, he was in New
York, in contact with Margaret Anderson and Jane Heap,
editors of "The Little Review"; tutoring for college; writing;
already passionately and rather wildly living.

At this time, two almost mutually exclusive tendencies
divided the American literary scene. One was centered in Ezra
Pound, Alfred Kreymborg, the imagists, Harriet Monroe's
"Poetry" and "The Little Review": the other was grouped
about "The Seven Arts." Young Crane was in vital touch with
both. He was reading Marlowe, Donne, Laforgue, Rimbaud;
but he was also finding inspiration in Whitman, Sherwood
Anderson and Melville. His action, when the United States
lurched into the war, reveals the complexity of his interests.
He decided not to go to college and by his own choice returned to Cleveland, to work as a common laborer in a muni-
tion plant and a shipyard on the lake. He loved machines, the
earth tang of the workers. He was no poet in an ivory tower.
But also he loved music; he wanted time to write, to meditate,
to read. The conflict of desires led him, perhaps, to accept
what seemed a comfortable compromise: a job in the candy
business of his father.

The elder Crane seems to have been a man of turbulent
and twisted power, wholly loyal to the gods of Commerce.
He was sincerely outraged by the jest of fortune which had

given him a poet for a son. Doubtless, he was bitter at his one child's siding with the mother in the family conflict. But under all, there was a secret emotional bond between the two, making for the ricochet of antagonism and attraction that lasted between them until the father's death, a year before the son's. The candy magnate set laboriously to work to drive the "poetry nonsense" out of his boy. Hart became a candy salesman behind a counter, a soda-jerker, a shipping clerk. He received a minimum wage. Trusted employees were detailed to spy on him, lest he read "poetry books" during work hours. Hart Crane escaped several times from the paternal yoke, usually to advertising jobs near home or in New York. And at last, in 1920, he decided to break with both Cleveland and his father.

His exquisite balance of nerves was already permanently impaired. The youthful poet, who had left a comfortable household to live with machines and rough men, who had shouldered "the curse of sundered parentage," who had tasted the strong drink of literature and war, carried within him a burden intricate and heavy—a burden hard to hold in equilibrium. Doubtless the chaos of his personal life led him to rationalize the accessible tangent ease from the strain of balance which excess use of alcohol invited. Yet there was a deeper cause for the disequilibrium which, when Crane was thirty-two, was finally to break him from his love of life and to destroy him. Hart Crane was a mystic. The mystic is a man who *knows*, by immediate experience, the organic continuity of his self with the cosmos. This experience, which is the natural fruit of sensitivity, becomes intense in one whose native energy is great; and lest it turn into an overwhelming, shattering burden, it must be disciplined and ordered. A stable nucleus within the self must be achieved, to bear and finally transfigure the world's impinging chaos. Personally, Crane did not win this synthesis.

But the poet was clearer and shrewder than the man. His mind sought a poetic principle to integrate the exuberant flood of his impressions. The early poems, collected in "White Buildings" (1926), reveal the quest, not the finding. Allen Tate, in his Introduction to this volume, writes: "The poems . . . are facets of a single vision; they refer to a central imagination, a single evaluating power, which is at once the motive of the poetry and the form of its realization." But the central imagination, wanting a unitary principle, wavers and breaks; turns back upon itself instead of mastering the envisaged substance of the poem. That is why, often, a fragmentary part of a poem is greater than the whole: and why it is, at times, impossible to transpose the series of images into the sense-and-thought sequence that originally moved the poet, and that must be perceived in order to move the reader. The mediate principle, coterminous with the image logic of the poem and the feeling logic of the poet, is imperfect. The first lines of the volume:

> As silent as a mirror is believed
> Realities plunge in silence by. . . .

are a superb expression of chaos and of the poet's need to integrate this chaos in the active mirror of self. Page after page, "realities plunge by," only ephemerally framed in a mirroring mood which alas! melts, itself, into the turbulent procession. Objective reality exists in these poems only as an oblique moving-inward to the poet's mood. But the mood is never, as in imagist or romantic verse, given for and as itself. It is given only as an organic moving-outward toward the objective world. Each lyric is a diapason between two integers of a continuous whole. But the integers (subjective and objective) are almost never clear. This makes of the poem an abstract, wavering, esthetic body. There is not yet, as in the later work, a conscious substantiated theme or principle of

vision to stratify the interacting parts of the poems into an
immobile whole.

But in the final six lyrics of this volume ("Voyages")
there is the beginning of a synthesis. Its symbolic theme is
the Sea. The turbulent experience of Crane's childhood and
youth is fused in a litany to the Sea.

> . . . Sleep, death, desire,
> Close round one instant in one floating flower.

The sea, first source of life, first Mother, is death to man.
To woo it is to return to death's simple singleness. This solution from the burden of chaos is like the erotic mysticism of
D. H. Lawrence. Immersion—hence loss—of the burdenea
mystic self in perfect sexual union is a romantic myth, old
as the myth of the Sea. It satisfied Lawrence. But Crane was
intellectually too strong, and too robust an artist, to abide it.
"White Buildings" closes on the unitary theme of surrender.
But the poet is ready to begin his quest again.

In 1924, the poems of "White Buildings" written but not
yet published, Crane was living in Brooklyn, in range of the
harbor, the Bridge, the sea-sounds. . . .

> Gongs in white surplices, beshrouded wails,
> Far strum of fog horns. . . .

And now, the integrating theme came to him.

The will of Crane in "The Bridge" is deliberately mythmaking. But this will, as we have seen, is born of a desperate,
personal need: the mystic *must* create order from the chaos
with which his associative genius overwhelms him. The poem
retains this personal origin. The revelation of "The Bridge,"
as principle and myth, comes to an individual in the course
of his day's journey; and that individual is the poet. In this
sense. "The Bridge" is allied to the "Commedia" of Dante,

who also, in response to desperate need, takes a journey in the course of which his need finds consummation.

Lest the analogy be misleading, I immediately amend it. Dante's cosmos, imaged in an age of cultural maturity, when the life of man was coterminous with his vision, contains time and persons: only in the ecstatic last scenes of the "Paradiso" are they momently merged and lost. Therefore, the line of Dante's poem is clear, being forth and back in time: and the focus of the action is cogent, being the person of the Poet with whom the reader can readily graph points of reference. Crane's cosmos has no time and his person-sense is vacillant and evanescent. Crane's journey is that of an individual unsure of his own form and lost to time. This difference at once clarifies the disadvantageous esthetic of "The Bridge" as compared with that of broadly analogous poems of spiritual search, like the "Commedia" or "Don Quixote." It exemplifies the rôle played by the cultural epoch in the creation of even the most personal work of genius.

In "Proem," the poet exhorts the object of his choice—the Bridge. It shall synthesize the world of chaos. It joined city, river and sea; man made it with his new hand, the machine. Parabola-wise, it shall now vault the continent, and, transmuted, reach that inward heaven which is the fulfillment of man's need of order. Part One, "Ave Maria," is the vision of Columbus, mystic navigator who mapped his voyage in Isaiah, seeking to weld the world's riven halves into one. But this Columbus is scarcely a person; he is suffused in his history and his ocean; his will is more substantial than his eye. Nor does he live in time. Part Two, "Powhatan's Daughter" (the Indian princess is the flesh of America, the American earth, and Mother of our dream), begins the recital of the poet's journey which traces in extension (as Columbus gives in essence) the myth's trajectory. The poet awakes in his room above the harbor, beside his lover. Risen (taking the harbor and the sea-sounds with him), he walks through the lowly Brooklyn streets: but walks with his cultural past: Pizarro, Cortés, Priscilla, and now Rip Van Winkle whose eyes, fresh from sleep, will abide the poet's as they approach the transfigured world of today. The poet descends the subway that tunnels the East River (the Bridge is above); and now the subway is a river "leaping" from Far Rockaway to Golden Gate. A river of steel rails at first, bearing westward America's urban civilization ("Stick your patent name on a signboard") and waking as it runs the burdened trudge of pioneers and all their worlds of factory and song. The patterning march of the American settlers traces the body, gradually, of Pocahontas; the flow of continent and man becomes the Great River; the huge travail of continental life, after the white man and before him, is borne southward, "meeting the Gulf." Powhatan's daughter, America's flesh, dances and the flesh becomes spirit. Dances the poet's boyhood memories of star and lake, of "sleek boat nibbling margin grass"; dances at last into the life of an Indiana mother, home from a frustrate trek to California for gold, who is bidding her son farewell; he is going east again to follow the sea. ("Write me from Rio.")

There are no achieved persons in the universe, barely emergent from chaos, of Hart Crane; and this first crystallization—the prairie mother—is the first weak block in the poem's structure. Now, with Part Three, "Cutty Sark," the physical course of the poet (the subway ride has exploded into the cosmic implication of the River) returns to view, but blurred. The poet is in South Street, Manhattan, near midnight: he is carousing with a sailor who brings him in snatches of song Leviathan, Plato, Stamboul—and a dim harbinger of Atlantis. "I started walking home across the Bridge": there, in the hallucinatory parade of clippers that once winked round the Horn "bright skysails ticketing the Line," the poet is out again, now seaward.

Part Four, "Cape Hatteras," is the turning point of the poem. Thus far, we have seen the individual forms of the poet's crowded day melt into widening, deepening cycles of association. Columbus into the destiny and will of the Atlantic: two lovers into the harbor, the harbor into the sea: subway into a transcontinental railroad, into a continent, into a River; the River into the Gulf; the Indian princess into the Earth Mother, and her dance into the tumult and traffic of the nation; ribald South Street into a vision—while the Bridge brings the clippers that bring China—of Atlantis. Now, the movement turns back toward crystallization. "Cape Hatteras" at first invokes the geologic age that lifted the Appalachians above the sea; the cosmic struggle sharpens into the birth of the airplane—industrial America; the "red, eternal flesh of Pocahontas" gives us, finally, Walt Whitman. "Years of the Modern! Propulsions toward what capes?" The Saunterer on the Open Road takes the hand of the poet. Parts Five and Six are interludes. Part Seven, "The Tunnel," carries the poem to its climax. The poet, in mid-air and at midnight, leaves the Bridge; he "comes down to earth" and returns home as he had left, by subway. This unreal collapse of bridge into subway has meaning. The subway is the tunnel. The tunnel is America, and is a kind of hell. But it has dynamic direction. In this plunging subway darkness, appears Poe:

> And why do I often meet your visage here,
> Your eyes like agate lanterns . . . ?

If the reader understand Poe, he will understand the apparition. Of all the classic poets of the great tradition in America, Poe—perhaps the least an artist—was the most advanced, the most prophetic, as thinker. All, as we have noted, were content more or less with the merely transplanted terms of an agrarian culture. Only Poe guessed the transfiguring effect of the Machine upon the forms of human life, upon the very concept of the person. The Tunnel gives us man in his industrial hell which the machine—his hand and heart—has made; now let the machine be his godlike hand to raise him! The plunging subway shall merge with the vaulting bridge. Whitman gives the vision, Poe—however vaguely—the method. The final part, "Atlantis," is a transposed return to the beginning. The Bridge, in time, has linked Atlantis with Cathay. Now it becomes an absolute experience. Like any human event, *fully known*, it links man instantaneously, "beyond time," with the Truth.

The principle that Crane sought, to make him master of his sense of immediate continuity with a world overwhelmingly chaotic, gave him "The Bridge"; but in actual life it did not sustain him. The later poems, despite their technical perfection (and with the exception of "The Broken Tower"), mark a retreat to the mood of the last pages of "White Buildings." The Sea, symbol of the return to a unity of personal abolition, had ebbed while the poet stood upon his mythic bridge; now again it was rising. The periodicity of his excesses grew swifter; the lucid intervening times when he could write were crowded out. Crane went to Mexico, where individual extinction has for a thousand years inspired a cult and a culture. On his return to New York, heart of the chaos in his life, there was the Sea; and he could not resist it. As his boat was bearing him from the warm waters which fifteen years before had given him a symbol, he took off his coat, quietly, and joined the Sea forever.

c.

The beauty of most of Crane's lyrics, and of many passages of "The Bridge," seems to me to be inviolable. If I analyze this conviction, I am brought first to the poetic texture. Its traditional base is complex. Here is a music plainly related to the Elizabethan poets. And here, also, is a sturdy lilt like the march of those equal children of the Elizabethans—the pioneers. Although Crane describes a modern cabaret . . .

> Brazen hypnotics glitter here;
> Glee shifts from foot to foot . . .

always, there is the homely metronomic, linking him to his fathers. Hence the organic soundness of his verse. Its *livingness* it owes to the dimension of variant emergence from the traditional music, like the emergence of our industrial world from the base of old America. The entire intellectual and spiritual content of Crane's verse could be derived from a study of his typical texture. And this is earnest of its importance.

The structural pattern of "The Bridge" is superb: a man moves of a morning from Brooklyn to Manhattan, returns at midnight, each stage of his course adumbrating by the mystic law of continuity into American figures with cosmic overtones, and all caught up in a mythic Bridge whose functional span is a parabola, and an immediate act, of vision. The poem's flaw lies in the weakness of the personal crystallization upon which the vision rests, as the Bridge is spanned upon its piers. This flaw gets into the idiom and texture. Sometimes the image blurs, the sequence breaks, the plethora of words is blinding. There is even, in the development of certain figures, a tendency toward inflation which one is tempted to connect with the febrile, false ebullience of the American epoch (1924-1929) in which the poem was written. Yet the concept is sound; the poet's genius has on the whole equaled his ambition. Even the failings in execution help to express the epoch, for it is in the understanding and creating of *persons* that our rapidly collectivizing age is weakest.

Crane's myth must, of course, not be confused with the myth as we find it in Homer or the Bible or the Nibelungen. The Bridge is not a particularized being to be popularly sung;

it is a conceptual symbol to be *used*. And the fact that this symbol begins as a man-constructed thing is of the essence of its truth for our instrumental age. From a machine-made entity, the poem makes the Bridge into a machine. But it has beauty. This means that through the men who builded it, the life of America has flowed into it—the life of our past *and our future*. A cosmic content has given beauty to the Bridge, and must give it a poetic function. From being a machine of matter, it becomes an instrument of spirit. *The Bridge is matter made into human action.*

We may confidently say that this message of "The Bridge" will be more comprehensible in the future (not in the immediate future), when the functionally limited materialism of our collectivist era has, through success, grown inadequate to the deepened needs of a mankind released from economic insecurity and prepared, by leisure, for regeneration. For even as necessity, today and tomorrow, drives most men to think collectively in order that they may survive; necessity, day after tomorrow, will drive men to think personally (poetically, cosmically) in order that their survival may have meaning. When the collectivist era has done its work—the abolition of economic classes and of animal want—men will turn, as only the privileged of the past could ever turn, toward the discovery of Man. But when that time comes, the message of "The Bridge" will be taken for granted; it will be too obvious, even as today it is too obscure, for general interest. The revelation, in Crane's poems, however, of a man who through the immediate conduit of his senses realized the organic unity between his self, the objective world and the cosmos, will be accepted as a great human value. And the poems whose very texture reveals and sings this man will be remembered.[1]

1933

[1] This is a short version of the Introduction to "The Collected Poems of Hart Crane."

11. AMERICAN TRAITS

1. IN DEFENSE OF OUR VULGARITY

If refinement implies spiritual values, vulgarity might be called their *aggressive* absence. The values need not be individually acquired. They may be traditional, unconscious. They are not necessarily linked to personal traits like morality and learning. The Negro peasant in the Alabama black belt is illiterate and often drunk. But in his native state, he draws from the soil and sky in whose cycles he is seasoned, a grace which is refinement even if it be unconscious like the grace of a flower. Perhaps he is transplanted to some crude mining suburb of Birmingham. Probably, then, he loses his refinement. But if the loss remain passive, if it be not aggressive, he is not yet vulgar. Give him now a shrewd head by means of which he pushes north and lands in Harlem. Teach him that he is a free-born, American citizen on whom it is incumbent to amuse himself in metropolitan fashion. Hand him a little money and a good dose of our contemporary eighteenth-century notion of Equality. Now, his absence of refinement will grow aggressive. He will be vulgar.

We all came from Europe with a modicum of refinement. And the collateral descendants of our forebears have it still in the mines and farms of Britain, in the towns of Germany and Italy, in the ghettos of Galicia. No natural peasant of Europe is quite without it. For this refinement is almost as widespread as vegetation—as perishable, as passive.

Transplanted, we lost this leguminous bloom. But we were not vulgar until we had grown conscious of being great. American vulgarity is the sum of our spiritual loss and of our assertive energy. Were we less lordly, our lack of spiritual values would not make us vulgar. And were we spiritually full, our assertiveness might prove a virtue. Vulgar people exist everywhere. We are perhaps the only nationally vulgar people. And therein dwells not alone our predicament, but our hope.

Surely, this vulgarity is clear in all our words and acts, from Maine to Texas! In my optimism, I would have it no less than universal. I would not be cheated of finding it, wherever America and Americanism wave. Politicians of other lands may be merely corrupt or dull: ours are vulgar. There is naught vulgar about the servant of a European lord. But there is naught more vulgar than an American lackey at post before the barracks of Park Avenue—save the barracks themselves, and the millionaires they house. Our newspapers are vulgar. But so are many of our churches. Witness their aggressiveness, their display of results, their want of the sanctity of silence. Our evangelists are vulgar, being void of vision and full of advertising. But the Menckenites who rail against them are no less vulgar—for the identical reason. Chicago is doubtless vulgar: but so is Ben Hecht who hates Chicago. And the whole land has turned the motorcar into vulgarity's badge: since it has become an instrument of display, a means of elocuting at so many miles per hour the owner's social status up and down the country.

Now, if you analyze this universal vulgarity of ours, you will discover in it a constant element of *misplaced effort*. The European servant may be quite as spiritually void as ours; but he is less vulgar because he is less striving: what he lacks is precisely the unfounded aspiration which makes our lackey vulgar. Our advertisements are vulgar because they strive so commonly to be something beyond the nature of advertisements—sermons or homilies, editorials or art. Our newspapers

are vulgar because they presume to be arbiters of taste and
morals; and our churches are vulgar because they labor for
results of the spirit with methods of factory and salesroom.
Run down the list, and it will bear me out. This vulgarity
of ours means no intrinsic lack of spiritual will and energy;
it means the failure of that good will and energy. We dwell
in a confusion of impulses and forms. The spirit is exiled from
the deed. The deed hungers vainly for justification by the
spirit. That is why we are aggressive. And the spirit lacks
body. That is why we are wistful, credulous, neurotic. High
energy we have—energy of the kind known as religious. It
vaporizes for lack of a container; or it is misapplied in the
pushing of old creeds no longer fit to house it. Emptiness
grows emphatic because it strives to be full.

Now, all this is the due consequence of our past. For
more than three centuries, old forms of thought and life—
for the most part hostile to each other—were dumped upon
our soil. Not until about 1860 had they all rotted enough
to begin to come together; rotted enough for the first tender
shoot of a true America to rise from the fecundity of decay.
In our outward life, we are still committed to forms of living
which our nascent spirit has rejected. We lug around the
archaic body of theological pioneers; and by means of it we
attempt to stammer out the rounded New World vision of a
Whitman. The result, of course, is a botch. The result, also,
is a promise. This madness of ours, finding symbols in motors,
dramas in football games, art in advertisements, morality in
statutes, and sermons in tabloid papers, lacks only a working
method to become supremely sane. Deflect this misplaced
will to unity into some channel that will hold it; and we shall
see how the energy which mothers American vulgarity and
American folly can father greatness.

Nor must we forget that all these forms of life in which
today we express vulgarity, because they are not proper con-

duits for the clamorous spirit with which we endeavor to infuse them, are not American at all—are European. We may produce 90 per cent of the motors of the world; we may measure our progress by our physical power: but the machine and the gold-and-iron standard of value are fundamentally and historically of Europe. Our contribution has been not in the form, but in the spirit which *deforms* it. We have not made the machine: we have made of the machine the carrier of a Dream. Mr. Henry Ford may be more vulgar than M. Citroën of Paris, because he is a tuppenny prophet: but it is the prophet in him, not the mechanic, which is of our land.

The world wistfully senses this. Europe reads the book of Henry Ford and studies the vulgarest of American expressions through a deep instinct and a mastering hunger. It seeks new spiritual gold. It knows—although it may not analyze the knowledge—that our vulgarity is an ore which holds it.

1926

2. THE MOVIES AND THE MASSES

The American motion picture is a truly popular art. It has more than one audience, of course: Broadway patronizes it, and Europe, and Africa and Asia. But whereas it could get along without these more decorative plaudits, it depends vitally on the American masses. A film that will please only the capitals and languish in the locals, means little to Hollywood's master minds. It is the people who count: the workers.

It is, hence, fair to say that the sentiments, attitudes and dreams of the American masses will find, if not flattery and full reflection, at least some harmonious note on the American screen. The makers of our movies are, of course, high middle class, with all the ideals and prejudices of wealth. You may accuse them of "putting across" their standards in their work. But you give them a heroism which they lack, if you suggest that they would go to the length of imbuing their wares with unpopular ideas, just because they believed them. Much as they love success and armies, the makers of the movies would refrain, no doubt, from confessing their weakness in public, if such confession weakened their incomes. After all, these men have made money because they have pleased the public. They will keep their money only so long as they hold off from antagonizing their public. If you find in our motion pictures a set of standards, a gamut of values, not only bourgeois, but actually oligarchic, military, antiproletarian, the reason must be, not alone that these suit the bourgeois fashioner of the films, but as well that they do not too radically displease the proletarian patrons.

What the tastes and standards in the movies are, is plain enough. Films devoted to the depiction of labor or rural life are extremely rare. High life is the average film life. Or life in the rising provincial class which begins with a Ford and attains a Packard. Alternate with this is the romantic cowboy world of the West. But such tales are no more proletarian than those of Wall Street. Here also is a realm of the picaresque, sentimental, admittedly mythic, and aspiring to the one True Value: the money and position of the middle class.

Run over in your mind the movies you have seen in a year. How many dealt honestly with the life of a farmer, of a carpenter, of a factory hand? If the hero began as a mechanic, was he not an automobile manufacturer at the end? If he was a stableboy at the outset, did he not own the stable or marry the girl who owned it, at the fade-out? If Reel One found him a country bumpkin, was he not a magnate ere you left the theatre?

Our movie world, like any theatre of its audience, is a confessional of the masses. And what it seems to mirror very plainly, indeed, is that the achievement of bourgeois status is the heart's desire of the average toiling man and woman in our country.

This is nothing new. But the obvious conclusion, that this is what the masses really and positively value, is the conclusion we do not wish to make. Worship of big guns, military, financial, social, on which the American movie thrives, is indeed the tonal will of the moviemakers. This is what really moves the businessmen and women who distribute, produce, direct, compose and act our movies. But the true reason why the masses—above all, the plastic sons and daughters of the masses—accept such values is that they have not received a set of values of another kind.

The people must love, must worship, something. What school and church provide them, as substance for their dreaming, has gone so dim that it disappears in the brash glamour of our jungle. The movie gives an idealization of the powers and hungers of daily American life. Empty the people go from church and schoolroom. But the press agent of the silver screen needs only to give a twist to the actual presences of the busy street in order to make the shopgirl a lady and the laborer a millionaire.

The corruptly glamorous values of an exploiting class are absorbed by the people, not because the people are corrupt, but because they lack values and glamour of their own. They have no ethos, they have no myth, they have no simplest story in which the elements of the laboring life take on essential and intrinsic worth. Lincoln, let it not be overlooked, became a corporation lawyer—like any movie hero. And Whitman has not yet been translated into American speech. But when a poet does arise, inspired to sing, as Burns did for his people, the values and virtues of laboring men as men, rather than as aspirants to wealth, the masses will follow him—even in the movies.

It is significant that no one has yet given the movie audience a set of values other than the prevailing. Has anyone tried? We suspect that such a poet would not languish in the anterooms of all the movie magnates.

And one reason for our confidence is the unique case of Charlie Chaplin. The average moviegoer does not love Chaplin more than he does Doug Fairbanks or Harold Lloyd or Lon Chaney because he thinks that Chaplin is a greater artist. The average movie fan believes that the high art of the screen is in such stars as Swanson or the Gishes. He is likely to be a bit ashamed of his love for Charlie. There are a dozen more "admired" actors. But the average American loves Chaplin most tenderly because Chaplin on the screen is so often a poor cuss of the people who remains one: and who "puts it over," not by becoming a millionaire, but by remaining a human being. Charlie as waiter, bricklayer, fireman, bank sweeper, pawnbroker's assistant, convict, is not at the tale's end and in accordance with film formula, the owner of the restaurant, the contractor, the fire commissioner, the banker, the police lieutenant. He remains, fragilely, wholly, triumphantly, of the people. ("The Gold Rush," in which Charlie strikes gold, is an exception.) He is the frail and unutterably sweet beginning of a movie mythos in which the common man may absorb poetic values not by changing his class, but *by becoming himself.* And this is the true reason why the common man adores him.

Here is a first step in our American labor and farmer movement which remains to be taken. It consists in the creating of living values within the life of laborer and farmer. Only so will the extrinsic values of "getting ahead" and of "getting into another class" be displaced. When such living values exist, the radical movements organized to put labor into power will have something to work with.

1927

3. THE COMEDY OF COMMERCE

Industrialism's mood is tragic. In the early years, men's wonder gave to it the glamour of romance. Something of the delicious terror memorialized in "The Castle of Otranto" went to men's consideration of these new giants fleshed of iron and belching steam. But the monsters' bite was too hard; too dolorous was the displacement which they brought to good men's lives. These were no proper prodigies like the "Gothic," avenging merely wrongs and rescuing the noble. So the romantic mood grew swiftly dark. With the early socialists and anarchists, it took on the Doom note of prophecy. Zola made it tragic. In the muckraking days of our magazines, the tales of factory and mill were grey and ominous. They were, indeed, replicas of the infernos of our industrial towns. Laughter, like the hero-workman's little girl, languished and died in those swart caves whose breath was a blast and whose light was a sear of fire.

But as industrialism became more the usual circumstance, we began to react against it. And our reaction, having as its aim recovery, was comedic. That particular response to the grim industrial glower, which is the Comedy of Commerce, has found perfection in America. In England, the monsters' bite has been too cruel. There are no spirits left, there is no energy, for the recovering laugh. In the Latin countries, the monsters' sway is not bitter enough as yet to have provoked a systematic answer. (There are signs of it in France.) In Germany, as soon as industrialism flourished, the Teuton genius turned not to a balance of frolic or of smiles, but to an ideal compensation. The machine was drafted by neo-Hegelian argument into the soldierly service of Kultur. In America, we had no such metaphysical bent. The best we

could do with our industrial tragedy was to cover it up with a surface, coruscating and comedic.

The symbol of this new comedy is the electric light on Broadway. It is, of course, commercial and of industrial antecedents. It is bright, dazzlingly. It displays power and wealth, yet it does not reveal. Instead it covers, with its hard cold beams, the rather shoddy buildings. It distracts the eye from the beholding of sources. It is a light that blinds. Any artist will assure you that the electric light is *false*—in the sense that it deforms.

But thanks to such enterprise, it will soon be inexact to speak of our "industrial cities." Industry must continue, of course, to have its home. But industry will not continue to control the tone and nature of our dwellings. It will be disguised or hidden. It will become as the kitchen or the plumbing system of our social house, as the bowels of our social body. And we will be outwardly bedecked and bedizened in an obtrusive laughter the ingredients of which, indeed, will be the results of industry, and the purpose of which will be to deny its parent.

Already, not alone New York among our splendid cities has cloaked this tragic source of its greatness in the comedy of commerce. Forget the blare of the Broadway lights, and think of the shop windows. How gaily drugstores, hardware stores, delicatessens, shine with their myriad cavorting forms and colors. Think of the newspapers whose columns of dour news are plentifully (and profitably) balanced with the comedic patter of the advertisements. In our popular magazines, the reaction is complete. The mill town is disappearing from them; the honest workman's daughter languishes less in print. It is the doughty salesman, the go-getter of commerce, with his steed a motor and his muse a flapper, who commands the pages not already commandeered by "National Advertisers." Our more sophisticated books reveal the same aversion. Our "first-line" critics must, above all, be comic—if not clowns. They must provide the sedative of laugher. And the books they tout do likewise. Tragedy is *nefas*. The tragic stuff about us has cowed our spirit from the enterprise of making it a means for that joyous confrontation of truth which is tragedy. We glance off into comedy—if not farce. And the cleverism, the anecdote, the epigram, the swift cartoon—so close to the heart of the salesman—clutter as well the minds of our intellectual classes.

It is so with the theatre. In such a typical success as "The Show-Off" (called our best comedy by many of the reviewers) a minor role fell to Industry. Not the boy mechanic who actually *invents* is the hero; but the salesman, the show-off, the man who by empty bluff and in utter ignorance of the product he is pushing, *puts over* the invention. The industrial source of wealth remains wistfully indulged and sedulously hidden beneath the noisy comedy of commerce.

The comedy of commerce is a comedy of display. It is a denial of the industrial gloom by a boast of brightness. And yet its materials and its very rhythms are conditioned tragically by the tragic world it aims to deny. It is only a disguise; often frenetic, often wistful, never more than momently successful. Nowhere is this more plain than in the music of the comedy of commerce—Jazz. I do not desire to discuss the music roots of jazz: whether they lead you back to the Barbary Coast of San Francisco or to the Argentine or to the Congo. The product we have naturalized is the song of our reaction from the dull throb of the machine. Jazz syncopates the lathe-lunge, jazz shatters the piston-thrust, jazz shreds the hum of wheels, jazz is the spark and sudden lilt centrifugal to their incessant pulse. Jazz is a moment's gaiety, after which the spirit droops, cheated and unnurtured. This song is not an escape from the Machine to limpid depths of the soul. It

is the Machine itself! It is the music of a revolt that fails. Its
voice is the mimicry of our industrial havoc.

You will find this irony in all corners of our successful
world. Industry is the source of our power and of our sorrow. We are ashamed of its ugliness, hurt by its cruelties. We
will employ the power it gives us to escape the sorrow. We
seem so adept! We have ten thousand gay contrivances, all
born of industry, to hide it. But all of them are like that
paragon, the motor. Its chief purpose, of course, is to carry
us away from factory smoke: ourselves figuratively, and the
laborers whose Fords stand parked outside the mill, literally,
when the day's work is done. But alas! the machine that carries us away from industrialism carries its spirit along. The
clever story in the *Satevepost*, the bungalow, the radio, the
song and dance—all the little acts of the comedy of commerce—hold the bitter taste, essentialize the spirit and the
forms of the industrial discomfort they are supposed to combat.

The Comedy of Commerce is a failure. It is an antidote
brewed of the poison it would save from. We must go deeper
for a healing laughter. Laughter that heals must come from
health, not from the disease. It must spring from the whole
vision and whole experience of life, not from a mere shrewd
juggling and twisting of any of life's products.

                                                        1925

4. JAZZ AND FOLK ART

In "The Comedy of Commerce," I referred to jazz, not in
uncomplimentary terms, but critically as an instance of the
art of a commerce- and industry-ridden people. Many readers
gave protest. So far as I could see, the chief point against me
was that I had dared be critical of a folk art. Jazz, went their

sentimental plaint, was the expression of a people. (I had not denied it.) Hence, hands off! Hence, down on worshipful knees!

There has, indeed, been abroad for a full century the curious notion that folk art—as once the king—can do no wrong: that folk art is necessarily good art: that the critic who dares to question folk art commits the unpardonable sin.

This is a point I would examine briefly, forgetting jazz as the mere pretext for it. The notion, to begin with, seems to be quite modern. Before Rousseau, folk art was known, of course; was appreciated; was, indeed, taken for granted. It was neither idealized nor despised. It was the art of the folk: the elite regarded it with the same relative eye with which they looked upon the people. The people was the mass, the soil, the loam, whence they had sprung; the body, if you will, for the aristocratic spirit. It was indispensable and it was causally, if not finally, good. No tyrant could think otherwise, without deleting the very substance of his power. Molière, in the first act of "Le Misanthrope," expressed the common philosophic attitude toward folk art. To excoriate the precious nonsense of Oronte, Alceste quotes a popular Parisian ditty, and declares it vastly better than the sophisticate's sonnet. He shatters the courtier with a point which today would be altogether lost. For he is uttering a paradox. Here, in our language, is the gist of his attack: "This popular Parisian song—you know its class—may not be much; but it *is* sincere, sweet, lovely. And your sonnet, M. Oronte, which should of course be an improvement on such primitive traits, shows but their total loss."

The crowning of folk art is a corollary from Rousseau who preached a "return to Nature"—as if civilized man were somehow miraculously out of nature; and "a return to infancy"—as if his own doctrines had not been the dream of a weary adult. If you accept the Rousseauistic premise, the modern notion follows about art. The best art, then, will be the least cultured, the most primitive, the most childlike. And poor man, addicted hopelessly to beauty, had best pursue his weakness in the art of folk who, thinking least, are least attainted. If, however, you reject the creed of Rousseau—which does not mean that you deny his value and his genius; if it seems clear to you that civilized man belongs as much to nature as a tree does, and that man's need to live well, to know true, to aim high, is as healthy and as natural a function as the tree's to grow good roots and blossom, then this indiscriminate adoring of folk art, merely because it *is* folk art, is nonsense.

Dante was once ten years old. He was a remarkable child. He babbled sonnets and rondeaux which revealed his nature. Do you put the prattlings he produced at ten before the "Divina Commedia" he composed at fifty? If you are the usual folk-art worshiper, why not? Were those lyric works of Dante's youth not the pure Dante? the untrammeled sign and substance of his soul? Were they not Dante's folk art? And the "Divina Commedia"! what alien and sophisticate and unoriginal matters dulled the raptures of his early years to this! Aristotle, Aquinas, Virgil, the apocalypses of Jerusalem, the pseudo epigraphia of Alexandria—the whole theology and logic of the school-men had to "debauch" the pure Dante, ere he was ready to write his intricate, conscious poem. If you are a real lover of art, surely you will turn with mild disgust from the "Commedia" to his childhood singing.

I do not think this caricature of the folk art fad is too unjust to sharpen a just point. It is literally true that if greatness be ever in a man or a race, it must potentially have been there at the outset. Therefore the beginning expressions of that man or race will hold the germ of their significance. Most men, moreover, fail (perhaps most races also) to fulfill their spiritual promise. The promise universally exists. No child, no child-race is without it. Only the mature achievement is rare. And so it follows that the search for spiritual values among children will be, by and large, more fruitful than among men and women. But to say that the art expression of all children gives more than the art expression of all adults, because children all have the germ and adults seldom the flower—only this bad logic can lead us to conclude that child art and folk art are best, or even always good. Folk art is the seed of great art: seeds are more numerous than flowers. To cultivate the seed at the expense of the flower is a defeatism and a folly we are not quite cured of.

But folk art is not naïve in its elements, any more than are the babblings of the "purest" child. It is, more often, the naïve mirroring and mimicry of ideas caught from above. The emotions of folk art are childish. Yet they are the result of unconsciously inherited ideas, imposed by ruling classes. Take, for instance, the folk arts of medieval Christian Europe, the spirituals of the American Negro slave. Did the folk invent the intricate theology and philosophy on which they rested? Rather, they vulgarized the product of intellectual minorities—Prophets, Plato, Plotinus and the Patrists: made it a pabulum, at last, which later intellectuals could re-employ for the creating of more cultivated art. Another example: Russian folk music reveals traces of liturgical and synagogical music. Now, a new group of cultivated artists—Rimsky, Stravinsky, Ornstein—reforms this popularized pabulum of older minorities into a fresh intellectualized music.

Or consider our jazz. Jazz is not so much a folk music—like the Negro spirituals—as a folk accent in music. It expresses well a mass response to our world of piston rods, cylinders and mechanized laws. The response is of the folk and is passive. The nature of our world itself is due to the work and temperament of minorities alien to the jazzmakers. Jazz expresses a personal maladjustment to this world, righted by sheer and

shrewd compliance. And this, doubtless, is why the races at once most flexible and most maladjusted—the Negro and the Jew—give the best jazz masters. Since the rhythm of our age is not transfigured in jazz, as in truly creative art, but is assimilated, the elements of the age itself which we may disapprove will appear also in jazz. In other words, a folk art—being so largely an art of reaction and of assimilation—will contain the faults of the adult minorities that rule the folk, as well as the pristine virtues of the people.

And we have other folk arts. "The Rosary"—jazzless, European saccharine—is as truly a folk art as any of the Berlin or Gershwin ditties. Harold Bell Wright's books— messes of Victorian notions in decay—are also an American folk art. The New York "Daily News" is the daily art of a folk numbering several millions.

The adorers of folk art in its own divine right need but observe what they adore. That will be enough to cure them. Nor should they forget that in all culturally early epochs, dissatisfaction with folk art is one of the incentives for the production of great art.

1926

5. STRAIGHT STREETS

What is the meaning of our cities of rectangular streets? What is their effect on our souls? It is plain that Nature likes curves. You may find rough angles in rocky mountain wastes, or in the sort of creature that a microscope makes vaguely visible. But the Nature of man and near to man is a sinuous, rounded being. Think of our bodies and of the bodies of animals—not a Euclidean angle in the lot. Think of the shapes of flowers, plants, trees; of the configuration of the hills and fields; of the sweep of waters; of the globe. Now think of our interior worlds. Our physical dynamo has not a straight line in it. And our mental digestion is tortuous as our intestines. Logic may proceed theoretically like a plummet; but there's nothing natural in such logic. Draconian justice might be called rectilinear, but it, too, does not exist in Nature. Uprightness when it is not tempered by the curves of mercy is repellent. Man's mind moves in curves. His thoughts arch, vault, melt into reverie. Dream and sense swerve into each other. His heart, too, is full of arcuations. And the heart's desires are parabolas. There is naught angular within us. Nor above us. Space, we have learned from Riemann, has a crimp and a curve. The "straight gravitational line" of Newton proves to be the "Einstein shift." From the detour of solar systems back upon themselves within a spheroid Space, to the devexities of dream, man has a universe full of everything but angles. And yet, the American urbanite has elected to spend his days in a gridiron.

The towns of the Old World were and still are curved creatures. From Iceland to the Cape of Good Hope you will not find an ancient city that does not gyre like a heart or twist like the intestines. Indeed, the European links angles with humanity only in his thought of death. Christ was killed on a cross. St. Laurentius was roasted on a grid. When the fanatical Felipe of Spain built a monastery to express his contempt for life and his withdrawal to the grave, he patterned it after a gridiron.[1]

Curves rest: angles tire. How often the American abroad lets his eye float down the gentle swerve of a street and is soothed sensuously, and is moved as by a freshet of pleasant impulse. It is the curve! The jolliest street in Manhattan—the one that is most human, most laughing, most restful—is Broadway, which has a curve or two; and even at its straightest runs diagonally to the ruthless grid, thus giving the delusion of a

[1] El Escorial.

flex. No wonder it has become the avenue of shows, the road for informal saunterings clear up to Harlem. No wonder the automobile, our pathetic symbol of escape, has made Broadway its home.

If straight bobbed hair delights, the reason is that it sets off the curves of our girl's face. Her straight dress has value in so far as it reveals the rondures of her body. American civilization has revolutionized the shape of cities. It may yet appreciably alter the shape of man.

For we seem to be angularized in almost everything else. Not alone our streets are straight and stiff. Our houses are as rigid as if they were made of the building blocks of Brobdingnagian babes. Where else is there a spectacle like the recently grown splendor of Park Avenue—that parade of pompous tombs, shutting in wealth and shutting out the sun? Is it possible that the disfavor of Riverside Drive as a residence street among our leaders is due to the swinging rise and fall of that untypical parkway? Our laws, like our houses, become more rectangular and upright. Our morals are strait like the gates of Ellis Island. Even our faces . . . If there be in all the world a human countenance made of angles instead of the immemorial curves, it must be that of Calvin Coolidge. So perhaps biology will give way after all to the rectangular will of our American world. Perhaps the flapper of tomorrow will have pyramidal breasts. . . .

There is a reason for all this, and a good one. If you care to go to the heart of the matter you entrain by the Santa Fé and alight in some New Mexican pueblo.

The Indian's culture is prophetic of what our culture must be. His nature is a guide to the understanding and achievement of our own. This does not mean that we are going to give up motors, and dress in paint and feathers, nor that the skyscraper will dwindle to the wigwam, nor even that our women at some distant date will be swinging their papooses across their shoulders. But it does mean that there is something deeper than these discrepancies between the Indian and ourselves. Something deeper, which we share.

The Amerind was profoundly, beautifully adjusted to the land. If you study him in his demeanor, his dance, his music, his pyramiding pueblos or his simple tepees, in his flinted arrows, in his decorations, you will find that the general symbol of his expression is a curve so sharp and so severe that it barely escapes being an angle. The curve is the way of acceptance: the angle is the way of resistance. America is a feverish world. Its geological tempo is not like that of Europe. It is far more terribly intense. I am certain that when the ancestors of the Indian crossed to America from Mongolia (or Atlantis) they resisted this atmospheric fury, as have we, with an angular restraint. That reaction was not a culture, any more than our present reactions from Europe or from mechanical civilization constitute a culture. The Indian culture began when his innate spiritual and intellectual values formed a solution with the world about him: his culture was achieved when the responses between his soul and the world had rounded into a unified *life* which expressed both fully. After many ages, the Indian's first reactive restraint toned down, and became the subtle and fertile curve of the Indian music, the symbolic gesture of his dance, the exquisite reticence of his demeanor.

Recently Dr. Jung of Zurich was in this country and made a visit to the pueblos in which he had been rightly advised that he would find archetypical remains of classic Indian culture. Dr. Jung had psychoanalyzed many Americans, and found in them all (whether their ancestry was Nordic, Latin or Semitic) a unique alliance of *wildness and restraint* which did not exist in the European nature. Dr. Jung's intuition told him that he would find this combination, so hidden in our souls, culturally expressed in the Indian pueblo. He was right. Despite the ponderous luggage with which we came from Europe and which so differs from what the Indian brought along, we must inevitably go the Indian's way in the spirit, since we have come his way in the flesh.

When Babbitt tells us that American towns are laid out "regular" because it "pays," he does not know how deeply he is right. Regularity and angularity pay, indeed, because such is the beginning of our self-assertion against a cosmic factor. In our straight streets, in our jazz, in our dress, in our morals, in our lantern-jaw Puritans, in our raillike girls, we manifest the first stage of resistance to the furious fire which is the nature of our world. The rigid angles will smooth out, will take on the curves of life—will become the forms of our American culture.

1925

III. IDEAS

1. SERIOUSNESS AND DADA

(An Exchange with Malcolm Cowley)

a.

It is possible in small space to touch but briefly, and upon one of its phases, the complex and defunct Dada movement. Its immediate progenitors were the Italian heirs of Athens and of Rome—they called themselves futurists: a restless Jew whose ancestors had settled in Rumania brought it to Paris. It had behind it, therefore, the ripe Mediterranean littorals and the full growth of Europe. It was a salutary burst of laughter in a world that felt itself too old. Europe was crystallized and desired a solvent. It creaked in stratified forms and laws and notions, and it yearned to explode.

The War was a violent but unsatisfactory excursion of a similar sort. The ponderous machinations of diplomacy had prepared this laughter of young millions rushing to a bright shambles from the straitened gloom of ordered cities and inherited farms. But the war was too superficial. Jaded Europe learned the inconsequent effect of such inebriety as death and murder. The deep spirit of the land was unmoved by columns of men miles long and by guns that raked cities. It was the esthetes of France—the solemn romanticists, the shrill Parnassians, the symbolists, the votaries of Bergson, it was the pragmatists of Germany and the rhetoricians of Italy, who invited the release of Dada by their formulations, hedgings-in and dogmas. There is no doubt that the face of Europe yearned for the smashing of a few cathedrals. But also the heart of Europe hungered after the battering of a few spiritual laws.

Dada was an emanation of this will of a too sober, too mature, too sanctified rationalist church. Scampering in disarray against metrics and the still more cloying bondages of "freedom," imping against the roll of such millstones as Truth, as Unity, as Beauty, Dada was as logical as the most Freudian hallucination. It was an eruption, a breakup, a shower: it was a jag and a reversion. And having cooled the face of the old land and made Europe forget her uncomfortable age, it disappeared.

Good jokers, the Dadaists were: wistful creators, against sour sense, of sweet absurdity. But they did nothing more ridiculous than the installation of the Dada mood in American letters. Europe called for Dada by antithesis: America for analogous reasons calls for the antithesis of Dada. For America *is* Dada. The richest mess of these bean-spillers of Italy, Germany and France is a flat accord beside the American chaos. Dada spans Brooklyn Bridge; it spins round Columbus Circle; it struts with the Ku-Klux Klan; it mixes with all brands of bootleg whisky; it prances in our shows; it preaches in our churches; it tremolos at our political conventions. Dada is in the typical Western university that spends $50,000 on cows and $200 on books. It is in the esthetics of Mr. Bryan, whose favorite work of art is any old Madonna. It is in the commercial comedy of our advertisements. (DO YOUR DUTY: CHEW MIXLETS GUM. BE AN AMERICAN: THROW YOUR RUBBISH HERE.) It is in the counterpoint of callow Hollywood and the immemorial desiccation of the California desert. It is in the medley of strutting chimneys and bowed heads, of strutting precepts and low deeds that make America. We are a hodgepodge, a boil. We are a maze of infernos and nirvanas. Our brew of Nigger-strut, of wailing Jew, of cantankerous

Celt, of nostalgic Anglo-Saxon, is a brew of Dada. No wonder they imported our essential chaos to lighten the regularities of France! But we are young, and what we need is a bit of mature action. We are fantastic ourselves, and what we need is integrating thought. We are the most fecund joke on earth—for the overserious others. What we need, by way of rounding our lives into livableness, is a bit of seriousness for ourselves.

Our complexities provoke strange paradox in our deeds. Ourselves a spontaneous combustion of contrariety and antithesis, there grew up in us a fear and a shame of the spontaneous. (This is, of course, a trait of adolescence.) In order to become unspontaneous, we turned to Europe. Our attention was caught by a lot of youths of age on a "bust" of spontaneous laughter. In all solemnity, we artificed their spontaneity, crowning thereby the best of the Dada jokes. But we did not create Dada art. Dada art arose from the traditional maturity of Europe. The intellectual stuff and stamina, in our own case, were lacking: and what we got were weakling strains of the European pose muddled with American incompetence and lost against the background of American bewilderment.

A healthy reaction to our world must, of course, be the contrary of Dada: it must be ordered and serious and thorough. Dada worked well in overmature Europe. We, by analogue, must be fundamental, formal. That, indeed, is the proper mood of youth. The young cutup in the literature of our land is the bromide. We need him doubtless, but humbly in the rank and file. To be coruscant, smart and swift in the American language is to be platitudinous and banal. Therefore it is that the literature which poses as most advanced in the United States is for the most part quite the contrary—is as undifferentiate, indeed, from the common wallow, as the Mecca Mosque on Fifty-fourth Street, as the Hearst headlines, or as were the jokes of Josh Billings. Our cosmopolites who think that they are emulating Aragon and Cocteau and Firbank, our local realists and shockers who think they are reforming us, are all in reality but sweepings of the immense centrifugal action of the American world. Our surface twists and scintillates and shrieks. They are caught in it, they are slavish functions of the American mass which they profess to lead. They are the reflections of a world that is Dada and that is in danger of becoming narcissistic: of growing infatuated with its own twitching image.

The first step in the absorption and control of our Dada Jungle is the achievement of a serious, of a literally religious temper. The academies are turned away from America: their earnestness is frivolous. The neoclassicists are turned away from America: their nostalgia is anemic and their grace is shallow. The realists are submerged by America. The pragmatists are bluffed by America. The clever and decorative boys who clutter our "serious" magazines are reflecting not even America's surface, but Europe's thirsty reflection of our surface. None of this is serious, although doubtless all of this has its place in the chemistry of ferment. . . .

If we can produce a handful of serious creators—men unafraid of unpopular words like philosophy, profundity, saintliness, devotion—and if we can keep them alive and at work a score of years, perhaps there'll be a start toward integration: and after several hundred years, we may be mature enough to inspire a Dada of our own.

b.

Dear Mr. Frank:

The progress of literature (and here progress does not imply a betterment) is largely a series of reactions, a passage from one extreme to the other: romanticism succeeding classicism, realism against romance, estheticism against naturalism and Dada against the esthetes. But given the fact that every national literature starts from a different point and follows a different course, their reactions of a given moment can hardly be the same. For American writers to revolt from the tradition of Remy de Gourmont or Mallarmé is empty imitation, a gesture with no more significance than could be given to a French protest against anticigarette laws in the state of Kansas.

To this measure your attack, in the last issue of 1924, against a hypothetical group of American Dadas was completely justified. It would have been more valuable, however, less obviously biased, had you gone on to consider that the progress of literature is also a discovery of new principles, involving a rejection or reaffirmation of the old; and that such principles are international.

To call Dada "a 'bust' of spontaneous laughter" was absurd. You were on safer ground when you spoke of it as a reaction against European writers whom you listed as "the solemn romanticists, the shrill Parnassians, the symbolists, the votaries of Bergson . . . the pragmatists of Germany and the rhetoricians of Italy"; or when you added that since few of these schools were represented in America, a similar American reaction would be stupid.

But Dada was also a discovery: that nonsense may be the strongest form of ridicule; that writing is often worst when it is most profound, saintly or devoted and best when it is approached in a spirit of play; that associational processes of thought often have more force than the logical; that defiance carried to the extremes of bravado is more to be admired than a passive mysticism.[1] Dada was the sense of exhilaration

---

[1] Bertrand Russell says, "Traditional mysticism has been contemplative, convinced of the unreality of time, and essentially a lazy man's philosophy." It has always seemed to me that the mysticism of Mr. Frank's novels was of this traditional type.

which was born when our old shackles were tested and found to be rusted away.

There was nothing geographical in these discoveries. But you prefer to play geographer.

You have been to Paris and carry back the gossip of Monsieur X the poet and Monsieur Y the novelist. Other American writers (I was one) have been to Paris. Some met Paul Fort and wrote polyphonic prose in his manner, some met Paul Valéry and became classicists, some met Soupault or Tzara and wrote a Yankee Dada, some met Jules Romains and his little group, studied his treatises, adopted his more solemn faults with some of his virtues and are proud to be called the Unanimists of America. There were a few Americans who met many writers of many schools, took the best of each and retained enough personal force to write about their own surroundings in their own manner, but you, Mr. Frank, are not generally included in their number.

Neither am I. One tries to keep free of the ten schools and two academies, but in this day of slogans we must all be ticketed, must possess a little slip of red, white or yellow cardboard printed with a name. I was in doubt which name to choose, but your article decides me. Let me therefore be considered as your butt: the clever but not coruscant, smart or swift young man who clutters our more serious magazines, the American Dada.

MALCOLM COWLEY

Dear Mr. Cowley:

It was good of you to send me a copy of what you consider your answer to my article "Seriousness and Dada," with the invitation that I—as you phrase it—"continue the debate." I have read carefully what you say; and I am forced to conclude that if there is to be a debate upon the principles suggested in my little essay, it has yet to begin. Until it does, I rest.

Many questions of fact rather than of theory are brought up, it is true, by your letter: but they are irrelevant to the issue. I might point out that your definition of the progress of letters is a good juvenile one, defining nothing. I might suggest, after your linking of the term "mysticism" with the adjective "passive" that you study a mystic, taking your choice from Hosea, Plato, Paul, Plotinus, Gabirol, Abélard, Aquinas, Bernard, Roger Bacon, Dante, Spinoza, Pascal, Teresa, Calvin, Blake, Dostoevski, Whitman, or any other who may appeal to you, and explain to us why and how this mysticism is passive. Finally, I might refer to your allusion to myself as having "been in Paris and returned with the gossip of M. X. and M. Y." or to your veiled reference to my American "unanimism," as convicting you of an impertinence which in turn is the result of an ignorance so essential as to disqualify you in your present temper from true intelligent discussion.

However, all of this is aside the point of my paper which sought by no means to destroy American Dada, but merely to put it snugly in its little place. The one statement in your letter which has the force of relevance is that in which you volunteer to be considered an American Dada. Of course, one must accept you so, since you insist upon it. I admit, however, that I for one could accept you in this guise with less regret had not my acquaintance with your poetry convinced me that you will be fit for better things when you achieve the moral courage to confront the reality of our world, and the spiritual energy to take issue with it; instead of permitting yourself to be flung off by its centrifugal action, in the fond belief that because you fly off to Nothing in a graceful pirouette and with a foreign oath upon your lips you are being any the less booted and beshat by the very elements of life which you profess to despise.

W. F.

*This exchange appeared in the December issue of 1924, a little
magazine edited and published by Edwin Seaver. . . . Of course,
out of Dada have come the surréalistes; and the best of their leaders (Tristan Tzara, Louis Aragon, André Breton, etc.) combine
their romantic creed with communism. Malcolm Cowley has
moved in a similar direction. At least one of the important writers
associated with Dada, Pierre Drieu La Rochelle, has moved into
fascism, like Marinetti and other earlier Italian futurists.*

2. MR. MENCKEN, KING OF THE PHILISTINES

America, which protects its deer and partridges, still has
perpetual open season for philosophy hunting. Dr. Durant
turned "The Story of Philosophy" into a best seller by the
shrewd device of leaving philosophy out and putting in its
place anecdotal stories, whole chapters on nonmetaphysical
authors, and his own not too subtly diffused contempt for
the entire silly business of "ultimate problems." John Dewey,
the most characteristic American mind of his generation, has
always been an antiphilosopher at heart (with unconscious
vestiges of the poor side of Hegel). And here is Mr. Mencken,
tripping upon the autumnal scene, all decked out in leather
jerkin, hunting cap, cartridge belt, and his usual supply of
automatic popguns.

"If you want to find out," says Mr. Mencken, "how a
philosopher feels when he is engaged in the practice of his
profession, go to the nearest zoo and watch a chimpanzee at
the wearying and hopeless job of chasing fleas. Both suffer
damnably and neither can win." The "fleas" in this case, you
realize, are truth, the absolute, any ultimate concept of the
real world, any distinction at all between reality and appearance. Elsewhere, in the same lofty Menckenian column, the
same matter is called "bunk." "For the absolute, of course,"

he absolutely assures us, "is a mere banshee. No such thing exists. Philosophy in the narrow technical sense"—read, in the sense of the whole silly lineage from Pythagoras to Whitehead—"is largely moonshine and wind music."

At last I know, from Mr. Mencken's rigorous definitions, what is his secret desire: the unsated hunger which all his literary work has struggled to fulfill. Since, to his mind, philosophy is bunk and wind and moonshine, is it not clear that Mr. Mencken looks upon himself as a writer of philosophy? And if he strives to sharpshoot all the other philosophical fellows off the field, who can blame him, since he knows that his own particular brand of brass fanfare is the best for us?

Let us therefore take him as a philosopher: take him seriously, I mean, of course. And consider the matter of this "bunk" of metaphysics. A moment's inquiry should make clear that if the philosophical "woolgathering" of man is to be judged merely by practical results—by results in the way man has lived; in contrast with the metaphysicians, the builders of temples were builders in sand, the makers of empires were but furious blowers of bubbles.

Of course, the findings of metaphysics—the logic of reality, and of epistemology—the logic of knowledge, are disputed, disputable, relative, impermanent. What is not? Even the term "eternal" is a pitiful, anthropomorphic thing, having no life and no sense save in the mouth of the evanescent creature who knows himself for mortal. If you will have nothing less than the eternal, what will you do with language, music, economics? what with religions, empires, arts? Do these outlast philosophy? On the contrary, they rest and have ever rested upon it.

Take the age of the Upanishads, nearly thirty centuries behind us. Do we speak the language of that day? We speak its philosophical thought. Do we live by its arts, its customs, its gods, its laws? Yet its metaphysics is a cogent factor in modern psychology, in modern letters. The era of the Upanishads is living for us, solely through its professional philosophers—those "idle" *sitters-about* who spent their days spinning webs about Absolute and Will—webs so marvelously strong that they have outlasted cities and cultures.

What exists now of the Greece and Magna Græcia of the sixth century before Christ? Chiefly Pythagoras: and through him a good deal of history, ancient and modern, of science, ancient and modern, of mathematics, of physics, of religious doctrine. From his philosophy of number came the science of numbers: came Euclid: came the whole forever adumbrating realm of physics and mechanics, the modern mathematics of analysis, the modern critical realism (via other philosophers, of course, like Descartes and Leibnitz) which in men like Mach, Einstein, Russell, Whitehead, is once again transfiguring the world. From the abstractions of these technical philosophers of preclassic Greece came Plato (even as Aeschylus and Tragedy came from the Eleusinians): came Aristotle, came Plotinus: came at last such fairly practicable structures as the whole civilization of Christian Europe. From the moonshine of such men as Pythagoras, Protagoras, Plato, Heraclitus, Democritus and Zeno, tough-minded men managed to build states, churches, sciences, atomic theories, machines. Similarly, the prophets of Israel, the wise men of India and North Africa—questers of that Absolute which, in their ignorance they called God or Atman, whereas Mr. Mencken in his more modern language calls it bunk or fleas—gave to man a concept so very real that he has dwelt in it, builded from it his art, his ethics and his state, for many thousand years.

Mr. Mencken probably forgets that Bacon's preparation for modern science was possible to him only because he rested wholly on a metaphysical faith: the assumption of an absolute Order without which, as Hume points out, there could be no science, because there could be no deduction from particular to general, from appearance to Law, from passing effect to eternal Cause. So Newton, also, rose from an intricate, profound, world-satisfying structure of metaphysical faith which a whole lineage of "professional flea-chasers" from Plato to Aquinas had molded at last into the Christian Cosmos.

Perhaps Mr. Mencken does not know that Dante, Cervantes, Shakespeare, Goethe, had their metaphysics—had, above all, their masters, technical and abstruse, in metaphysics. Has not his careful study of the philosophical classics, which he assures us he "rereads every year when the weather is too hot for serious mental work," revealed to him that his favorites, Conrad and Nietzsche, are romantic versions of Schopenhauer who, in turn, rests upon Kant and the philosophers of India? If he has no use for Kant, his disgust with the post-Kantian idealists (Hegel, for instance) is utterly beneath words. Yet, from these sources come psychoanalysis, Marxism, the Nietzschean anti-Marxism: come the non-Euclidean and n-dimensional geometers (Gauss, Riemann, Lobachevski, Minkowski), who in their turn nourished Lorentz, Einstein, the critical realists—makers of the modern world. And straight from Hegel is derived the impressionistic style in criticism which Mr. Mencken so adorns—since it is, indeed, his own.

It is one of the burdens of philosophy that lesser men turn its noble doubts into dogmatic denials: chip from its high structure of critique little stones to fling against it. In all ages, heedless people accept what the great past bequeaths them, live by it, and betray it. The man who is most proud of his Buick is most contemptuous of the thinker whose intricate thought made his car possible. The man most at ease

in his Zion sneers most at the makers of the concepts which
built his state and his morals.

1926

3. PSEUDO LITERATURE

The term, I believe, is Schopenhauer's. He declared that
there are two streams of writing, for the most part indis-
tinguishably merged save for a very few. One of these, the
effect of creative thought and of creative vision, he called
literature; and all the rest, however pleasant and respectable,
he outlawed. To go back to any flourishing epoch is to be
convinced that Schopenhauer was right and that our present
status is not essentially unique. The modish ladies of Weimar
forsook Goethe for the "more modern" Kotzebue. Pradon and
Quinault outbid Racine for favor. Alexandria, Rome, Athens,
Jerusalem, had swarms of writers who were so close to the
contemporary clamor that they have died with it into as whole
a silence. The printing press and the mock crowning of
demos have merely aggravated an immemorial condition.
Where only a minority could read, only a minority could
be idle readers. Now that everyone is forced to read, the
flood of words without creative source is stintless, and there
are organized for it great armies of "distributing agents," of
which an unconsciously servile group call themselves reviewers—even critics! The swollen plethora of pseudo literature has perhaps lowered the visibility of the real through
its sheer mass. But if this be argued an increased deterrent
to the life and health of literature it is more than overcome
by the increasing of the potential public for what is good.
The more persons who can read at all, the more may read
what is authentic.

There is then no good ground for the friend and writer

of literature to complain. He has traditionally addressed a minority in a minority; and it exists for him today. The new presence of hawkers and bawlers purveying printed goods to the mob has not altered his position any more than has the deformation of the democratic doctrine into the myth that everybody is as good as everybody else. If the writer hungers after enormous sales, he is the victim of confusion: unconsciously, he desires to leave his true domain. If he feels that he is entitled to the royalties of a Michael Arlen or to the popularity of a Fannie Hurst, the urgence of his vision must be very weak. For it is the glorious compensation of the wooers of beauty and of truth that all other of life's guerdons are by contrast dull. To have heard clear, even once, the word of God is to hear it forever in all the calls of life.

More serious and more concerning is another phase of this mutual attraction between the real with its rigorous solitude and the false with its populous cordialities. The purveyors of pseudo literature are so many that they fall into classes. They have their snobs, too, their social climbers. And there is among their readers an ample group sufficiently emerged from the rest to desire "culture" even at the cost of thrills. These persons are aware of the term "literature" and want their share in it. Their conception, of course, is derived from shallow study of the past. Incapable of recognizing the essence of an art, they dwell on its external traits and manners. And the contemporary writers who most flatter them are the emulators of these imitable parts. Such authors are competent in style, they are elegant, they reproduce in terms of up-to-dateness the forms and virtues of previous pioneers. Most of them will be novelists, dramatists, even poets. But they must have their critics. And to them falls the dangerous task of establishing a rationale for their kind; an aggressive apologia for all their sterile wares.

The creative, the heroic, the religious spirit of true literature is by such critics utterly ignored; and by repeated omis-
sion comes to be regarded as nonexistent. The novel which
flows well, the tale which is pleasing, the construction which
reflects current thought or current passion is hailed as *good*,
and the more reflective, hence passive, it is, the higher is rated
its importance. Unconsciously, it is assumed that literature
has no independent body: that its real substance is the public
taste. From this fallacy it follows that criticism becomes a
solemn discussion of secondary traits—timeliness, grace and
color. The primary creative stuff of literature without which
these secondary qualities can have no true existence is for-
gotten. The terms of what is genuine are borrowed for what
is false. And the confusion grows.

What hungry common reader could dream, from contemporary criticisms of Mr. Hergesheimer, of Mr. Cabell, of
Miss Cather—supply your own names from the current columns—that these are makers of books with an essential lack:
a lack as crucial as that which parts organic death from life?
The books of such novelists are competent in so far as they
are elegant reflections of styles in form and thought and language. As contributions to the creative life of the mind and
of the spirit, they are inept. Their source is neither a luminous
vision nor an authentic knowledge; but rather the shrewd
perusal of past masters and present moods. Neither their purpose nor their substance adds one iota to the experience of
man. To call them literature is to degrade the name.

And it is precisely urgent that the name "literature" be
not degraded. For there is much in a name: much directing
of intelligence, much shaping of powers. And we possess
an age in which intelligence is not small, but confused, in
which powers are lavish, but debauched. A critic of our day
as aware as were Abélard and Anselm, would be as concerned
as they were with the pragmatic virtues of the Name. He

would know, as they did, that a confusion in words is the symbol of confusion in continents and souls. Much of the dangerous condition of our time springs from the fact that in the readjustment of social and spiritual forms, names have become the prostituted playthings of any fool or knave who wishes to mouth them.

Thus, the gigantic reaches of pseudo literature from the Hearst papers to Harold Bell Wright, being allotted their proper place, do no great harm. They touch only the senses they appeal to; they convince only minds incapable of conviction; there is no formidable claque to name them other than they are. Far more pernicious is the snob class of pseudo literature; for it sails under false colors and of late it proceeds almost unchallenged.

The challenge of other days was a competent tradition. Pseudo literature has always thrived on pretension. But an audience to whom the classics, holy or profane, were valid had an incessant standard to protect it. If a French academician extolled Quinault, there was Euripides to answer. If an Alexandrian put out a bad pseudepigraphia of Ezra, the Chronicles could face him. Our situation is more arduous. In the general liquidation of old forms, the esthetic tradition has dissolved. We must build up a new critical standard not only within, but from the current chaos.

1925

4. "UTILITARIAN ART"

It is revealing that the notion of "art for art's sake," of art sprung from itself and for itself, arose with the utilitarianism of the nineteenth century. If you will read the conversations of Goethe, the prefaces of Racine, the notebooks of Leonardo, the prose works of Dante, and finally trace back to Aristotle and to Plato, you may marvel (if you are a "modern") at the ethical bias in all our classic art. Not alone Milton believed that he was writing "to justify the ways of God to men." It is safe to say that if a respectable goldsmith of the Renaissance had been cornered for a "reason" for his work, he would have professed some moral or some religious purpose not too remote from that which moved the Alexandrians and the prophets. While theology was hale, esthetics was its handmaid. Later, art went into the service of the God of Reason; and later still, took on the harness of metaphysics when that logic had assumed the imperatives of revealed religion. Only when modern man has debauched the ideal of spiritual progress—old as the Hindus and the Hebrews—to a bare functional or mechanistic pattern do we come upon art so divinely considered that it may have no "purpose."

The reason for this is not far to seek. While man's fate was still linked with gods or with godlike values, the arts could honorably serve. When that fate was mechanized into some economic or utilitarian or biological "design," art rebelled and set up a church of its own. The dogma of "pure poetry" and of "art for art's sake" is a reaction from the dogma of vulgar materialism and of "man for his belly's sake." Being a reaction, it partakes of the nature of the source whence, however obscurely, it has risen.

The doctrine of utilitarianism had two esthetic offspring. One is obvious: it is the art which in devious ways aims to "get results" in actual life. The debased condition of such art is coming to be suspected even by the bourgeoisie. The other offspring is the art of the Ivory Tower—the art of "esthetics"—the art of "purposelessness" and of aloofness. And I wish to make clear that these two are radically one. However they may differ in the intelligence that makes them, they are both utilitarian: they are both debased from art's full function.

The philosophy of utilitarian materialism defined life in terms of the pursuit of specific material values. (I speak of it in the past, for it still lingers only in the minds of tyros.) It committed the fallacy of taking some "end" or process *within* life—economic or sexual, personal or biological—and setting it up as the Cause. Like all geneticisms, it was illogical and was, indeed, refuted in the texts of the very philosophers whose shallow disciples had invented it. Now, the same point may, of course, be raised against the nugatory notion of "utilitarian art." Whereas art in its full sense is an organic event of life, sensorily formed, autonomous and yet contingent, like any individual, on its living context, utilitarian art disavows this individual organism of art, and aims to reduce art's essence to some specific effect within the world of men.

Examples of this class of instrumental or utilitarian art are everywhere about us. Such is the "art" of advertisement, of exhortation: such is the play "with a thesis," the fiction of reformers like Upton Sinclair or H. G. Wells. Such, too, are the industrial "arts" whose purpose is to turn out *salable* machines, rather than *livable* ones, as was the purpose of the ancient craftsmen who worked for an intimate, spiritually harmonious client. The arts of the popular magazines are no less utilitarian. A story which strives simply to amuse is kin to the story which endeavors to reform. The novel that "cleaned up" the Chicago Packingtown may have been more laudable, it was not more utilitarian than the tale that aims merely at killing a few hours' boredom. In both instances, you have that organic life process called art narrowed and debased to meet some specific sensory demand. Whether the demand be for clean meat or a vicarious amour, esthetically your books are of one class.

And as "utilitarian art" must be grouped—and condemned also—the current works of the esthetes. Mr. Cabell's fancies may be more refined than Mr. Sinclair's: they are as remote from the whole province of art which can "help" in life by no less fact than that it *is* life. Mr. Cabell, engineering an escape from life, is not in the lineage of the masters: he is an epigone of the materialists who lowered the whole life process into a "struggle" for comfort or for survival. I see no essential esthetic difference between the schools of Mr. Cabell and Mr. Aldous Huxley, and that of Pollyanna. In the latter case, you get sugar instead of a whole experience of life; in the former, you get some acrid opiate. If this is in any way the revelation of a superior taste, then the jaded adult who adores rotted cheese is superior in taste to the child who calls for candy.

The organism of art is, of course, constructed of physical materials with sensory and ideological associations, even as is the individual life made up of physical substances. In life, these materials—chemical, mineral, vegetable—are mysteriously organized into the unitary, indivisible *living organism*. And in true art, the same holds. The sensory appeals—to eye, ear, appetite, memory, emotion—are the materials which the artist has composed into the organic whole called art: which differs from its elements, even as life from its ingredients. A utilitarian philosophy of life might be called one in which some group of these materials in life is made more causative than the whole. A utilitarian art, by analogue, is one in which the main matter (instead of the means) is some appeal to the senses.

Purposely, my definition lumps with the commercial, the pornographic, the dully sensational artists, a whole school of haughty favorites: for instance, Virginia Woolf. Analyze "Jacob's Room," and what do you discover? A sensitive woman (the authoress) with deft hands picks to pieces the banal story of an English boy. Upon her nerves, its fragments register sensations. She is not, like James Joyce or D. H. Lawrence, composing these sensations into organic life.

They are her end and she is using them for a personal sensory delectation which her reader may share. She is not creating at all: she is transposing.

You may apply, for yourself, the same criterion to our music or our painting. Is the composer building the sensory ingredients of his music into an organic life which transcends bare sense, as life transcends inorganic matter? or is he *using* his theme—transposing it perhaps from a well-known tonal to a striking dissonance—in order to get a sensory appeal? If this is his end, even though his name be thrice Russian, he is as completely a utilitarian artist as the man who writes a Buick advertisement.

1927

5. ART IN OUR JUNGLE

When you have done with the latest work on relativity or the theory of quanta, and the once so solid universe has melted into a mere congeries of spaceless, timeless, substanceless vibrations, go to some modern art gallery and bask in the certainties of our painters. For the best of these are men who hold to a reality or are resolved to re-establish it.

From Picasso to Weber, from Marin to Orozco, it is amazing how harmonious most of these painters and sculptors are, in their formal purpose, even in their formal use of color. They are builders of *structure*. Not of architectures or machines: not even, for the most part, of such designs as the fugue or the canon. The structure which they seek to produce is the answer to the chaos which they find about them. It is as if they were plunging through a liquidated world; and as they fall they build—in order to cease falling.

The best of them are workers in a crisis. Confusion of fundamentals is our atmosphere. Emergency in danger is their temper. Their response to the carpers who expect them to be pretty and pleasant is: "We need ground to stand on!" Would you criticize the manners of the man who rescued you at sea? or judge by metropolitan standard the costume of the fireman who led you from a blazing building? If not—and only then—are you in the proper mood to appreciate the contemporary artist.

Let us hope that the modern gallery director has interspersed a number of pretty or "academic" paintings among the works of the creators and of the seekers of form. They establish a curious dissonance. Who shall quarrel with dainty ladies flimsily attired and dancing to a rose? or with excellent gentlemen silk-hatted and promenading with a spaniel? But what if you find them at their peaceful antics on the walls of an embattled city? In some such way are men like Charles W. Hawthorne, Childe Hassam, Henri Martin, most of the British, out of place in a serious exhibition.

The capacity of any generation for misunderstanding its art is not mysterious: it is equal to, for it is the same thing as, each man's capacity for ignoring the essence of his soul. How long is it, since you last heard the usual Wise Word about the whole esthetic movement since Cézanne? "Oh, ho—a Saturnalia of decay! These wistful little artists, so out of touch with the great world; reflecting their defeat, their impotence, their despair. These inadequate anarchists glorifying their own chaos! How lucky it is that we have Solid Science!" Well, your too-solid scientific world has melted. Gone is the atom, gone is ether, gone is the whole Mechanism in which, from Aristotle to Newton, man dwelt irrelevant and complacent. The conclusions of our physicists hurl us back, through three thousand years of certainties, to the "vagary" of the Upanishad: our universe is but the Breath of Brahma.

Relation, Vibration, entity of Movement, conformity of

impalpable motions into a dream called substance—these are the lean relics of our centuries of science. And these are the precise materials with which the contemporary artist is creating truth and beauty! The age which produces Picasso, Maillol, Brancusi, Derain, Braque, Marin, Juan Gris, Rivera, Orozco, is not alone an age of art: it is an age of classical and of religious creation. Only the labelmakers, the "wordmen" are lacking, in order that we may know it. These artists are, if anything, too somberly intent upon their basic purpose. Were the saints more pure to their ideal? Man Ray extracts the essential line of jazz, and has no time for dancing. Picasso establishes the formal counterpoint in a woman's body, and has no eye for the woman. Brancusi's Bird is the bird at its height: a sort of hero-bird which neither mates, sleeps nor builds its nest— a bird, a bird which soars, which is sheer soaring. One and all, these men make a demand on nature as heroic as their own temper of salvation. One and all, they seem to say: "You, bird; you, woman; you, farm; you, landscape—you are doomed: all of our glamorous dream of earth, sky, men is doomed. Unless you are transfigured—unless you will permit that our spirit of the god burn you pure of your phenomenal dross—of your associations of sentiment, of hierarchy—unless you go to your allotted place as parts of an essential Whole, you are doomed. For we assure you, O bodies and sights of nature—you do not exist save in that Whole. The old men who sought to build up their Whole, by adding you together one by one, as you appeared to yourselves, were wrong. You've crumbled and disappeared. The very atoms of your bodies—the very words of your consciousness, have vanished. All that remains is God. If we can reinterpret our tragic memory of you—O bodies and colors of existence—in terms of God, perhaps we can bring you back to life."

Of course, I am saying this in words: the painters are

creating this in paint. Spaniards, Frenchmen, Rumanians, Americans, Orientals, all are tending toward a single declaration. And it would be a shallow error to believe that this symphonic kinship is due simply to the influence of the schools or of certain men in Paris. Paris for fifty years has been the focus of so much modern art, because men from all the world *were looking in one direction.* Paris is not an influence, it is a confluence. The reason why Cézanne rediscovered El Greco, and why French Colonials brought African sculpture to their metropolis, is aside my point. The significant is that the arabesque or body-language of Picasso, the plastic lyres of Maillol and Brancusi, the mosaics of Braque and of Marin, the rituals of O'Keeffe, the revelations of Julia Codesido and Sonia Brown, the mass equations of Derain and Walt Kuhn, and the instinct rhapsodies of Walkowitz and Epstein, are so many personalized departures from a common experience and toward a common purpose.

The common experience is that the old static formulas and bodies wherein Western civilization dwelt are gone; that only relations and the movements of relations are real and are immortal. The common purpose is, to produce from these immediate experiences of relation new bodies (unities) and new forms (faiths and ideas) wherein mankind may dwell and thrive again. And the achievement is already of sufficient stature to presage a modern classic art.

1926

6. THE ARTIST IN OUR JUNGLE

Gilbert Seldes has revived what might be called the classic debate of American culture: Should an American artist stay at home? Mr. Seldes holds that the artist is at home wherever he chooses to settle. And he cites instances in favor of his contention. He is indirectly seconding Edmund Wilson who reproached Van Wyck Brooks for writing an admirable book about Henry James without more than a word about the novelist. Mr. Brooks, of course, was writing about Henry James the exile; and employed him as a symbol in his own thesis which is contrary to that of Mr. Seldes. It seems to me that the considerations and examples presented by both sides have suffered, because they were neither specific nor general enough. Perhaps the exiles of Joyce, Stravinsky, Picasso, were successful; perhaps the pilgrimage of Henry James meant failure. If a law or a rule is to be sketched from these instances, the elements that enter into them should be essentially understood. One might study the basic idiom of the arabesque which Picasso brought with him from Málaga, or the basic folk voice with which Stravinsky came away from Russia; and plot the intellectual transfiguration of these primary materials by the schools of Paris. Or one might attempt to correlate the chaste designs which Henry James desired to produce, and the American chaos from which he escaped in order to produce them. One might at the end decide that James was a shrewd tactician, saving his art by retreat; or that Picasso was a brilliant culturist, enhancing his art by transplantation. Yet the general and haunting problem of the artist in America, which unconsciously inspires all these arguments, would be as untouched as ever.

This problem of the artist is, after all, not unrelated to the question of his materials. In some manner, the successful creator organizes a fusion between what we call his will, his vision or his experience, on the one hand, and what we call life, on the other. Both the creative will and the workable objective material must exist, else there will be no art. Now with this simple idea to illumine us, let us venture into the specific dilemma of the American artist and the American world.

The first thought to occur is that this material of ours is still inchoate; it has not been digested by the conceptual activity of previous generations of American artists and thinkers; and in this it is abysmally apart from the native material of the European. The arabesque, for instance, has been an essential form in Andalusian life for so many ages that Picasso must have absorbed it as instinctively as he did his language. Ages of cultural selection have simplified the expressional background of European peoples; these simplifications beget traits and provide tools for the European artist which he can take with him: moreover, the relation between these concepts in different European countries is so close that deeply a European artist remains at home, wherever he is, in Europe. A concept is an essence; and it can be transported. Or, to shift the figure, if one belongs to a world which has culturally refined its gold, one can leave that world yet take the gold along. But if one has had the fortune—good or ill— to be born upon the scarce-scratched surface of an unmined treasure, and if one indeed wants that treasure for his own— then, it is necessary to get down and dig.

This, it seems to me, is the very human crux of our classic problem: Should an American artist stay at home? The answer may be left to him. He will seek the material fitted for his creative will. To the peculiar will of Henry James, of Whistler, of Ezra Pound, it seems clear that the right material was best available abroad. The point of vision of these artists was static; they required a fixed focus wherefrom to trace in leisured sureness the Apollonian intricacies of their designs.

The creator who yearns to weave ever more intricate glosses upon a given fundamental statement of life is fortunate if he is born across the water. France, for instance, will provide him with a completely conceptualized experience which he can build on and variate forever. And if such a man is born in America and yet feels drawn to the, after all, not too-distant cultures of Europe, it is idle to begrudge his departure.

But there is another kind of artist: he who rejects the fixed limits of any established cultural status, and whose will it is to forge the parabolas of chaos into unitary form. This creator might broadly be termed the religious artist, in so far as his purpose is to bind together what appears confusion, and to make whole what strikes the sense as multiform and diverse.

If an artist of this kind is born in America, he is fortunate indeed. For he inherits a world particularly apt for his purpose. The *life* of America is a stupendous symbol of the human chaos which such an artist beholds in all life ere the transfiguring magic of his unitary vision has been worked upon it. And yet the implicit *idea* of America is symbolic of just such a unitary will. America, in other words, is a multiverse craving to become One; it both challenges and invites the purpose of the religious artist.

This American will to be One is manifest in every noble chapter of our history. More encouraging still, it is the very theme of our follies, the essence of our most ignoble social acts. It is the ideology shallowly applied, of our bar on immigration. It is the unconscious factor in our sumptuary laws, in our pathetic efforts to legislate uniformity of morals. We are not One; and we desire to be One. The whole American scene is, hence, a symbol on a human plane of the sort of activity which takes place in the mind of the religious artist. It provides him with the challenging material; it energizes him toward creation.

The Middle Ages in central Western Europe established a similar apt symbol for the religious artist. Europe was a turbulent chaos in material and fact. Yet it possessed in the ideal Body of the Catholic Church a unitary will. It was this marvelous conjunction of material and will in the objective

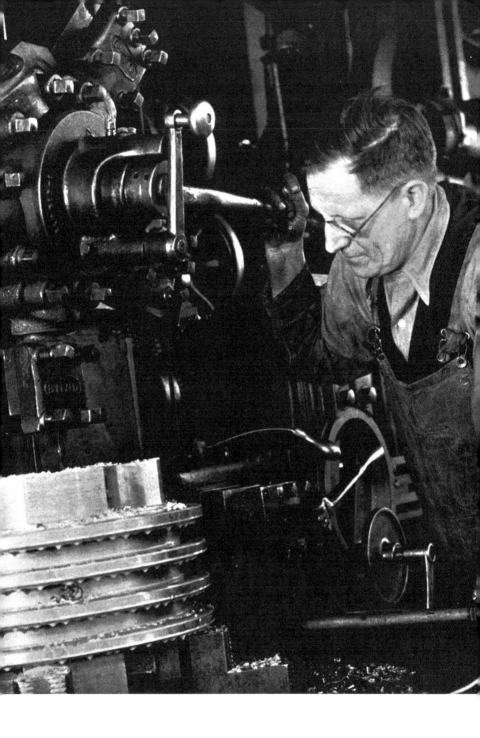

world, with material experience and will within the artist, that made possible the success of Dante, of Aquinas, of the Gothic architects, of the polyphonists—a success not equaled in the modern European epochs, whose art has been for the most a wistful echo or a frustrate fragmentation of that last great Synthesis.

The American artist whose will is to join in the tristful litany over the dissolving body of European culture does well, like T. S. Eliot, to live abroad. The American artist who feels within himself the power to add to the intricate glosses of that culture does well, like Ezra Pound or Henry James, to live abroad. But the artist who is tempted to the task of forging new organic life from chaos may bless his stars if America is his home. For in all the world there is no symbol of this chaos so potent and so pregnant as our American jungle.

Moreover, the failure of artists of this high aim heretofore in our land need dishearten no one. It is true that the athletic will of Poe was not supported by a consonant strength of nerves. It is true that Melville broke down. It is true perhaps that Whitman sounded little more than a summons. But failures of a kind so heroic—and all within a century—will, we may be sure, discourage only those whose intimate desire it is, for their own comfort's sake, to be discouraged.

1925

7. THE MACHINE AND METAPHYSICS

At first thought there seems an insoluble difference between the machine and the tool. The tool is passive in the hand of the workman, and by that fact comes to express his will both intimately and directly. The tool is, indeed, an extension of the hand. The crude laborer has a crude tool and does crude work. The subtle craftsman becomes an artisan, an artist: the tool holds close to his nature and works his will in ways so immediate that the instinctive love attaching limb to mind goes over, consciously, into the brush, the knife, the hammer.

With the machine, this alchemy inspiriting a thing of wood or stone is gone. The machine is set in motion and achieves therewith a somewhat autonomous life. Moreover, the nature of this life does not depend upon the man who works it. Its qualities and its powers are fashioned for it and are inevitably determined, at a source to which the machinist has no access. An inventor, abstracted from his products, designs their future acts. The machines go forth. And the mechanic by a series of rote behavior sets them going, runs them, stops them without for an instant coming into creative contact with the thing by which he lives. A crude man may work at a delicate machine: a blind or illiterate man may print a book: a man with no sense of texture or design may run a machine which manufactures lace or turns out decorations. And conversely, the delicate man—the creative man—can find no immediate channel for his will in running a machine. Whatever creativeness or delicacy it possesses has been ordained for it and is aloof. He cannot swerve it from its stubborn independence. All he can do is care for it. Attendant, doctor, nurse—however you look at it, he is the slave of a creation which in its act and its idea remains beyond him.

Now all this is clear enough and from it philosophers deduce our woes, rightly—and wrongly our despair. If this state of things were final, we might forsee man's downgoing in sterile servitude to a too-exterior, too-permanent grandeur. For, indeed, much of our common misery has sprung from man's loss of tools which were his own and through which in myriad ways he did express himself. With the tool came beauty, because it was a subtly extended and yet obedient hand bringing between subject and object that harmony which is beauty's norm. With the tool came contentment, because by means of it the humblest worker put his seal on his craft; and came pride and those births of pride—morality and value—since the work of the tool was the man himself, and so must be good, and so must be regarded. Finally, with the tool came fullness: for that man alone is unified and full who has spent himself in self-expressive labor. And by contrast, the man is empty and disrupted who has been spent in labor which excludes his deep co-operation. Thus far the pessimists of the machine are right. But here their rightness ends. Could they look back upon what must have been the experience of man ere he mastered the tool, they might more sanguinely look forward.

The primitive man, wielding an artifact, paddling a dugout or making an instrument of a horse, had to undergo a profound psychological revolution ere this element in his hands, stone or wood or flesh, could become an extension of his personal will. He had to grow. How far he had to grow you can see symbolized for yourself by comparing your own hand with the paw of a dog. The step was inscrutably vast: so vast that once man made it, he dared not look back, and soon he forgot—and still he fights to forget. Who shall say what tragic ages went to the transition? to what insanities and despairs men plunged with the strange tool in their bewildered hands, with a wild horse beneath them? Surely, those unmastered weapons must have committed follies; must have broken the measure of men's life; must have inspired the wiseacres of that day to gloomy forecasts. We do not know the names of the Rousseaus of these desperate generations in which man's brain had not yet instinctively grasped the tool. But nothing is more certain than that they existed.

Now, with the machine, we are once more primitive. The

tool is ours: we have tamed it and made it part of our dominion by a step in consciousness. Before the machine, we are still barbarian or savage even like early man before a horse or a stone. Through a failure to make a certain further step in consciousness, before the machine we are still external.

Of course, there are differences. And it is precisely they which point to a new departure in man's life. If the machine were merely a more complex tool, there would not be this new element to our exciting day. The machine is a new part of nature: one which did not, like the stone or the horse, exist before. There is in the machine a marriage of what we call the old elements and what we call the human. The domestic animal, in this sense, was a tool: its elements were outside of human nature. In dominating it, as with any other tool, we mastered a part of external nature. And this was comparatively simple, since in our use of the tool we did not come in conflict with any human will. But if we dominate the machine—make it part of ourselves—we shall have won control over a realm of nature which includes mankind; for man's will, other men's wills, are constant and determining factors of the machine. We shall have won a victory of consciousness not merely over the nature of the external world—but over our own nature.

The problem was one of consciousness in the days of the stone artifact; and it is again of consciousness today. It is a problem profound as human destiny, inscrutably complex. Yet I think the heart of it can be thus simply stated. The animal, so far as we can see, is incapable of the idea of any part of nature becoming part of itself. Man, with the tool, achieved this: fused unto himself the animal and the stone. Call the process what you may, this attitude of his toward portions of the physical world was metaphysical. And no savage could paddle a canoe without this metaphysical inheritance, made instinct.

We flounder before the machine, we are features more or less groveling of its external life, because we lack an instinctive metaphysical consciousness to make us master and absorb it—to fuse the machine with all its elements of will and act into our own expression. Such consciousness, of course, must be evolved vastly beyond the childish metaphysics beneath the use of a tool. In the machine are adumbrated the will of the inventor, the will of the owner, the will of many workers, the will, indeed, of an age and of a world. Only when the individual worker experiences that these wills are not alien to him; that these elements of life contained in the machine fuse, in a higher synthesis, together with his own, into a unitary act—only then will his spirit in participation be able to go out through the machine, so that it and the whole mechanized world may once again, in his joy, in his beauty, in his human pride, express him.

But such a mechanic would possess the consciousness of a Spinoza? No less! No less is needed, in order that the human world may not go down before this new Nature—the free-spawning mechanical invention. The modern machine converges with the wisdom of the ages to force man ahead. From India, from Judea, from Greece, from Germany, has come the single canon: that life is unitary, that experience is One, and that the human consciousness in one form or another must know and be this One. The machine will compel us, at this human crisis, to experience what heretofore merely great men have known. The machine again makes metaphysics man's most practical engagement.

1925

THREE: BOOKS

1. POE AT LAST

Perhaps the classic figures of American literature should be regarded chiefly as actors in the epos of the American birth. With one or two exceptions, they did not produce great books. Yet all of them were heroes; were characters who in their defeats as in their victories fleshed and fixed features of our nascent world. Their lives—like the careers of the patriarchs of Genesis—may prove more current in our future mind than any of their works.

This certainly will be the case with Poe. Despite his influence abroad, despite the range of his activity, he wrote neither verse nor prose intrinsically great. His significance is not to be extracted from his situation. And the construction of the creative Poe—the *true* Poe—has lagged, precisely because this situation was misunderstood. Poe paid bitterly for his youthful Byronism. From his neighbors and the Bostonians, it shrouded him in sentimental horror; from us, it has quarantined the man in an equally blinding sentimental glamour. His first biographer, Griswold, was incompetent. And Professor Woodberry inherited this incompetence for all his scholarly good will since crucial features of Poe's life were hidden and since without them Poe's work, unlike organic great art, lacked an entire dimension.

There has now been published a sheaf of letters [1] which will mark the true birth of Poe as an authentic, working figure in our cultural world. For the most part, they are notes written by Poe to his foster father, with brief notations

[1] "Edgar Allan Poe Letters Till Now Unpublished," in the Valentine Museum at Richmond, Virginia; with introductory essay and commentary by Mary Newton Stanard.

or replies by Mr. Allan. They give us at last the young
Poe, the crucial Poe, and the world which he went forth to
live in and to conquer. The first of them dates from the
University of Virginia which the poet entered at seventeen;
the last reveals him, seven years later, abandoned for the final
time by Mr. Allan who has remarried and is soon to die.
The years—from seventeen to twenty-four—are the years of
Poe's confrontation with America. Prior to them, he was a
child—what manner of child, nurtured and spoiled in the
Richmond mansion of the Allans, his words reveal. And after
them, there come the open pages of his books, of his trafficking
with editors, of his relations with Mrs. Clemm and with
his wife, Virginia. These letters form the link that makes the
whole. Their appearance is a major event in American letters.

The career of Poe becomes a scene in a symbolic drama.
He is creative will, nakedly let loose upon the American
world. Who shall say America did not summon him? He
rises like an impulse from this land which cannot act him
out. Between America and Poe, as between Poe and his
foster father, are the chains of a need unrecognized. Without
his adopted son whom he bred to hyperesthesia and left to
starve, whom he set high and then cast down, John Allan
would be a clod. And without John Allan, Poe would have
been altogether disembodied. In the tortuous recriminations
of these letters, there is the plea for love as well as bread.
Transpose the family quarrel into general terms, and you
have the full years of Poe: Poe, the most highly potential
intellect of a land whose hour of realization had not struck.

In this failure there is no object lesson, no call for a
morality. It is too inevitable and too right. It is true that,
with the intellectual range of a Goethe, Poe gave forth but
a few shriveled and glittering pages. And yet, in his hour and
for his hour, he gave the ultimate, since he gave a Symbol.
An imagined Poe, petted to old age in the rich library of

an adoring foster father, would have been less—far less—than the frail, fierce, frustrate Poe we have.

Unarmed, unguided, he went forth to create in the American desert. His masterful will found no immediate object upon which to work. He had absorbed haphazard the philosophers, the metaphysical poets, the occultists and seers of the Kabala, the chroniclers of exotic journeys. But he did not stay in *their* world. His constant effort was to refocus and apply this chaos of ideas to some absolute experience of life. Witness his treatment of the values of poetry and music: his making metaphysics out of the relation of facts or out of the forecast of facts: his use of the machine, or airships, of mesmerism, of physiology and mechanical contrivance, to express the widening consciousness of the human soul. Even the wanderings of Arthur Gordon Pym end in a revelation. Of course, Poe failed. Grub Street in Baltimore and New York—this remained the stage for his apocalypse. And the hazard crumbs from the intellectual banquets of Asia and of Europe were but manna, in no wise transfiguring the Wilderness which for forty years he wandered.

Yet the lofty impulse of his work is lodged, forever. Poe's theory of pure poetry holds the intuition of a great esthetic. His "Eureka" gives the glimpse of a vision deep as that which is imagined in the Kalpa and the Brahma of the Hindus. A half dozen of his tales, "Eleonora," "Ligeia," "Morella," "The Fall of the House of Usher," etc., are variants of a single theme which envisions the mystery of the Person as close as any prophecy of Blake. Hard, shut, shrunken work it is: and yet it holds a vaster sense of life than do the amplitudes of Whitman or of Emerson. Holds it, however, as a seed the tree. In Whitman and Melville there is life's blossoming. Poe belongs less with the creators of art than with its prophets.

His creative impulse, first to last, was metaphysical and religious. Behind these horrid trips to Ulalume and Usher, these dogmatic repetitions of telltale hearts and reincarnate lovers, is the man's will for a world timeless and absolute. That his materials were the shoddy "seconds" of the romantic Gothic, we may leave to the pedants to assure us. Poe's impulse was no more romantic than was Goethe's. He had a flair for the Real: he lacked the power to establish this reality from the world about him. Hence his defeated flights to other realms. But in his Poetics and in "Eureka," it stands proved that the glancings-off which constitute his "works" were but his trial flights: that Poe was resolved to found his revelation within the visible, audible, beating world. Unlike the Bostonians, Poe was no transcendentalist by choice or reason. The confrontation of experience and then the act of alchemy upon it, by virtue of his vision, was beyond his powers. And was beyond him not, as seemed manifest, because of his harried and brief life: was beyond him symbolically, inevitably, since it was beyond the America of which he was so high, so near, so unachieved an impulse.

Let us make *this* Poe ours. Let us not twang semi-sentimental plaints about his failures. Let us not fool ourselves as to his triumphs. Let us not blame the symbolical Mr. Allan for acting so well his ungrateful role in a Scene so vastly without his canny ken. Let us, above all, not split Poe—as is the fashion of the day—into pseudo-scientific fragments of psychologic and sociologic terms. Let us take him whole— the man and his work: Poe the embodied impulse of an Organism which holds not only him, but us; Poe the impulse of America to transfigure the worlds within it into a world more real. And let us proceed to the Adventure.

1925

2. FRANCE AND THOREAU

Since Bernardin de Saint-Pierre, French literature has come variously to America for materials and forms wherewith to re-create itself. The greatest instance is still perhaps that of Chateaubriand whose impossible Indians may outlast the too-possible Frenchmen of Flaubert. The sustenance which Stendhal won from contemplation of our scene for the esthetic of his novel of the modern will is less widely recognized. We are aware, however, of how the symbolists transfigured Poe; and more recently of the enthusiastic creation by the Dadaists of a romantic America of cowboys, skyscrapers and jazz. Romantic movements in classicist France are ever forages for nurture rather than voyages of discovery. Like Greece, France is omnivorous and egocentric. In every period of influences her writers are like a family consuming beefsteak. That beefsteak will become, let us say, part of a lanky father, a fat mother, a bad pagan boy, and a noble Christian sister. At this moment, we may behold America turn into Louis Aragon, Valéry Larbaud, and Bazalgette. . . .

Bazalgette's translation and biography of Whitman had a dynamic share in the slow stirring of French letters, away from the Narcissus mood which led to the masterworks of Claudel, Valéry, Proust, toward a new gesture of spiritual excursion whence a good range of fresh romantic stuffs will accrue for the young classicists to work on. His Whitman was a biography that held fairly close to the narrative form, save that a lyrism illumined it and made it speak with emphasis and fervor to the imagination of the French. In "Henry Thoreau," however, Bazalgette stands revealed more clearly: a poet himself, and a prophet, he employs a certain spiritual experience made manifest in America because less assimilated here than the experience of Rousseau and of Tolstoi in their lands; and he makes of it his own spiritual Word for France. This technical analogy between Bazalgette in sophisticated Paris writing of Thoreau, and Chateaubriand in rationalist Paris dreaming of our virgin forests must not be strained too far. Bazalgette is less a poet than Napoleon's noble hater, but he is more historian and critic. His book has the lilt and passage and effect of a packed personal paean; and yet it is perhaps the best of all pictures of our great New England. There is no phenomenal relation between Chateaubriand's America—or that of the Dadaists—and ourselves. Their work is, therefore, not negotiable beyond their immediate needs. But clad in the fine English of Van Wyck Brooks, Bazalgette's "Thoreau" responds to our experience. It becomes an American classic as surely as it is a French one.

The method is not narrative: it is a composite of allusiveness, colloquy, lyrical projection and dramatic scening. A hard method to follow unflagging through three hundred pages; and at first the frail figure of Thoreau seems insufficient for it. The author has sustained his tone with ruthless logic that at times may pall. One would occasionally welcome passages in a more direct, conventional prose. But the consequence of the author's lack of mercy is an esthetic form the more remarkable when one considers the, after all, comparative slightness of Thoreau's stuff and the frustrate colors of his milieu. At the end, one realizes that this unsparing method was the inevitable right one for the subject. Thoreau's greatness did not loom like Whitman's. It was the consequence of impacts on a small living nucleus, of the organic yet reactive growth of that nucleus within an inchoate social envelope. When he created his Whitman, Bazalgette had but to follow Whitman. Hence his use of narrative was correct. Even the Civil War fell into place as a sort of objective scene for the hero's progress. Creating Thoreau, Bazalgette creates primarily the New England town, and the woods and the rivers and the birds, creates the astringent air of Emerson and Alcott, creates Mr. Greeley and his *Tribune*, John Brown and his raiders, lyceum audiences and village ne'er-do-wells. A superb massivity of America bounding Thoreau gives him his dimensions by indirection and by the dynamism of the man's responses. It was a subtle task, and Bazalgette has done it. It required a complete mastery of the American scene; and the extent to which this Frenchman who has never visited our land knows it—its past, its present, *and* its future—is uncanny. Where did he learn what a New England village feels like, what winter is in a Canadian wood? How did he catch this scent of the Emersonian family, this shuttling rhythm of Broadway, this dark deluvial stain in the Judge's house in Staten Island? No mere thorough scholarship can explain it. Chateaubriand's Indians, Baudelaire's Poe, are alien and exotic. Bazalgette possesses a true intuition of America. Strange as it may seem, he loves us—loves our promise, our struggle to evolve it. But his love is clairvoyant: his mind has stratified his vision of us with analytic understanding. He knows the heartbreaking husk of social and psychic life in which our promise stifles. Bazalgette is a Roussinean romanticist in that he chooses to bring to Paris our Thoreau as a reality *for it*, from the New England town. But he is no romanticizer of the town. Nor of Thoreau who emerges from the book as a true hero almost by a process of survival. Thoreau is a hero of his age, we gather, because his age was otherwise unheroic.

The book is a new type of novel, if you please, rather than biography in the strict French sense. There is a new novel form—the Proustian—in which the hero is literally "I." An example of it in our language is Sherwood Anderson's "Story Teller's Story." Here is another kind of novel—a sort of Crocean history—in which a real personage is drawn ruthlessly as regards the facts and yet with Dionysian freedom in spiritual emphasis and in esthetic.

A work like this dares to contain anything: and there is to be found here a bit of literary criticism so original in form that it must be mentioned. Thoreau and Whitman meet. Their talk is a failure. Walt is distrustful of this highbrow Yankee who has so consciously turned away from Harvard. Bazalgette records the futile dialogue and adds to it, by way of antistrophe, an imagined dialogue consisting of responses gleaned from the two men's work. The effect is powerful and convincing: a contrapuntal fugue that does more to prove the nuclear energy of the American mind and its unity, in variety, of direction, than a score of essays.

Mr. Brooks's translation has a tendency toward "toning down." The original title, as an instance, reads "Henry Thoreau, Sauvage." This might be faithfully Englished as Henry Thoreau, the Untamed. Mr. Brooks has preferred to substitute Emerson's "bachelor of Nature." Perhaps he shares somewhat Emerson's Apollonian attitude toward this nature-drunk, nature-sweet, neoprimitive neighbor. But the translation is very far, indeed, from a betrayal. It is the process whereby Bazalgette's book becomes indigenous and takes its place in our American literature between the old and the new. Thoreau stands with Whitman and with Melville for the creative transitional gesture between that new America, inheritor of Old World forms, and our old America, creator of a new world. Of this hazardous long birth-hour in whose travail we persist, there is no lovelier expression than the prose of Van Wyck Brooks.

1927

3. FAIRY TALES FOR THE OLD

Our country was not young from the beginning. It had to achieve youth. From the Old World came old shoots: the transplantation as often as not aggravated their antiquity. Ere we could be young, our elements had to rot and to be remingled. This took time. And it may broadly be said that only with the opening of the West and the demise, in civil war, of our old sectional cultures, did America become at last a single sprawling infant.

Even then, the sectional elderships persisted. They took many forms. None more pleasant than the glowing second childhood of New England which stands expressed in the stories of Sarah Orne Jewett. These are tales mostly of Maine in the later decades of the nineteenth century. And rightly enough the best of them are about old women. The occasional story of a child is sicklied over with an aged cast: for instance, Sylvia of "A White Heron" is an old woman's child, and lives with an old woman. And when there is a wooing in "The Country of the Pointed Firs" the maid has grown grey in service of her mother; the man—son of the almost centenarian Mrs. Blackett—is a simpleton past fifty. But whether the scene be the Poor Farm or a spruce island home or the tiny palace of Queen Victoria's Twin, there is ever a single glamorous illusion making the substance and life of these sweet tales. And it is the manner of illusion that dwells in the hearts of folks who have grown sweetly childish, rather than sour, in their senility.

It is not necessary to insist that the farms painted by Miss Jewett are about as "realistic" as the England of "Alice in Wonderland" or of Tennyson's "Idylls." Yet these uniformly charming people, so pure of thought, so innocuous in action, so redolent of lavender and lace, are true, although the theatre of their verity is the poetic fancy of Miss Jewett. We may all snatch from our coming decrepit days the nodding wish to turn from the rot of our world into a sweet-scented realm of senile wishes, in order to enjoy Miss Jewett.

The Maine of a mature mind, contemporary with these

stories, must have revealed men and women more like the
persons of Robert Frost, more like those one feels, rather
by reaction than by direct creation, in the works of Thoreau,
Hawthorne, Margaret Fuller, Melville. And yet these kind
and well-groomed vagaries of Miss Jewett's are no less a
result of the crass facts—no less respectable. The spirit of
them is a sort of iridescent mist rising from the shut pools
of that life.

Of course, stories with substance so wistful and so misty
cannot rank high as art: and we must not permit the present
mood of American reminiscence to which are due so many
biographies, so many re-editions, so many reconstructions, to
blind us to their frail value. The fairy tales of youth have
greater destiny, because they have harder substance. The
child transcends his world: his ebullient vaulting energy despises a mere unmastered round of fact and with parabolic
power brings Mystery to earth. But with second childhood,
reality is too much and is avoided by a sharp reduction.
Energy, exhausted, draws back in catatonic gesture; re-creates
smallnesses to dwell in as a comfortable offset to the no longer
challengeable world.

Willa Cather, a feeble daughter of Miss Jewett, has had
the fondness to compare her tales with "Huckleberry Finn"
(a fairy tale of youth) and "The Scarlet Letter"—one of
the maturest dreams of American romance. But these per-
fumed pictures of the land of pointed firs are a gross reduction of the truth. All the primary lines, colors, forms, are
missing. Indeed, all life-welling passion, all organic substance,
have been mulcted out by the desire for Peace: and what remains is a predigested brew of natural descriptions and carefully balanced converse—a true diet, indeed, for old and
toothless gums.

Yet, although their stuff be small, these tales have loveliness. And one rereads them, after all these years, marveling

at the grace with which their frailties have aged. The scenes of nature are good lyrics. Although Miss Jewett's sea has become strangely gentle, like a parlor pet, it is still living: it is captured somewhat as life is captured in certain two-dimensional prints from old Japan. The dialect has the mark of absolute perfection; and yet is musically mannered so that none of the conscious stress on veracity is there to irk one. But above all—those women, those adorable, impossible old ladies, brewing tea, gossiping, sewing! They are there, not like our grandmothers, but like our childish vision of them—like what our grandmothers would have liked to be, to our rapt young love. Even this sentimental splendor is reduced to a kind of loophole glimpse. And yet the lens is never blurred and the effect has all the negotiability of art.

There was a strength in old New England which passed maturity without losing all its power. There are wild flowers still in these rock-bound fields that go to seed hardily: they do not scatter or fall with the first turning away of the summer sun; but wraithlike they stand aloft upon their stems and let the autumn air run through them. Something of this prowess is in Miss Jewett's stories. For all their simplification, for all their romantic refusal of the true stuff of tragedy—finally, hence, for all their subtle denigration of New England which deserves greater and more athletic art, these tales bear well. They may be tales of senescence—of a soul's twilight: but this is a soul not impotent even in decay.

Most of them appeared in magazines well over forty years ago. As one measures them with what has followed, one is dismayed. For hidden in their glamour is a sinister seed. True enough are tales which spring from a felt illusion. But it is only the lie which has brought forth progeny. The hallucination of Miss Jewett, making her see such paragons of peace and sweetness in the New England farms, causing her in all solemnity to compare the "Bowdoin reunion" with "a company of Greeks going to celebrate a victory, or to worship the god of harvest"—this peculiar magic of old age could not be copied and has not been transmitted. Only the trick of reduction, only the simplification, only the falsehood. And the consequence, patented and standard, swarms within our fiction magazines and in our novels.

The fairy tale turned formula—the fairy tale without the motive of youth or of old age—becomes the harsh, cold, mechanical, nugatory art which makes up most of our current "competence" in fiction. It marks the extension into literature of the processes of mass production which belong to an industrial age. It is responsible for the factories and sweatshops whence reading matter is turned out for the million. How it came to be born you can trace in the soft, warm, gradually shallowing and self-repeating art of Sarah Orne Jewett.

1925

4. DUSK AND DAWN

The basis for any criticism of a book by Lewis Mumford must be respect for the author and thankfulness that he is at work in our country. Rare, indeed, are American critics who, like him, venture into the realm of general ideas; and rarer are the men who, with his good will, possess his rounded equipment. For Mr. Mumford tries to be no specialist save in the task of seeing and interpreting life whole. No less than all the works of men shall be his laboratory; no less than the search of values for "the good life" his aim. He can write of archaic Utopias and future city plannings, of modern books and ancient pictures and medieval guilds; he is at home in all subjects since he has gained awareness that all of them are one.

Mr. Mumford's "The Golden Day" sustains this sense of
him. It is in many ways a beautiful book. It flows easy,
brilliant, poetical, from the store of its maker. It has style, it
has form. There is no reason to doubt that it will take its
place in the sparse critical literature of our uncertain era.

Mr. Mumford has written an essay in interpretation of
the American past. With this purpose, he has utilized an
analysis of our customs, of our ideals, principally through
the medium of our writers. But the standpoint of his study
is the present. He has not written history; he has established,
as his focus, not alone our day, but as well our need. His
retrospect receives its dynamic rhythm, one might almost
say its *life,* from the author's mastering interest in "What
next?"

The general theme, viewed as a series of facts, is plain
enough and has been proposed in similar terms, before. Europe's state since the Middle Ages is regarded as a disintegra-
tion. Of this profound breakup America is a conspicuous
symptom and expression. America was colonized by forces
of Europe's decomposition; and America itself, determining
such states of mind as pioneering, hastened the deliquescence
of that spiritual world which man raised up in Europe and
whose tearing down had no deeper symbol than the emigra-
tions. Howsoever, before the final breakup of Europe in the
American West, new shoots of the transplanted European
culture rose on our Eastern seaboard. In the Golden Day of
Emerson, Thoreau, Whitman, they reached a splendor fresh
and unparalleled in the contemporary hour of a Europe less
swiftly, but as essentially decadent. Thereafter, the American
West, in which the disintegrated force of the Old World and
the barbarizing condition of the New came to a climax, gradually prevailed. Already, with Hawthorne, Melville, Poe, the
Golden Day was waning: the good elements of old Europe
were rotted by unconscious "new" American factors. The

"pragmatic acquiescence" marks America's rationalized slump into the barbaric mood of the industrial pioneer. William James, John Dewey, are good men ennobling the sterile cause. The descent, now, is swift. The muckrakers are social critics themselves submerged in the muck, failing of any principle to catapult them free. Novelists socially and spiritually submerged are Mark Twain, Jack London, Theodore Dreiser—scavengers whose true function is to pick to pieces what still remains of a once noble structure. And not deeply otherwise are the wistful "pillagers of the past" of whom the finest are Henry James and George Santayana; their retreat into Europe or to "philosophy" is motived by as forceless an acceptance of the barbaric day as the rationalization of the pragmatists. Finally, Mr. Mumford brings us to ourselves. After this ebb, we are sunk so low that naught could remain but a new rising. Mr. Mumford is hopeful, one feels, for sheerly tidal reasons.

Of course, to state in a paragraph what the author himself has athletically stripped to but three hundred pages is to leave out much and to denature more. This book, it seems to me, is chiefly a personal essay—a confession by a significant man. You will find, here, excellent pages on the "romanticism" of the pioneer, on the genius of Emerson, on the limitations of Dewey and Santayana. You will find other pages less adequate: as the discussions of Whitman, Melville, Poe and Dreiser. What interests me most in "The Golden Day" is not its assemblage of interpretations, but its focus.

This focus is external. Mr. Mumford is outside his own book. He depicts superbly the Platonic, pagan and mystical glories which in America's Golden Day were called Emerson, Thoreau, Whitman. But they are experientially remote from Mr. Mumford: as remote as Dante and Aquinas. Ideally, of course, we share all greatness and find its recognition in our souls. Yet those medieval worlds were not actually ours:

their source, their form and their behavior differ. Mr. Mumford depicts, also, and with no less eloquence, the horrors of the American scene: the barbaric frontier, the Protestant decadence, the tyranny of the machine and of the job, the fallacies of materialism, utilitarianism, experimentalism, pragmatism. But he is outside the experience of these also. When he praises the age of Emerson, there is an aloofness of elegy. When he exhorts the young men, his contemporaries: "Allons. The road is before us!" there is an aloofness of rhetoric. What is the matter with Mr. Mumford?

The matter is that he has considered us, rather than experienced us. He has gone deep to behold our past greatness, our present miseries; but not deep enough to establish the vital connection between them, and between them and himself. America is an organic subject. Mr. Mumford, for all his studies in causation, treats as a series of isolate manifestations, "good" or "bad," "tasteful" or "disgusting," what are really acts of a single spiritual Organism, yet immature, yet basally "in the making." The Golden Day whereof the author so wistfully sings was not a day at all: it was not even a dawn: it was, if you insist on solar terms, *a* dusk of Europe. But only in its ideologies and cultural forms! More accurately, it was a moment in the American childhood when the spirit spoke lyrically, before the whelming demands of body—of nutrition and of growth—plunged America more fully into chaos. The fact that this age was not a Day is plain in its shimmering, surface passage over the American mind: and in the sequence when America transformed the idealism of its transcendentalists and poets into immediate adolescent matters of expansion and of self-indulgence. Mr. Mumford makes Emerson the hero of this "day." Yet if ever a man was a congeries of lovely echoes, of wistful longings, of fleeting and unfleshed intuitions, Emerson was he! His intimations of immortality were almost literally those which the great Wordsworth beheld on the visage of a babe! Emerson *was* such an intimation on America's huge child face. He was our first, unfleshed, undifferentiate glimpse of manhood—of a manhood still very far ahead.

In Whitman this intimation is no longer the tremorous glimpse so well symbolized in Emerson's frail and evanescent prose. It is a roar of adolescence: a true hunger call: no more. Now, note Mr. Mumford's basic misunderstanding of Poe and Melville. These men were the first to try to *flesh* what we might style the Emersonian intuition in American life. Mr. Mumford calls them figures of the twilight. And yet, from the standpoint of a study of the American Organism, they are more advanced than such more successful artists as Whitman and Thoreau. Poe's mystical attitude toward the mechanism and applied science, his marvelous attempt to add a dimensional sense to the inherited experience of life; and Melville's tragic effort to wed God and whaling—these are the first organic *acts* after the childhood intimations of the men whom Mr. Mumford esteems as makers of our Noon.[1] And the author fails to recognize them, because he has no organic experience in America to guide him. He is in love with the gesture, the dream, the childhood faëry of our past: yet he rejects the *body*—our present interim of the Machine and of the romanticisms of the Machine—whereby alone this promise from our past may be organized into a living future.

Therefore, finally, his book brings the flavor of a plaint: his envoi is wistful and vague, his call to future action has no ring. For American future spiritual action must rise organically from the facts of our hideous present, since these facts are an insuperable sequence from our past ideals. Mr. Mumford, in this book, is a man sincerely, prophetically in

[1] I feel moved to recall that in "Our America," a work with a kindred theme published in 1919, Poe receives even unfairer treatment than that accorded him by Mr. Mumford; and Melville is utterly ignored.

love with the sweet spirit of childhood; yet turning from the physical, often bestial process whereby alone the child can grow in order to express that spirit. When the child America lisps purities half understood, Mr. Mumford blesses. But when the child America gulps food, wallows in mud, slugs and robs comrades, adventures, bullies, cheats—Mr. Mumford merely scolds.

1926

5. ELEGY FOR ANARCHISM

a.

I hoped to glean from the autobiography of Emma Goldman four experiences, each of them worth while: the intimate life story of a remarkable woman, the history of her ideals and thoughts as an anarchist, a portrait of toiling America during the past four decades, and an account of the years of military communism in the U.S.S.R. I got what I wanted, although in each case the net gain in light is different from what I had supposed it would be—different, I feel certain, from what Emma Goldman herself believes her book has given.

The most enlightening point, for me, in the first volume where the author describes her girlhood, her marriage, her entrance into the anarchist ranks after the Chicago executions, her love affairs, her friendships with Johann Most and Alexander Berkman, is that her narrative is almost bare of experience and ideas. The pages fly with gusto, Emma Goldman holds back nothing. But she has, rather amazingly, almost nothing inward to give! Intimately, for all her good will, she appears to remember little of her own sensations; and if there was a period of doubt and inquiry before she accepted Kropotkin and Bakunin, she takes her own thoughts for granted, giving us the bare conclusion. I had a sense of

Emma Goldman writing these pages of her youth; but it was a sense of the mature woman the author, not of the young woman the subject. And this very fact: that Emma Goldman describing her loves, her factories and sweatshops, her cities, her encounters with magnates and policemen, gives no direct experience of her feelings and thoughts, helps to reveal the nature of the woman. One must make one's own deductions, as one might if one were actually speaking with the author. For Emma Goldman is a presence in her book—a deep, hearty presence. She is never the analyst or integrator of her story.

Her chief traits are goodness and energy. There is something abstract in her élan vital, since she is unaware of causes. The Freudians would doubtless call her career a flight from a cruel father (who became symbolized as authority and the state). More obviously, her life was a simple escape from the intolerable pain of inhibitions (personal and social) and a blind rush toward that freedom which the word "anarchism" convincingly evoked. In a life so purely dynamic, there is no pause for thought, hence her book's total lack of ideology; there is no room for emotional contemplation, hence its author's want of vivid memory. Emma Goldman cannot be said to remember her girlhood, and its record, pictorial or sensory, is absent from her pages. Which is to say, that her first thirty or forty years were lived not on an intellectual, not even on an emotional, plane; but were instinctive. Instinctive action (if I may use this obsolete term) is automatic, and leaves no memory.

But Miss Goldman's instinctivism must not be confused with that of others. It is paradoxical, being extremely good and brave. Most women who live on this level are self-indulgent, cowardly, shallow. Miss Goldman, although she seems never to have thought, has a nature both good and profound. At any moment of her youth, it is clear that she was ready to give herself to her Cause. Even her sex life, one feels, was the response of a motherly heart rather than of a lusting body. And if she followed the dictates of her body, the wonder is that even selfish impulse moved her to constant sacrifice and the acceptance of suffering.

This paradox convinces me that there are really persons in the world like the "free souls" on whose actual existence Rousseau, Proudhon and the other romantic anarchists based their theories. No wonder Emma Goldman was an anarchist—and without having to think about it. Her innocent nature predicates and incarnates the anarchist creed. Even in her appetites, she is a woman instinctively good and pure: a woman whose blithe spirit only the alien contacts of official law could poison.

The pages are, of course, full of references to anarchist comrades. Directly, she analyzes them no more than herself; but her own vitality imbues with life her portraits of men like Berkman, Reitman, Brady and Most. Like the author, these figures belong to the romantic movement. They are an issue of the same social forces which gave the Atalas, Renés, Adolphes and Werthers. The key to these characters is a deliberate return to "self"—a return which is a reaction from a system, social and intellectual, that was losing its vitality: so that the romantic return to "self" was literally the escape of "life" from the old Western order. In the profounder romantics (Rousseau, Blake, Beethoven, Stendhal, Balzac, Whitman, Nietzsche, etc.), this return to "self" was sufficiently thorough to reveal the self's cosmic implications and therewith the nucleus of a whole new social fabric. Intellectually weaker romantics did not go so far. They discovered their own yearning ego, and loved it, and regarded the world as a mere bar to its divine trajectory. Their ideas of social justice were rationalizations of their lyric need of freedom. They were the anarchists. They knew nothing of the objective world, save that it got in their way. They knew nothing even of each other, since in the last analysis they knew nothing of themselves. They were "pure being," and since "pure being" is a rationalized fantasy, their own lives have an abstract air, a lack of body and of reason. This *unreality* of the anarchists is perfectly revealed by Emma Goldman. It is epitomized in the *attentat* on Frick by her lifelong comrade Berkman. Young Berkman (a very different man from the mature Berkman of later years) is as good as his girl friend. He *knows* nothing, either: not how to make a bomb, not how to speak English, not the crucial differences between an American magnate and the lords of Tsarist Russia; not (at the end) how to aim a pistol. His act is a "pure act" in a cruel, complex world that has thrown him off, so that he wills to destroy it. The anarchist is a tangential force from the social center, but in his naïve egoism he conceives himself as the center. Thus, by immediate logic, the legalized social world becomes the centrifugal tangent—and he erects a philosophy or builds a bomb, to wipe it out.

Volume One of Emma Goldman's story might, then, be called the premise of anarchism: there are really born in the world persons instinctively good, whom the complex tissue of laws tortures and maims. Volume Two is the conclusion of anarchism: the fate of such persons in the real world that persists. In her record of the past ten or fifteen years, the author is closer to the subject. We no longer have a woman of sixty trying to recreate a girl. We know what the young Miss Goldman was, by what she failed to record: we have the contemporary in a more positiv₃ record. For this other woman has been forced, by her frustrations, from the instinctive rush of her élan vital to the emotional plane. The natural mother blindly fighting for her children becomes the contemplative mother who can no longer wield arms, who can only suffer. The bud of the young woman's goodness blooms into a dark flower of pain. Now Emma Goldman has memory. Her last pages, in which she gives us a War America and a Russia of her own, are suffused with tragic light.

b.

I do not wish to appear to minimize the intellectual contribution of the great anarchist writers. They established a theory of the state which Marx accepted. Indeed, the bitter war between anarchism and communism is one of methods toward a common goal—the classless and stateless society. As anarchism evolved, however, it became an unrealistic fixation on the end, whereas the Marxists assumed the task of establishing the ideological and technical means that might bring the end into existence. The anarchists (in the contemporary jargon) became a dissociation from the context of life: they represented that extreme of social suffering which touches madness in so far as madness is a dislocation from the whole. And against them, Marx brought his organic rationale to the cause of revolution. He counteracted the instinctive anarchist flight from an unjust world by making reasonable the relation between the rebellious impulse and the capitalist system, and by integrating social revolution as an organic (dialectic) issue of our social order. In this effort, it is natural that all the leading Marxists—Engels, Plekhanov, Lenin, etc.—should have made conscious war against the anarchists. But it is a beautiful stroke of fortune which led a leading anarchist, like Emma Goldman, into articulate contact with the first Marxist nation.

Her bitter rejection of bolshevism is well known. She went to Russia in 1920, ready to defend and to collaborate. A year and a half later, she and Berkman left, heartbroken by what she names the betrayal of the Cause for which she has given her life. Her record is full, and is—for reasons unknown to herself—the most significant part of her book. It is the final revelation of the utter unreality of her own kind of revolution. Emma Goldman found in Russia a ruthless state employing repression of all kinds—censorship, imprisonment, execution —in the effort to survive both the inherited chaos of the Tsarist regime and the seventeen White armies that were attacking it. This was enough for Miss Goldman: the old hated state at its old methods. She had never stopped, in her assaults on bourgeois society, to understand it; why, now, should she stop to understand the real problems of the proletarian dictatorship in Russia? Contexts are beyond Emma Goldman, whether they be White or Red. The whole activity of relations is beyond her.

Her book, in its finality, becomes the tragedy of good will and a good heart unguided by a sense of the Whole. The impulse that had made her a rebel was generous; her methods of rebellion were brave and pure. But rebellion became the automatic habit of her life; her one positive response to the objective world of men and of values. If she had *understood* the evils of bourgeois society, she would have understood the inevitability of their survival in the transition period which she witnessed in Russia. Her descriptions of what she saw are factual enough: Emma Goldman is incapable of deliberate falsehood. But she is also incapable of truth, which is the placing of facts in their vital context.

Her failure to understand Russia is the anarchist failure to understand and hence to work upon the world. Her story of a great anarchist (there is something about this woman that is great) becomes the most eloquent defense of communism. If the revolutionary impulse can go so far astray through blind emotion, become so hysterical, so impotent, so unjust, and finally so destructive, the Marxian method is imperative.

But if the lesson of this book went no further, it would scarcely deserve the space that I have given it. Anarchism as a system and method of revolution is dead: communism has killed it. What remains in the revolutionary world is the menace of a fixation, different but as deadly as that which in a hundred years turned the fertile beginnings of Godwin and Proudhon into so pitiful an end. Anarchism has died of intellectual dry rot induced by its eccentric emotionalism. There are signs that orthodox communism is threatened by a dogmatic rationalistic creed (by no means discoverable in Marx) whose inadequate depth and breadth would ultimately exclude the creative energies of mankind.

The intelligent communist will not gloat over the tragic story of Emma Goldman. He will bear in mind that a revolutionary cause must be constantly creative, and that to this end it must be vigilant against mental or emotional habits that exclude the right of fresh discoveries. To bring a new mankind into the world is a long act of birth menaced at every instant by the nearness of death.

1931

6. THE BOOK OF LEO STEIN

The man whose conversations about art have gone into the nurture of most of the important artists of our day in Paris has written a book. For one who knows the author, it will be hard to dissociate these printed pages from the voice of the man who wrote them. To have had acquaintance with this tireless seeker, watched the beautiful curves of his mind moving for hours of uninterrupted discourse upon a mental action, and to have relished his piquant admixture of spiritual humbleness, intellectual passion and ascetic distrust of all passions, is not the sort of experience to be overlooked, just because one of the best talkers of our day has turned to writing. Mr. Stein's work is, moreover, in the best sense, conversation. From beginning to end, his curt and quiet tone is a manner of speaking. The color of the man stands in his most abstracted thought. He has written a volume in which all thinking and all topics are so securely focused to a personal rhythm, that—whatever else—his essay is a work of art.

Mr. Stein has a poor opinion of philosophy, and of what esthetics, at its hand, has suffered. Mr. Stein, moreover, has loved art. He has, in consequence, attempted what might be called a "rescue." The sentimental mists of philosophic thought must be cut away from his beloved; the basis of the esthetic act must be presented in simple, matter-of-fact, assumptionless terms. This is the program. Actually, what Mr. Stein has achieved is a statement as subjective as Amiel's journal: a self-portrayal which is both beautiful and significant, since its hero is so archetypical of his time.

With the purely technical part of his examination of esthetics, there can be no quarrel. It is superb. Mr. Stein has studied the *picture* with a combined sensitivity and intelligence of which I, at least, can name no even approximate equal. To read his discussion of focus, interval, the physiology and analogies of rhythm, distortion, tension, composition, is to be aware of mastery and to know what sentimental perfume most literary art appreciation—from Goethe to Elie Faure—consists of. Mr. Stein's technique for the practical taste of art seems to me to be perfect. His chapter, for example, on "Pictorial Seeing," in which he makes clear how the eyes can turn a dish into a picture, how this ideal act is the basis of esthetics and must inevitably determine the distorting, flattening and focalizing, is a masterpiece; and the man who understands it is ready to see pictures. Moreover, the book is filled with apophthegmatic observations on life, the ego, civilization (which, to Mr. Stein, is yet far from dawning), that should make his volume precious to all lovers of delicious talk. Indeed, the work is so complete in its foreground—the physiology of the esthetic object—that its utter lack of background—the matrix, causality and dynamics of art—becomes the clearer. Mr. Stein makes plain how in a picture it is upon the depth dimension that esthetic success hinges: how, indeed, much European art has failed because of the failure to throw the focus organically back and to make alive the planes which support and enact the forward action. And in this criticism he has given the measure of himself.

If, having so amply learned from Leo Stein how to transform the dish before our eyes into a picture, one were to ask him: (a) why one should do this; (b) why anyone has ever done this; (c) why and how this act is universally linked with the entire history of man's spirit; (d) why feeling and value accrue from this act, and (e) what is the nature of this process whereby the self is enhanced, one would receive no answer. As I have said, Mr. Stein is "against" all philosophy and metaphysics. He takes furious pride in telling us that he has never been able to understand the writers on these subjects: and he makes clear that, if you think you have understood them, you are suffering from a delusion. "Philosophy," he tells us, "is a pseudo-knowledge which attempts to add a dimension to human capacity." "Mysticism," he adds, "is sentimentality taken seriously." The entire effort to establish truth from facts, or the real from our complex of thought and sense and act, being "philosophical" or "mystic," is inadequate and acrimoniously barred from his discussion of esthetics. "Esthetics gives us fact, not truth," he tells us. The work of art is a cognitive object, an object by means of which men may know but which they must "stay outside of."

Mr. Stein sticks about as heroically to his backgroundless thesis as he could, without becoming inarticulate altogether. What value exists in that rhythmic synthesis of ingredients intercepted by self, and called art, unless the unity achieved conveys an experience beyond the matters abstracted? Why should we care to know a Cézanne landscape, if this especial focusing of hills and houses is a mere unification of themselves? Mr. Stein, in refusing to ask such questions or to place his facts in a context that inherently transcends them, dislocates every fact, every question he discusses; as assuredly as he would dislocate a dish (in a picture) if he essayed to represent its planes without the planes that intersect them.

To render art intelligible by isolating it from those causes and associations which invade the philosophic realm is just about as wise as it would be to employ a language after abstracting the meaning of the words. (This, by the way, is not far from the method of Mr. Stein's illustrious and ridiculous sister, Gertrude.) In his fear of unproved assumptions, Leo Stein has made a two-dimensional picture of esthetics. For the expert, his study of the traits of art in analytical cross section is instructive. But for the reader who is really seeking an alphabet of esthetics, the result is arid.

Leo Stein represents, in his attitude, the philosophical defeatism of our day. Because so many little boys have burned their fingers, he will eschew fire and live cold. There is something positively heroic in this spectacle of a man aborting the creative process of his mind, because so many births in the past (as he sees it) have been abortions. Even worse, Leo Stein, having no sympathy with the birth pangs of the world, decides there shall be no more birth at all. To this end, the work of art is reduced to a mere rationally cognitive object, with self as a static co-ordinate of the cognition; and that entire process of dynamic osmosis between self and not-self, *which is the history of culture*, is put away as sentimental nonsense.

His subject has its revenge upon him. You cannot trace more than a diagram of the means of esthetics, unless you know that the configuration of facts in any work of art establishes for both artist and observer an experienced entity called truth, which as radically differs from these facts as water does from H_2 and O, or as a human body differs from the sum of inorganic chemicals within it. And—unfortunately for Mr.

Stein—you cannot talk about anything with perseverance, without having to choose between a philosophy of your own (which is at least alive and yours) and a philosophy that is unconscious and not yours and uncontrolled. This is the fate of the antiphilosophic Leo Stein. He says, for instance: "Some believe there are quite a lot of emotions. Some believe there are only three. I doubt very much that there is more than one, which is just emotion." This sounds like a brave refusal to "assume." It is really an assumption based on an atomistic philosophy whose tenet was that you must split up psychic states just as physicists split up matter into atoms. I might respond that there are no emotions —only organic contexts from which the mind may abstract analytic elements which partake solely of the mind process and which it has called emotions. I don't say my organic philosophy would be truer. The point is that Mr. Stein, in disagreeing with me, is as philosophical as I am.

Throughout his book, such unconscious philosophical assumptions are present: and they are inadmissible because *he* does not admit them. He says, for instance:

Esthetics gives us fact, not truth. But fact to be interesting to adults in the long run must be true. Only science and practice can judge validity beyond the mere aspect. The world as it is scientifically known is not a whole world, but the nature of that world is such that it can find in science a partial reflection that is true enough to work. Our esthetic perception of the world must not contradict this knowledge.

If this is not philosophy—philosophy of a very classic mold —then Aristotle was a landscape painter.

I have here no space to isolate the assumptions which color the esthetic of Leo Stein; nor to work out the inadequacy of his definition of art as a cognitive object. The task would be the more difficult, in that he forbears from the method of statement of his first principles—a method which makes it so easy to attack the systematic thinkers. I detect, under Mr. Stein's abnegation of first principles about the "real" and the "true" and the "good," the cowardice of our epoch. Every man who lives should know that his *life* is an assumed, rationally unproved first principle. The real and the true are categories of our existence and enter as functions into all our acts. Our sole choice is between a creative and a passive attitude toward the first principles thus *given*. So far as I know, the one honest, if vain, effort to reject first principles is suicide. Much of the brilliant intellectual activity of our day is a comfortable surrogate for self-destruction.

1927

7. REFLECTIONS ON SPENGLER

Oswald Spengler's "The Decline of the West," from 1918 to 1926, sold in Germany almost a hundred thousand copies. It would be inspiriting to believe that a profound historical and philosophical work could have so large a sale in any modern land. But the originality of Spengler does not reside in his erudition; it is poetic. The book's metaphysics is eclectic rather than sound; its historical research is vast rather than uniformly deep. "Der Untergang des Abendlandes" is an epos, a myth. So, if Germany has not bought a hundred thousand copies of a great philosophic work, it has at least welcomed a personal mythos of deep interest: one whose elements are philosophy, history, esthetics: one whose comprehension requires of the reader a great familiarity with comparative history and comparative religion.

I think at once of "The Outline of History" of H. G. Wells, which had an analogous popular appeal in America and England. Wells, like Spengler, under the guise of writing history, offered a thesis and a myth. Here the analogy stops. The story in Wells is a vulgar, obvious narrative of "events": his thesis is the most illiterate notion of "human progress" and his myth is a mere flatulent, optimistic dream. Spengler's work is formally beautiful. He builds, not by storytelling, but by the presentation and analysis of analogies. And he concludes on a note as darkly glamorous as it is pessimistic. The Winter is upon us, he declares in doom words that are closer to the note of the prophets than he would care to admit. Our salvation is to perform, nobly and perfectly, the work of Winter: to understand ourselves, to set down as the Seal of our glorious dying life a ruthless scrutiny of what we were.

I shall criticize Spengler harshly enough. Let it be, however, always clear that Spengler has written a work of heroic poetic power. The land that dared to welcome such a volume still possesses culture.

The book's main thesis seems to be disguised in the title. "The Decline of the West"—is it not a misnomer? Has not Spengler really written a history and a morphology of Cultures? But no. Though the title may mislead—may, indeed, have misled its author and its readers, it is a true self-confession of the poet's veritable purpose. Spengler has composed this erudite, overpoweringly brilliant thesis on the anatomy and physiology of cultures, in order to prove that *his* Culture (the Culture of the West) is dying. This is where his heart lies. He has written a swan song. And since he is a citizen of the world whose most valid mythic material is no longer the personal legend, the hero, the war, the romance; is, on the other hand, metaphysics, history, epistemology and science, Spengler has employed these elements to make his tragic tale.

And the value of the book lies not in its thesis and its proof. This decline of the West is obvious enough. Spengler shares his conviction of it with a great measure of good Europeans. For several generations the disaster has been in the air. The Great War was but an episode. Rousseau had some ideas on the subject. No sooner had the Germans after Kant invented the notions of Culture, Progress, Spirit, than the critics rose to prove that their culture was moribund and their spirit sleeping. Since Schopenhauer and Nietzsche, Europe's religious decline has been taken for granted. Tolstoi and Nordau from contrary directions met in calling modern art the herald of the fall. Rimbaud, Blake, Dostoevski, Whitman, were the sort of prophets who declared the death of Western Europe, although it was to predict a new spiritual rise. Long past its zenith is the myth that the "modern age" is a height rather than a decline from the medieval. The notion that the Middle Ages were "Dark Ages" is relegated to Chautauqua.

Spengler's value (and it is very real) lies in his attitude toward this decline of the West and in the method whereby he establishes it. His attitude is poetic. He despises the Superman construction whereby Nietzsche cheated his despair of tomorrow: he is closer to the marvelous poet Rimbaud who accepted the complete negation of all values, without hope of heavens or nirvanas, and who, yet, made of his acceptance a last song. Spengler is in love with winter. So bitter-passionate is his embrace of the death he feels in his own soul that he has written a vast book to prove the inevitability of his love. The romantic "proves" the perfection of his lady by showing how the birds and the trees and the winds sing her praises. Thus has Spengler bent the art and mathematics of the Greeks, the religion of the Jews and Arabs, the cultures of Egypt, India and China to his one loved purpose: he has made them over into ineluctable signs of the winter upon Europe.

Before such thorough passion one must be respectful. This is a song—a death song the Prussian is singing. The work of art is a matter of focus. Here a man with the whole world's learning in his hand has *focused* it to make refrain for a great downgoing. He has seen mankind whole, in order to make that whole the accomplice of his own particular end. He has warped history, maimed philosophy, chain-ganged science, perverted art. But he is an artist himself. He has written a book which is poor history, worse anthropology, perhaps. So was Dante's "Divina Commedia."

Spengler, I have said, is a poet, his metaphysics eclectic rather than sound, his historical research vast rather than uniformly deep. Spengler's masters, as regards the material with which he works out his conception, are almost legion, nor has he always done them justice. The notion of a culture-organism, independent, impenetrable, yet somehow mirroring the universe within its autonomous self, and moved only by God in the mysterious shape of Destiny, is very close to Leibnitz with his Monads. Spengler, indeed, is an instance, with Whitehead and Bertrand Russell, of the revival of Leibnitz, whose realistic, pluralistic universe was for a time submerged under the idealistic waves of Kant and Hegel. To this Leibnitzian base, Spengler adds a good measure of Hegel. His treatment of mathematics, science, history, all the attributes of culture from geometry to esthetics, as expressions of Spirit and as subjective, is Hegelian or Kantian idealism. On the other hand, his radical differentiation of mathematical time (which is reversible) from the irreversible Time which he calls Destiny brings to mind Bergson who opposed creative Time, the signature of Life, to the false, spatial, materialistic time which he condemns as a constructed figment of the intellect. Spengler's anti-intellectualism, whereas it is as logical as Hegel, springs from Bergson, as does, likewise, his hostility to the geneticisms of Darwin and of Marx. His treatment, however, of the art-phenomena of any age as physiognomic traits of its people is a brilliant evolution of what Taine and Renan themselves derived from Hegel.

Spengler avows Goethe as his master. He is forever quoting Goethe, appealing to him as the scientific and philosophic source of his conception. And he is right, in so far as both these men are poets. Spengler is very far from the ideas of Goethe; but in his use of ideas toward an absolute, mythmaking end, he is allied to the creator of Faust.

Goethe's philosophic master was Spinoza. This manifest fact would be inadmissible to Spengler who regards Goethe as the last master of the Faustian soul and Spinoza as an anomalous survival, out of time and out of place, from the alien Magian or Arabian culture. Spengler's thesis of intact, autonomous culture-organisms does not allow that a master from one culture can do more than impede the evolution of another. Spinoza, he declares, shows his strangeness from Western (Faustian) Culture in that he lacks the *force-element* which is that culture's primary trait. Faust denotes force tending toward the infinite. But why cannot the same be said of the personal nature of any of the Hebrew prophets or of Prometheus? In Spinoza, it is true that this trait of personal force is assimilated—or, rather, it is equated—in that balance of individual wills whose sum is God. The point is that whereas Goethe as artist depicted personal force in Faust, he transcended it as a philosopher precisely in his acceptance of the Spinozistic synthesis of forces. Goethe, maturing as a thinker, transcended the concept of personal will as ultimate. Spengler has taken Goethe's esthetic creation of the individual, *willing* Faust, and made of it a philosophic symbol for an entire culture.

Let us take Spengler for a while, as he demands to be taken, critically. My notes of specific disagreements with the Spenglerian presentation of facts and of conclusions would cover many pages. This is no place to print them. Yet I cannot avoid some minimum of analytical discussion.

The major thesis is the critical issue. Spengler considers the culture as an organism. He discerns in history a number of such cultures. He examines the Chinese, the Egyptian, the Indian (Hindu), the Classical (Greek and Roman), the Magian (Jewish-Persian—early Christian-Arab), and the Western or Faustian (roughly Western Europe since 900 C.E.). He discovers in each of these cultures a regular life span of four seasons: spring, summer, autumn, winter. They sum to about one thousand years. The form and length of this course never varies. Each culture has a *soul*: this it expresses through a chief spiritual attitude, through an individual vision of life and through a specific symbol. The mathematics, science, art, religion, political, financial and economic forms of every culture express its soul, its vision—are symbols of its attitude toward life. These expressions go, with the culture itself, through the seasons to decrepitude from youth. Each epoch in any culture is strictly homogeneous with the "contemporary" epoch of any other culture. In the spring, that is, of Classical culture, you will find manifestations in every activity of man which are analogous to those of the spring of Western or of Chinese culture. Each culture lives out its own destiny, dies its own death. No other culture can do more than impede it, even as one tree may impede another's sunlight. There is no interpenetration. There is no mutual understanding. It is an illusion on the part of the Western soul to believe it understands the Chinese, the Arabian, the Greek. The inherent growth of each culture is a matter not of geneticisms and material evolutions, but of Destiny. There is no cause and effect; there are monadlike cultural units, mapped through irreversible Time from birth to death.

Now, the trouble with these organisms is that they are placed *in vacuo*. They are described as evolving their destiny sheerly out of themselves, without relational struggle, drama, reaction, interference. And yet they are also described as having the nature of biologic organisms: i. e., they have youth, maturity, old age; they have a specific lifespan. But no organisms known to man exist in this utter isolation. One and all, they arise from other organisms like them, they live in a continuum of interaction with other organisms like them, they give birth before death or in death to other organisms like them. The culture-organisms of Spengler do not seem to be really alive: they are mere synthetic constructions of the author. In order to prove them alive, Spengler has been forced to a progressive and virtuosic deforming of the facts.

When I say that the Spenglerian culture-organism, absolute, monadlike, impenetrable, does not exist, I do not mean that there is no valid view of cultures as organic within their rise and fall. Before I can come to this, I must examine in at least one detail the Spenglerian proof.

Each culture, Spengler undertakes to show, has a soul unique and radically different from that of any other culture. (If this is so, why is there such strict analogy in the forms, seasons and lifespan of all cultures?) This soul's Weltanschauung is its own. And its prime symbol is its idea of space or of extension. From this symbol each culture-soul constructs its mathematics, its sciences, its religion, its architecture, etc. They are all expressions of the prime symbol. Therefore every mathematics, science system, religion, etc., differs radically from every other. Moreover, there is no one mathematics, no one system of physics, etc. There are as many as there are cultures. Each is true, and true uniquely for *its* culture.

To prove his thesis of the individual prime symbol of each culture, Spengler bravely ventures to establish that Greek "number" and "space" and "mathematics" differ radically from the Western. The Classical prime symbol is the finite unit, the entity, the *here and now*. It denies infinitude, past, future. It considers space as the mere emptiness between objects. Therefore it looks on number (Pythagoras) as the essence of all things: and by all things it means literally things perceptible to the senses. From this prime symbol has come the Classical esthetic unit—the human body: the Greek tragedy of episode and exterior fate: the political unit, a small city (polis): the coin, etc. But the Western (Faustian) soul has infinity as its prime symbol. Space for it is infinite and comes prior to the objects which have their being *within* it. Western mathematics is, therefore, one of function, analysis, relation. Its geometry is non-Euclidean. Its State is a cosmic empire. Its money is credit, not the coin. Its signal art is not sculpture but atmospheric painting and contrapuntal music. Its architecture is not the interiorless Greek temple, but the infinitely soaring Gothic church.

To make his thesis absolute instead of merely suggestive, Spengler is forced to explain away the Dionysian (anti-Apollonian) element in Greek culture and the Renaissance in Western Europe: to ignore the mystical in Pythagoras and Plato, together with the Aristotelian elements of medieval thought and modern science. The idea of the infinite and of aspiration toward it existed, indeed, in Greece. It came over. organically, from Egypt. Classic Greece did not lose it, but formed it, rather; and transformed it. Moreover, the modern mathematics is different from the classic and the Newtonian only in so far as it is a growth. Infinity was a problem evaded by the classical geometers: admitted as insoluble by the Cartesians: and *eliminated as solved* by the non-Euclidean mathematicians of the nineteenth century. The Classical attitude toward ultimate problems was a status of childhood. It admitted only the object and the material. So it evolved materialistic systems like those of Thales, Democritus, Heraclitus; or turned the abstractions of ideas into quasi materials called essences, as in Plato. The Faustian attitude was one of adolescence. It stressed the unsolved and aspirational: the concept of infinite space, the autonomy of the personal will. Faust is a growth from Œdipus; even as the Cathedral is a growth from the Temple. To differentiate the prime symbols of cultures which so obviously were interpenetrated, not alone one by the other, but each by still other cultures (such as the Egyptian and the Hebrew), is to do them violence. It is an unnecessary abstraction. Why Spengler wanted to make this abstraction we shall see in the sequel.

Here is a book packed with intricate allusions. To criticize it in detail would take almost page for page. I must confine myself to one more example. One of the cultures discussed by Spengler is the Arabian—the culture of the Magian soul. Its prime space-symbol is the *world-cave*. It lacks the force element of the Faustian, and the unit-object notion of the Greek. The individual, here, is a mere passive emanation within God, as within an aloof yet immanent and defining Cave. The Arab arch, the mosque-dome, the mosaic painting, are alike expressions of this symbol. As are also algebra (the arithmetic of indefinite number), the arguments of Talmudry, the fatalism of the Moslem. The Magian culture-soul was born about the first year of our era. Precultural to it was the whole pre-Christian history of Judea, Persia, Arabia. Now, as "springtime scriptures," come the Gospels, come the philosophies of Origen, Philo, Plotinus, Iamblichus, Mani. With Augustine and the Nestorians we are at the summer. Mohammed marks the decline into the autumnal dryness whose strawlike flowers are the Arab and Judaic thinkers of Babylon and Spain.

Perhaps this amazing violence done to such various spirits as ancient Hebrew prophet, Berber mystic, Alexandrian pseudepigraphist, Arab Moslem and Granadan Moor, in the attempt to enclose them all within one organic cultural conception, born at the birth of Christ, reaching summer about 400, drooping in 800 and dead with the *rigor mortis* of "civi-

lization" at the year 1,000, will most briefly prove the dangers
of the Spenglerian method.

Of course, there are analogies between St. Augustine and
Ibn Gabirol. Are there, then, none between Faust and Job?
between the writers of the Upanishads and Whitman? between the sculptors of Egypt and the painters of Spain? If
Maimonides is a "Magian Winter man," why is Aquinas a
"Faustian Spring man"? If kinship of "prime symbol" bring
Philo, Plotinus, Mohammed, Rabbi Akiba and Jehuda Halevi
together as seasonal expressions of a single culture, why not
prove for the entire world one spiritual Body, one organic
culture—with its systoles and diastoles, of course, its tides, its
shifts, and yet as well with its deep unity of purpose, its continuity of form and of method of creation?

Death is a breaking up; a lapse from unity into multi-
plicity. When a human being dies, only his unity is gone.
Disease means *dis-wholeness*. Spengler breaks up the world
into these absolute cultures which are really fragments, because there is the tendency toward death—toward dis-
unity—in his own high Prussian soul. *He* is breaking and so
is his particular portion of the world. Let him, therefore,
make conscription of all the wisdom of his world to prove
that his experience is the Law.

Nowhere is the man's will to see crooked plainer than in
his virtual ignoring of the Jews. The whole Scriptural era
before the Gospels is set aside as "inorganic"—not cultural at
all. Now, Spengler's thesis is that the pure mystical religious
ethos is the trait of the birth of a culture. Legalism, materialism, socialism, communism, the various systems of utilitarianism, mark that culture's end and herald the "state of suspended
death" which he calls civilization and which, with all its
wintry signs, he declares now to be upon the European and
American worlds. But if, hypothetically, he had deigned to

consider the Hebrews and Jews as a culture, what would he have found? Mosaism (read: materialism, legalism, utilitarianism) came first! "Civilization" or death came before culture or birth. And from this winter a gradual unfolding toward the spring of the prophets. He would have found matter even more disquieting than that. For this "organism" of the Jews is hopelessly irregular: its seasons and states recur and are intermingled. Nor does Spengler's millennial limit for the entire story tell one-half of its creative tale. He would have found, moreover, that this hypothetic culture interpenetrated with others: revived and created others, was revived by others.

And, looking from the Jews back to his Greeks and Faustians, he would have found a similar intricate story. He would have found, in other words, hope in lieu of his dear despair. Wherefore he looked elsewhere, reasoned otherwise.

The culture-organism is a notion abstracted from human life. It *is* an abstraction. And abstractions are needed for intellectual work. They are right when they are fruitful. To regard the life of Greece as a strict cultural whole is wrong: yet pragmatically it may be correct to do so, since it enables us to get the results which observation in isolated status alone brings. The danger rises when we forget that abstractions are of use qua abstractions. Take them for real and they turn monsters.

Indeed, the idea of the periodic rise and fall of man is probably a similar abstraction. Yet it is justified so long as we employ it either to criticize the past or to envisage a greater future. Both of these acts require the analytic method: and analysis *is* abstraction. And now we are at the root of what ails Spengler. His "cultures" are counters of the analyst. And these he has turned into a poet's bodies. This is why his book, although its impulse is poetic, cannot rank as great poetic art. He tells us a good deal about the cultures which have filled the world. And much of what he says is true and is profound. Nowhere, for instance, have I encountered better comment on German music, on the deep significances of Classic and Gothic architecture. Yet the cultures themselves, whereof he speaks as breathing entities, do not become plastically real. We learn much in detail about their traits. *They* neither breathe for us nor move. They cannot. For they are not persons of a drama: they are tools of an argument.

Human spirit takes forms, of course, and all forms die. But the *constant* is the human spirit. And it is poor philosophy to take its forms as really abstracted from each other. Even the painter of a group of persons must relate them, one and all, upon his canvas if he aims to achieve esthetic truth.

Among the forms of human spirit are the arts which rise and fall; are social entities like state and city, which are builded and broken. But the Spenglerian assumption that the human spirit has no other life than in the splendor of great buildings, great realms, great arts, is a profanation. To prove that the abstraction called Rome was "decadent" in the year 400 is not to prove that Man, then, was less great than in the days when Caesar strutted. It may require a peculiar conjunction of poetic genius and social readiness to produce a Vergil. But there are other ways to the light. And some of them are always open.

Spengler feels death in his own soul. Wherefore he marshals a whole retrospect of life to funeral him in true Prussian glory. But human history is subtler. Man is a variable constant. He can achieve greatness with the ruins of a world as his sole instruments, as well as with the aid of outward fortune. Here, too, the evidence of the Jew might have saved Spengler—from the writing of his book! Variant circumstance has infinitely varied the expressions of this people. They have been warlike and humble; unphilosophical and, later, abstruse beyond the Greeks and Hindus. They have had no drama and flooded the stage: no worldly arts at all, and later supplied such arts for all the world. They have been pastoral, and adverse from the soil. They have been creators, politically, of Greek polis, of Oriental empires, and of invisible, Platonic Zions.

Only in so far as Man remained alive among the Jews was Jewish culture a constant. And this is true of any culture. The undying kernel is humanity: this is the locus of organic growth and of organic permanence which Spengler should have studied. For cultures are never isolate. Cut them off from their immersion in other cultures—in Life, they will die uprooted. They move upon and within each other: they fall to rise, fade to be transfigured.

Above all, the human spirit, in any cultural body, is capable of *unprecedented transformation,* provided an unprecedented new element of life comes fertilely upon it. This is the destiny of evolution. And evolution is true, however discarded the mechanistic form of it may be which Darwin degraded from Lamarck. *And this crucial fact—that the culture, if to be regarded as an organism at all, must be taken as a transforming organism; an organism related to the genus, not to the individual, to the possibly infinite genus, not to the sharply delimited and mortal person—is entirely ignored by Spengler.*

Look on cultures, not as biologic bodies with their youth and age, but as indefinite series like those in mathematics, and you have a fertile abstraction in lieu of a dead one. These series have, each, their inner laws, perhaps, but they are intertwined and any figure belonging in one place to one series may differently occupy other series. Paul, then, who in the Spenglerian sense was a "winter man" for the Jews, could be a "spring man" for Western Europe. And Jesus, his strict contemporary in time and race, could have in him all seasons.

Or take America. Spengler would rightly say that America was born of the dying of European culture. So he condemns us to the *rigor mortis* of civilization; to a noisier Egyptian fellahdom. But what of the new mythmakers, the springtime men, those creatures of pure ethos—Whitman, Lincoln, Melville, Thoreau? In an organic body, shut by Destiny, they have no place, and Spengler doubtless would deny them. In a life series, self-contained yet indefinitely progressing, they are in place. For with such a series each integer is at once the conclusion of what came before and the outset of an infinity beyond. . . .

1926

8. THE MODERN DISTEMPER

(A diagnosis through Joseph Wood Krutch and Bertrand Russell)

a.

In the days when all men of a nation shared a view of life —worshiping Jehovah and obeying Torah, dwelling within the cosmos of the Catholic Church, accepting the divine right of their king or of their reason—it was possible for the author and critic to make his individual contribution without explicitly stating the philosophic ground on which he rested. The base of his point of view was common, and was commonly understood. The personal variation was what mattered. This, of course, is the contrary of our modern state. It is precisely the foundations of human vision—hence of human thought and of language—that have shifted. In place of essential harmony in the premises of intellectual action, there is chaos. But the American writer, despite this obvious fact, seldom honors his public with a clear-cut statement of what his philosophy and his religion are. He may even go so far as to deny that he possesses any, and make of his lack a virtue.

Yet, however negative and confused, each human being must possess an attitude toward life. Every thought is a judgment, every act is a judgment, the interpretation of every word is a judgment: and judgment implies a standard. If that standard is not stated, it may function contrary to the conscious will of its possessor. But it functions nevertheless. Current literary work is for the most part the expression of a philosophy and a religion that are not stated at all. The essential implications never come to light. The student could, of course, go to the complete works of each writer and discover the traits of his *Weltanschauung;* but most readers possess neither time nor power for such research. They are therefore constantly taking in, under cover of a stream of articles, biographies, poems, novels, plays, an attitude toward life of which they never become aware. And this hidden attitude works in them; shapes and nourishes, or corrupts them.

Joseph Wood Krutch is a well-known American critic. He is neither more able, nor less so, than a dozen others who write in our liberal magazines. But he has done what all of his fellows should have realized the need of doing; and what most of them have shamefully neglected to do. He has written a book, entitled "The Modern Temper," in which, with all the clarity and honesty at his command, he has set forth the philosophy behind his judgments—the *measure* of life that determines his specific critical responses. How far he is justified in calling his mood *the* modern temper, we shall see. Certainly, his is *a* modern temper, widespread and hence significant. His book therefore offers an occasion, exceptionally concise, to study the philosophy and spirit of some of the men who write our books and who review them.

In order to take fair advantage of this occasion, I must begin by setting forth in some detail what Mr. Krutch has said. In my summary I shall, without criticism, follow the line of the book in its exact progression, using wherever possible the words of the author.

Chapter 1. (a) Freud says that the unborn babe is the happiest of creatures; into his consciousness has entered no conflict, nor is there any limitation upon his desires. (b) As the babe grows up and experience and knowledge make life miserable, he invents myths of all sorts to recapture or protect his infant bliss. The realm of poetry, mythology, religion, represents the world as a man would like to have it, while science represents the world as it is. (c) Connections between parts of life, explanations of life, reasons for life—relations between the parts—are supplied by the imagination. Which means, they are illusions. (d) Only man has rationality; the universe is not rational. (e) Therefore man is an alien in the universe. His rationality, being "unnatural," is hence an illusion. (f) Our morality and emotional lives are adjusted to a world which no longer exists—because it has been destroyed by reason (science being the reasoning from facts).

Chapter 2. (a) The social virtues of the humanists—serving one's children and posterity, living for society, etc.—are really animal traits. (b) Don Juan is the real type of human. (c) An individualism that is antagonistic to and destructive of the social virtues is the highest human value. (d) Human individualism, the real human value, is perfect separatism of each soul. (e) Nature reveals no ends, only means for its own self-perpetuation. (f) Man in civilization strives for ends, and turns means (sex, thought, etc.) into ends. Therefore man is unnatural. (g) Apotheosis of the ant, as the ideal of nature; since the ant has no individualistic ends, living entirely for the anthill. (h) The antithesis between natural means and human ends is irreconcilable, for when man makes his own thought or sensation or life an end, he neglects the procreation of the species. (i) Therefore, all cultures no sooner ripen than they rot. (j) The alternatives for man are an antlike stable group, or recurrent death at the top. (k) Humanism is riddled with mutually destructive contradictions.

Chapter 3. (a) The generation of Huxley, Tennyson, etc., was sure that science was going to disclose a world in which man is perfectly and regally at home. (b) But science has revealed only a vast emptiness, in which, lost like Milton's Satan, we wing our way. (c) Scientific mastery of the inner life, the soul, leads likewise to no real mastery of it, but only to more confusion. (d) There is no ethics or morals. Anthropology and psychology reveal merely a variety of ethics and morals. (e) Yet man persists in being an ethical, moral creature. (f) There is no royal reason. (g) The reason in which Aristotle, Shakespeare, Spinoza, believed is revealed by science to be mere rationalization. (h) Science itself is doubtful. 2,000 years of epistemology have made it dubious if man can know any reality outside himself. (i) Science gives us one table—consisting of nothing but electrons. Our senses give us another table. The former we know as truth; but the second only can be of use to us in our experience. (j) Science gives us the real universe. (k) Huxley, etc., were deluded, thinking we could make this universe ours. (l) There is no relation between the outer world of science and the inner world of man's needs and emotions.

Chapter 4. (a) Love is defined as the sexuality of the individual separate ego. It is a discontinuous, physical phenomenon with no implications in reality beyond its naked self. (b) Since science and modern freedom have freed love of the old taboos and of the religious and poetic myths, love, as more than naked sexuality, turns out to be illusion. (c) Sex is a mere physical need, and hence has no values whatsoever. Man is simply cursed with this need and must make his peace with it, as he can. (d) We shall have to get used to a loveless as well as to a godless world.

Chapter 5. (a) Tragedy is based on noble action, and noble action is based on the belief (as Sophocles and Shakespeare had it) in the dignity of man's soul. (b) This dignity is an illusion; for it derives from the notion that man is the center of the universe, or at least that he belongs to the universe, and that his deeds have some universal import. (c) With the going of this illusion has gone man's dignity, his possibility of noble action— and Tragedy. (d) The art of the present can only distrust its own thoughts, despise its own passions, realize man's impotent unimportance in the universe, and tell no story except such as makes it more acutely aware of its trivial miseries. (e) Yet with the passing of Tragedy, our need of Tragedy (i.e., of dignity, noble actions, etc.) has not passed.

Chapter 6. (a) To medievalism, life was an exact science. The laws, rules, etc., of that science have broken. (b) Life regarded as a science is now and forevermore intellectually indefensible.

(c) The modern mind, realizing that there is no Peace unless each life is made into some self-sufficient pattern or order or whole of its own, strives to achieve this. Strives, that is, to make life an art. (d) For in science, there is only one Truth; but in art, there may be many truths. Many men have striven to make their lives an art: e.g., Cellini, St. Francis, the heroes of Henry James's novels, Anatole France. (e) In art, there is no standard except the artistic perfection of the individual work, according to its own rules. As an artistic creation, Othello is no better than Iago. (f) In art, there is no ethics. (g) To conceive of life as a group of works of art means, therefore, anarchy. (h) No society can live by such a scheme. Life lived as an art is pragmatically impossible, from the standpoint of mankind.

Chapter 7. (a) What progress did philosophy or religion ever make? None. It was only when the thinker discovered how small are the things he can do, that he did anything at all: only when he renounced looking for the key to heaven, that he was able to keep chimneys from smoking. (b) The world grows more comfortable, as man ceases to strive for anything beyond comfort. (c) But now, despite this progress, behold metaphysics is reborn! (d) It is typified by the neo-Catholicism of France, and the neo-Anglicanism of England. (e) Its essence is expressed by T. E. Hulme, who wrote: "One of the main achievements of the nineteenth century was . . . the principle of *continuity*. The destruction of this conception is, on the contrary, an urgent necessity of the present." The premise of the new metaphysicians is therefore *dualism,* or discontinuity. It says: "There are two worlds: one, the empty spaces of materialism and science, and two, the world of man—spirit, faith, ethic, value, emotion, God. And there is discontinuity between them." (f) But there is nothing of which we are so sure as of the *continuity* taught by science. To earlier, naïve men, the important thing about *living matter* was that it *lived:* but science can only be sure that it is *matter.* (g) We believe in matter, accepting *its* continuity, wiping out the merely hypothetic world of spirit, value, etc.—the world of the modern metaphysicians. (h) Metaphysics is but another petty effort to make life an art: it is a confession of its own despair and failure.

Chapter 8. (a) It is not by thought that men live. The less they think, the better they live. The more they think, the more willing they are to die. (b) The very need of thought proves that man's vitality is ebbing. An animal, a barbarian, has no such need. (c) Civilizations, constructed on thought, reach death; then the naïve barbarians rush in, the man begins anew. (d) The fresh hordes of barbarians destined to renew us are perhaps the Russians. (e) Communism, despite its sophisticated phraseology, is a new barbarism. In communism the individual does not count, only the anthill counts. No religious speculation is allowed. Life is perpetuated, unquestioningly, for its own blind sake. (f) But the inevitable despair of the modern man who, having learned to think, has learned the hopeless abyss between himself and nature, is not so bad after all: since he has physical comfort. Philosophical pessimism is not so hard to bear as cold or hunger. Ours is a lost cause, but we should rather die (in comfort) as men, than live as animals.

b.

Our next step is to examine the various elements of Mr. Krutch's philosophy of life: to test their quality, their typicality, and to compare them; to measure their cogency as the cause of such desperate conclusions. The references are to the divisions of his argument, as catalogued, omitting repetitions and minor points.

Chapter 1. (a) states with apparent sympathy that a prenatal, vegetable life, bereft of struggle or aspiration, is a possible desideratum. (b) asserts that there is a dualistic conflict between art, which is an illusory world, and science, which is the real world. Here is the author's doctrine: the relation between the unborn babe and the womb in which it lives is real; but the relation between the born man and the world in which he lives is illusion. Therefore, since life in any individual consists of the relation between it and its environment, and since no man could live an instant without some relation with the air and the world, what Mr. Krutch is really saying is: the life of the unborn babe is real; the life of the born man is an illusion. (c) implies that relations and connections between man and the universe, such as imagination supplies, are necessary for his welfare. But they are illusory, since the imagination is delusion. Yet Mr. Krutch has not even attempted to prove that imagination is delusion. This is his premise, so that, of course, this must be his conclusion. (d) and (e) invalidate man's reason, since the universe has no reason. Yet the author employs his reason to prove his alienness in the universe. Virtually, he says: "My reason is invalid, since the universe is not rational. Yet my reason is, miraculously, valid enough to *prove* that no relation between me and the universe exists." What he should have said, logically, from the premises, is this: "I declare my reason to be exclusively mine. Therefore it is not a cogent measure to determine any relation outside myself. To discover if I belong in the universe, I must employ some measure common to both me and it: some measure that I can move from myself to the universe." Of course, if he had relied on some such measure—a measure of mass, for instance, or of causation—he would have found *continuity* between man and the universe. Conclusion: the chapter assumes that continuity between man and the universe is desirable, but that absolute discontinuity exists. The assumptions are sustained by means of indefensible logic.

Chapter 2. (a) states that since man's social virtues are found also in animals, they cannot be human. This is tantamount to asserting absolute discontinuity between animal and man. Darwin, evolution, modern biology, are therefore flouted. The author unconsciously assumes an attitude more close to the early ascetic Christian and neo-Platonic concept of an abyss between man and brute. (b) and (c) lift up an old Spanish myth as the real human type. Don Juan was a "man" who could make love to countless women without ever becoming tired, without ever becoming attached, without ever changing, without ever feeling. Psychologists class him as the archetype of "fixated adolescent" and agree that he never existed, outside the realms of pathology. This insulate human "atom," the "perfect individualist," with no social relations or connections, this abstract fiction of infantile will, is the human ideal of our author. (e) and (f) carry on the thesis of discontinuity. Nature has no ends and is not moral: man has ends and is persistently a moral creature. The traits of nature are determined by studying the ant, etc.: they are by no means to be determined by studying man. For the ant, by some inscrutable right, belongs to nature, whereas man does not. This is really the premise of the argument: Mr. Krutch makes it the conclusion. His syllogism in its pure form is this: "Man is not part of nature: man has certain traits: hence these traits are not part of nature. Therefore man, possessing these (unnatural) traits, is not part of nature." However, let us grant the premises that the ant is in nature, man is not. The conclusion must be that man is different from the ant. From this, our author is inspired to conclude that man, to *succeed as man*, must behave like an ant! Man, to succeed like a man, must build anthills and—nothing else. Conclusion: the chapter declares, in the face of anthropology, biology, sociology, psychology, that man is utterly apart from nature and from animals, and that (even as the old ascetics and transcendentalists insisted) he is a separate creation. Here is the syllogism, transposed for clarity: "A tree is made of wood. Apples are not wood. Therefore, apples cannot belong on trees." But despite the organic difference between man and "natural creatures," he must behave—if he would succeed— just like the creatures whom he in no way resembles! (Here, the ascetics were more logical. Having posited man as different from the brute, they mapped out for him a totally separate course.) Assuming the organic difference, our author insists that the two relationless entities must go the same way. He builds up the definitions of his humanism upon illogical contradictions; and then dismisses "humanism" as full of the contradictions of his own bad thinking.

Chapter 3. (a) and (b) are repetitions. (c) looks for science to "master" the soul—and looks in vain. Pure science attempts merely to measure, from the outside. For instance, it weighs the sun and names its elements. It has no mastery of the sun, in the sense of controlling the sun. To a slight degree, science has similarly tried to "measure" the soul: i.e., to analyze its components. Pure science has never attempted more, leaving the application of its discoveries to education and religion. The modern effort in these fields is unknown to our author. (d) comes down to this: science has found that *noses* are not alike, in any two parts of the world. Negro, Eskimo, Malay, Nordic, have decidedly different noses. Ergo, science has discovered that *noses do not exist!* . . . To prove that morals and ethics do not exist, it would be necessary to prove that the sense of right does not exist or is at least very rare. But anthropology shows that this sense is universal. Its diversity of ethical and moral forms, of course, is due to the fact that morals are a product of the interplay between men and their environment. To say that morals vary is simply to say that men vary. To say that morals do not exist, because they do not agree, is to say that men do not exist because men do not agree. Chapter 1 revealed the genesis of the author's mood as the result of an exorbitant faith in reason. Now (f) and (g) call reason a bad name, and dismiss it. Chapter 1 illogically employed human reason to establish the preponderance of an external, irrational universe over man. Now the evidence of the mind is declared to be poor: the universe itself may be but the projection of that poor human's reason which (in another part) has no existence within the universe. Mr. Krutch has said: the table of science is real. The table of his senses, like the neo-Platonist dwelling in Tyre or Batanaea in the year 300, he rejects as unreal. But the old Tyrian was logical. He lived where his faith was: he utterly declined to follow his senses. This is too athletic for our modern. With one breath, he gives credence to the table of electrons; with the next, he confesses that the false table is the only one he ever hopes to live with! But the lack here is greater than merely one of logic. Mr. Krutch has the most childish notion of what science *means*, when it states that the table is a congeries of electrons. . . . The language of science is mathematics; and mathematics is a logic of *forms*. Everything that cannot be expressed in symbols of mass and motion is nonexistent within the realm of mathematics. Now, pictured in so far as it exists within the domain of science, i.e., in so far as it is a congeries of mass in motion, a table, of course, can be nothing but a congeries of mass in motion: a chart of electrons. In the precise same way a living body, pictured in terms of anatomy, can be nothing but an anatomical structure. But there are other domains; for instance, human behavior, which has qualities that the language of mathematics does not cover. In this domain, the description of the chair as a group of electrons will not work: but the notion of the child who has never heard of electrons, but who wants to sit down in the chair, works very well, indeed. To say that science is the *whole* truth, because it prophesies an event like an eclipse, is just as reasonable as to say that the ideas of the child are the *whole* truth, because the child prophesies that it is going to sit in that chair, and straightway does so. The eclipse takes place in a realm where human quality is largely extracted: so we are right to deal with eclipses in the logic of science. But man's experience of beauty, for instance, before that eclipse is largely in the realm of human value. Here, the language of poetry is more adequate than that of mathematics. To deny one of these measures in absolute favor of the other is as reasonable as it would be to say that the architect's blueprint is more real than the house. Mathematicians of high order, of course, are aware of the limitations of their language and therefore of the realm which their language expresses. It is only the weakling, desperately in need of an absolute Word, who speaks like Mr. Krutch, of the "certitudes of science." Not Poincaré, not Einstein. Not the typical Eddington who says: "There is a constant unknowable in science. . . . Scientific laws are merely truistic measurements of a single physical condition. . . . So long as the electron is not reacting with the rest of the universe, we cannot be aware of it. . . . A particle may have position or it may have velocity, but it cannot in any exact sense have both. An association of exact position with exact momentum can never be discovered by us, because there is no such thing in nature." . . . All of which is tantamount to saying, that the mathematical electron is an abstraction, that it is a mere plausible symbol; and that certitude can never exist in a field which is built up on the assumption of discrete, separate parts; since these parts do not exist—cannot exist in a continuum; and could not be observed by man, even if they existed.

Chapter 4. A display of the same dualism and an assumption of the same discontinuity between the various functions of man, and between man and his world. The author's attitude toward sex is worthy of the hermit in the Egyptian desert. Sex, as an energy expressing the whole man and woman, linking them in a full human relation, mobilizing their creative as well as their possessive nature, is unreal for the author. But unlike the antique gymnosophist whose rejection of sex he shares (while ignoring his science of self-control and despising his God), Mr. Krutch has not the courage or the will to carry out his own convictions. He considers himself superior to his sex; but he is quite willing to capitulate before it.

Chapter 5. The finest writing of the book is here. Mr. Krutch discourses on Tragedy "as it once was" with discernment and fervor. It is plain that he is attached to Tragedy, "dead child of fallacy and illusion"; he can write with loving observation about the body of a "fraud." (a) and (b) assume discontinuity, once more. (c) and (d) misread the modern status of literary art. Human dignity still exists, noble action and noble lives still persevere. The disappearance of the anthropocentric cosmos and of the personal heaven have enhanced man's sense of dignity within himself. He is responsible now, not as the child of a mythic Father, but as the father of himself. Yet more is needed than dignity and noble action for the production of Tragedy. Tragedy is a social form. It must enact man's dignity in communicable, common terms. These terms are wanting. The modern conscience of the world has not yet bridged from private into public symbols. There is nothing discouraging in this. There were ages of social preparation, also, before Sophocles and before Shakespeare: ages in which individual men had dignity, in which men lived nobly, and yet in which no great Tragedy was written.

Chapter 6. (a) begins with a dubious statement. The medieval science of life was inexact; it was, indeed, founded upon self-contradictory laws, and the dualism of these laws, which were supposed to conform to life but did not, eventually disrupted medieval science. In "The Re-Discovery of America," I have gone into this question at some length. Here it is not centrally cogent, so we let it pass. (d) and (e) again imply discontinuity and discreteness not alone between man and the universe, but between man and man. Men, says the author, have so little relation among themselves that (f) if each man lived his truth according to his essence, these multiple truths would sum to anarchy! If men are essentially related, if the reality or truth of each is a focus of the interplay of the whole (as philosophy, psychology and social sciences agree), then their living by the light of their individual reality and truth would bring them into active relation with one another, and would result in harmony. These premises are denied by Mr. Krutch. The rest of the chapter is less essential. It is interesting to note, however, that it implies the impossibility of man's ever achieving any inner principle of order or control, whereby he might integrate his life within the vicissitudes of the world. The chapter is the final admission of man's impotence. The artist is the creator of a kind of order. Man can be an artist, says the author, when he deals with words or pigment or marble. When he deals with life, man can be only an amoeba.

c.

But the reader has had enough of this dissection of a dreary argument. Let him give one final backward glance to Chapter 7, and I shall insist no more. There he will discover that Mr. Krutch, after desperately building upon the premise of *discontinuity* (of absolute separation between man and nature, between man and man, between certain traits in man and certain others), refutes the "new metaphysicians" on the ground that *they are the discontinuists;* while he falls back on the continuity of science! The reader will agree that Mr. Krutch has now sufficiently revealed himself as a befuddled man. If he were a thorough pessimist like Schopenhauer or Gautama, if he were a thorough transcendentalist like St. Paul, if he were a thorough materialist like Haeckel, if he were a thorough individualist like Rousseau, we could disagree with him and yet respect him. But he is thoroughly nothing, except confused. His thinking quavers between contradictory extremes of which he is not even aware; his values are a crazy-quilt of fragments pieced together from the worn creeds of Manichaeism, Puritanism, Rousseauism, Nietzscheanism,

Haeckelian monism, etc., etc. His emotions are infantile. His spirit is an aggressive fear that would deny to others the dignity it lacks. He has nonetheless been worth our scrutiny. For his argument contains most of the clichés and most of the implications of our current "culture." It shows the distemper of the modern mind, unable to bear the chaos of three centuries of ideological destruction, and unschooled to reform that chaos. If the average pundit in "The Nation," "The New Republic," "Harper's," "The Atlantic Monthly," "The Dial," were to put down, with a like candor, his philosophy of life, it would turn out a no less pitiful confusion. If our current literary arts were analyzed, they, too, would reveal a message as ill-founded. Behind the stubborn bewilderment of Theodore Dreiser, behind the lyric bewilderment of Sherwood Anderson, behind the bravado of Hemingway, behind the dandified despairs of Cabell and the earlier T. S. Eliot, behind the dainty froth of Thornton Wilder and of Carl Van Vechten— behind the materialism, the cynicism, the indifferentism, the impertinence, the impotence of most of our popular writing [1]—exists a failure to think straight from the facts, and to feel straight, not identical with the failure of Mr. Krutch, but essentially related.

The key to the situation—perhaps the basic cause of the "modern temper"—is suggested in Chapter 7 of Mr. Krutch's book. What the author calls the "new metaphysic" is merely the old transcendentalism. These men whom he attacks— neo-Catholics, sentimental mysticalists, spiritualists, deniers of the "flesh" in one way or another—answer the "certitudes of science" by declaring that there is *another world*—their world of value, spirit and religion. Here, you have transcendentalism defined. And Mr. Krutch rejects it on the proper ground of discontinuity. But he does not see that his

---

[1] The reader of "The Re-Discovery of America" will know that I find important exceptions to this general statement.

own argument—the separateness of parts and traits of man from other parts, and of man from men, and of men from nature—is discontinuity no less. And he does not see that he has blinded himself to the discontinuity of his own thought by the naïve method of calling *his favorite part of reality the Whole.*

Like the two ladies in Kipling's jingle, transcendentalist and materialist are "sisters under the skin." The transcendentalist (Platonist, Christian, Christian Scientist, etc.) starts by dividing the world into (1) spirit-value-quality-soul and into (2) matter-body-evil. Having begun this dualistically, he cannot go on. Unknown to himself, *he must reduce this duality into a whole.* This he does by denying the part he does not like—by denying matter. (He may be subtle about it, like the followers of Henri Massis, or crude, like the disciples of Mrs. Eddy.) Now, he has his Whole, which is all life, all good—which is All. But this All will not bear the buffets of the world: for it is really a fragment. And the transcendentalist begins his endless labor of corrupting reality, in order to make it fit his figment. . . . The materialist starts likewise. He, too, divides the world into (1) measurable matter and (2) the unmeasurable qualities of certain kinds of matter—good, value, love, spirit, color, poetry, dream, etc., etc. He, too, cannot abide this dualism, and must somehow manage to resolve it into a One. He simply rejects what the transcendentalist exalts, and takes what the other refuses. He sacrifices everything that is not measurable matter. Whatever cannot be measured, he says, does not exist. But the part of the Whole which he has legislated into nullity still "functions" in him. He wears himself out, denying the domains of emotion and thought which his petty "whole" has no room for. He becomes the tired cynic, like Mr. Krutch; or the arrogant pseudo-scientific clown, like Dr. Watson.

(Of these two sisters, it must be avowed that the transcendentalist is less foolish. Both find "living matter." The one rejects matter and retains the abstract living: the other accepts matter and denies life. But it is plain that we are more sure of the undifferentiate quality of *living* than we are of matter. Living without form does not exist, of course: living-matter cannot be divided. But there is a difference of degree in the folly of the camps.)

Between dogmatic transcendentalist and dogmatic materialist—each hoisting his "part" into a Whole—stands the agnostic, of whom Bertrand Russell is an illustrious instance. Mr. Russell understands the limitations of the language of mathematics, and how they must limit the scientific universe which mathematics symbolizes. He says that there are two general logics: the logic of quantity and the logic of quality or feeling. He says that both are right.[1] But since the logic of quantity (measurement and science) is within the mind of the observer who personally must follow the logic of feeling, Mr. Russell concludes that there is no way of measuring the *measure* value. So he decides that it is all no use: man can

[1] We have in America a logician who, obscurely and unaided, is working out the fundamental problem of the dualistic languages of modern culture, and who is relating them into a logic of the Whole. His name is Scudder Klyce and he resides in Winchester, Massachusetts. He has published three books: "Universe," "Sins of Science," "Dewey's Suppressed Psychology." In the first (which I have not yet read), he attempts to establish continuity, or the Whole, in purely empirical terms and to construct a logic to express it. In the second, he exposes (often brilliantly and at times wildly) the contradictory dualisms in modern thought. The third volume, as invaluable as it is unwieldy, reveals the failure of John Dewey to carry his own "infinite pluralism" to its logical conclusion: an explicit philosophy of the Whole. . . . So it goes in our America. Just as one is getting ready to despair of the current tendencies, along comes a man like Klyce who is doing work as essential and great as any I know in the contemporary world. I was not aware of Klyce when I wrote "The Re-Discovery of America." That is my excuse for not mentioning his contribution and its organic part in what I call the Great American Tradition.
P.S. Since the writing of this note, Scudder Klyce has died. The first work to acknowledge the greatness of his contribution has yet to be published. But it will come!

never know anything since in order to do so he would have to "get out of himself." And of this agnosticism he makes a dogmatic virtue.

The agnostic is not so different, after all, from the other two. He also has begun wrong: he has arbitrarily divided the world into two parts, of which one theoretically is "the truth," and its expression into two languages or logics. Having made this dualism, he also irresistibly is driven to seek his Whole: and this he does, not by the sacrifice of one part *to* the other, but—since he cannot separate them—by the sacrifice of both! For the Zero of the agnostic is a kind of Whole: nescience is an assumed omniscience. The man who *knows* that we cannot know is dogmatic also. Again, in this agnosticism,[1] there is the same false premise: the dividing of reality into two parts. Wherever this is done, there must ineluctably follow confusion and falsehood, agnosticism or despair. . . .

d.

The voices of confusion, agnosticism, despair, are the popular voices of today. The average American reader of the so-called educated classes has been brought up on literature and science that were crassly dualistic. He probably left a dualistic church when he was young. He has fallen at once into the camp of Rousseau (the individual as a separate, perfect atom), or into the camp of dogmatic science (only measurable matter exists), or into some allied camp like that of vulgar collectivism (society is real, but its individual integers are not). These statements, of course, are caricatures: that is why they express the distorting effect of modern doctrine on the average mind.

The consequence has been that the common reader of

---

[1] Not to be confused, of course, with the athletic *skepticism* that is the servant of positive knowledge.

books (the kind that calls himself an intellectual) is helplessly lost and helplessly confused. For his doctrine and the world will not go together. "Feeling" draws him imperiously one way; "knowing" another. He is miserable. And misery loves company. The literary art which makes that misery respectable by "proof" that there is no other course, and by decking out impotence in gracious gestures, becomes the popular art. Books have engendered the modern distemper. The least they can do, now, is to justify it.

The curative, recreative task is very hard. It is the work of the ages before us. And those of us who choose it for our own will have to labor in the cold of an unfrequented dawn. Yet, although it is the task of generations—of armies of artists, of corps of truly scientific thinkers—the essence of it can be stated very simply.

We have seen how even the dualist and discontinuist is irresistibly drawn to believe in a Whole, and to create a Whole (out of his favorite fragment). The concept of wholeness, the experience of wholeness, the living of wholeness are the unavoidable aspiration of human life.[1] This is so inevitable that even the intellectual denier of wholeness in the effort of his thought and deed belies his rejection. The right beginning, therefore, of our task must be to conceive a Whole *that will be the Whole*. Let us passionately refuse all dualism, all denials, at the outset. If science is so foolish as to say: "There is no color in the colored thing," let us challenge that science. If religion is so foolish as to say: "Man's soul is separate from his body," let us challenge that religion. If mathematics is so foolish as to say: "*x* and *y*, although they are in the universe, are not joined, but are discrete and separate," let us challenge that mathematics. Let us say:

"There is one and only one irrefutable truth: *the universe*

[1] The reader will find a development of this idea in "The Re-Discovery of America."

exists. Men differ about what it is, men differ about where it is. Some say it is all 'matter,' and outside; some say it is all 'thought,' and within. All must agree that it *is.*

"There is, to this one truth, one corollary that is irrefutable also: *the universe, for each of us, is focused from the self.* Self—whatever it is—looks out, or looks in, on the universe. Men differ about that. Yet must agree that self *is* that focus of the universe which knows the universe exists. Self, therefore, is *of* the universe (it may be the whole of it, of course) which self asserts.

"All my words, all my thought, all my action, shall be determined by this single common truth—this single common premise of existence. My words will be such that when they point to a 'thing' or a 'state' (as all words do) they will imply the tentative existence of the thing or state, within the certain Whole. For the thing is vague and fleeting: only the universe is certain. . . . My thought will be such, that when it represents a 'thing' or a 'state' or an 'action,' as all thought must, it will imply its tentative existence within the certain Whole; and its valuation of the 'thing' or the 'state' will be the relating of it with the universe which alone is certain. . . . And my action will be such, that it expresses this relationship of self and of all things involved, within the Whole that is the premise of all thought and all behavior."

If these few words, necessarily insufficient, suggest the revolutionary task that challenges human life—the re-creating of language, of society and of man in the image of the Whole which is God—they will have served their purpose. But the task is not impossible. The ant is born with the capacity to fulfill his function. Savage man was born with the capacity to fulfill his. Why should historic man alone, of all creatures in the world, be born without the capacity to realize himself? All history attests that man's nature is a striving toward the divine achievement: the focusing of the Whole in his thought, the enacting of the Whole (this is called holiness) in his deed. But whereas all art, all science, all religion, are the striving toward this consummation, they have always been too weak: so they have broken. Dualism, with its rejections, its denials, its corruptions, is the symbol of this breakdown. Dualism, in its twin forms of transcendentalism and materialism, has always brought a temporary death to man's immortal effort. History is a short tale. It has been just long enough to tell us what, as men, we have to do.

But let us Americans not delude ourselves. Only the Remnant lives. And this is so, because the way of death is easier than life. Mr. Krutch has stated well the inevitable end to which the dualist—whether he calls himself materialist or transcendentalist or agnostic—is ineluctably brought. "Ours is a lost cause," he closes, "and there is no place for us in the natural universe." So he elects to die. This is the death, indeed, of the race of men who look upon themselves as alien from the remotest star, and who put their loyalty in life upon one jot less than the Whole which is God. Let them die. . . . And for the race, still at its dawn, let Spinoza speak:

A free man thinks of nothing less than of death, and his wisdom is not a meditation upon death, but upon life.

1929

9. THE "UNIVERSE" OF T. S. ELIOT

The collected essays of Mr. Eliot provide a portrait of a mind that for the past twelve years has prominently played on the American literary scene. The volume contains theoretical chapters from "The Sacred Wood," eleven papers on the Elizabethan dramatists, the entire brochure on Dante, essays on the Metaphysical Poets and on Dryden, Blake, Baudelaire, Swinburne. It represents Mr. Eliot's social and theological position in the studies of Lancelot Andrewes, in "Thoughts after Lambeth," and in the two essays on Babbitt et al., which did so much more to discomfit the new humanists than the lunges of their foes. And finally, it reveals the more casual man—delightfully—on topics like poetry in drama, Wilkie Collins, Dickens and Marie Lloyd. The book portrays a sensitive, finely endowed person. Itself an accumulation of comments on many matters, it suggests a review of like nature: one is tempted to pass from page to page detailing, comparing, dissenting. But the place of Mr. Eliot as a literary influence in our time, and the cultural crisis of our time, make this method inadvisable. It is important to employ the book as a means for seeing the man whole; and, having done so, to deduce a measure of his values as a leader and thereby a measure of the time which took him as a leader.

The first revelation is of a man with an exquisite, almost infallible, taste for the stuffs of literary art. Whether he touches a line of Dante or of Swinburne, a melodrama of Cyril Tourneur or of Wilkie Collins, the prosody of Baudelaire or of Blake, Mr. Eliot evinces an esthetic delight which implies true contact with his subject. This first trait is particularly distinguished in an age in which the field of literary discussion has been almost monopolized by writers who may know something of baseball or economics but who ignore the nature of literary art. The second trait of Mr. Eliot, not less pervasive but more subtly entextured in his book, is his moral sense; and this, coupled with his first, is even more rare. We have had plenty of moralists—More, Mencken, Lewisohn, are examples—writing on literature and totally insensitive to literary esthetics; we have had a few "estheticians" disclaiming the moral sense (as if esthetic form were some kind of insubstantial absolute and not an organic configuration of ordinary human experience and motive), and therefore writing with even worse futility on books. When

Mr. Eliot compares lines in Massinger and Shakespeare, contrasts tropes in Dryden and Milton, draws a prosodic sequence from Donne to Shelley, he reveals, in his taste and judgment, the moral integer: he knows the *human nature* of esthetics. This moral sense is organic in the man; it is no mere acceptance of rules, it is not moralistic. Being the permeation, within his specific literary experience, of his general view of life, the moral quality in Mr. Eliot is religious. Everywhere, although he may be discussing merely a choice of verbs in Middleton, he reveals a general and definite attitude toward existence taken as a whole: and this attitude, when logically formed, becomes religion.

T. S. Eliot, then, is portrayed by this book as a man with a sense of the whole, with a conviction of his place in the whole, as a man engaged in an activity (literature) for which he is fitted and to which he gives his entire equipment. Such a crystallization comes close to what Nietzsche meant by a cultural act; and in an epoch whose literary critics have been insensitive and incompetent men, it makes Mr. Eliot an exceedingly welcome figure. If, however, we turn from those contemporaries in contrast with whose nullity he looms, and measure him rather by his own subjects and by the literary exigencies of our epoch, Mr. Eliot dwindles. No single major essay in this book, for instance, can be said to be organic either as a presentation of its subject or as a literary essay. Consider the "Dante" in whose study he is at his best: every observation is exact, many a phrase stands forth a luminous gem; but the observations merely mount arithmetically into so many pages of running comment. Dante and his work are never objectified, never dimensionally re-created either in the world of Dante or in the world of T. S. Eliot. Or consider the justly admired pages on the Elizabethans: they contain glimpses both precise and profound into the art of the theatre, into the poets and their world. But none of the plays, none of the dramatists, is made to stand whole, either in the epoch, in the drama, or in some total conception of the critic.

If, then, as I have stated, there is wholeness in Mr. Eliot, we are led to question what kind of wholeness it must be that can focus so superbly on details in a dozen poets and a dozen epochs, and yet fail to envelop any one of them. It is true that this failure is not always complete. In the "Baudelaire," for instance, or the "Swinburne," we obtain a kind of two-dimensional cross section, built from the prosodic study, which we can place for ourselves in the organic milieu of the nineteenth century. But in the essays on the more cosmic men there are no dimensions beyond mere points of light. And in the studies of dynamic but little-discussed figures, the failure is disastrous. The pages on Bradley, for example, proceed without the faintest evocation of the two ideological worlds—Hegelianism and English individualism—which Bradley sought to synthesize. The chapter on Lancelot Andrewes is a mere ringing of personal responses to the old priest's music, which become sentimental and pretentious, since there is no effort to place this music in the symphony of Roman Catholic, Jewish and Arabic exegesis, from which it was never truly independent.

T. S. Eliot, it becomes plain, is a man of integrity in the real sense of the word; but his vision is such that it can never hold more than details; and his energy is too weak to give organic form either to his subjects or to his essays. Unlike most of his fellows, who suffer in a chaos, he lives in a "universe." But this "universe" of Mr. Eliot's is evidently small and minor. It is achieved by huge and deliberate exclusions. It scarcely contacts with the modern world—the world whose radical transformations in physics, psychology and economics have dissolved all the old formal values. Nor does it really embrace the past worlds with which Mr. Eliot is so sympathetic: Dantean Europe or Jacobean England. This failure of mastery even on Mr. Eliot's chosen ground is revealing. No one can understand a living past who is not actively engaged in the living present. For any past age is an integer in the creating of today, and only by conscious sharing of this creation can the past, as part of it, be understood. Fundamentally, Mr. Eliot's subjective love of the Anglo-Catholic tradition leaves him as remote from what England really was as his distaste for modern problems leaves him remote from us—and for the same reason.

That reason brings us to the heart of our portrait. Any living world, whether it be Seneca's or Shakespeare's or our own, in so far as it lives, is dynamic; and Mr. Eliot's world is static. Wherefore, in confrontation with a chaos of dynamic forces like our modern era, a chaos which our dynamic will must meet, grapple with, and mold, Mr. Eliot can only ignore; and in confrontation with dynamic worlds of the past, he can only rather sentimentally adore. His own static vision picks out details, reflects them and variates them into a kind of series, like the stills of a cinema, whose total effect may be sensitive and delightful, but cannot be organic.

This same static quality explains Mr. Eliot's loyalty to a class and a class creed. A static universe does not evolve, cannot believe in evolving. It does, however, accumulate, and its "additions" make a quantitative change—the one kind of change and of cultural contribution which Mr. Eliot admits (see his essays on "Tradition," "Individual Talent" and "The Function of Criticism"). In a static universe, transfiguration and revelation, and the capacity for these, are all stratified in the past. And this is another way of saying that Mr. Eliot's spiritual experiences, from which issue his moral and esthetic taste, although they are real, have the form not of life, but of an inherited convention. Thus Mr. Eliot, with a religious sense, conceives of no religion except the orthodox Christian;

with a tragic sense, conceives of man's struggle exclusively in the cant meanings of Original Sin; with a sense of the spirit's need of discipline and order—both in society and in the person—dreams of no method but that of a moneyed class ruling through church and state.

Are such views valid, in the sense of having a relationship with reality? Is there a position from which the universe is static; in which transfiguration and revelation are past; in which Good, Evil, and the given political and economic forms are absolute? The answer is Yes, in the sense that death, being real, is valid. The living world of the mind is as dynamic as the material world (they are one); there, too, the individual life must partake of the dynamism of the whole, and when it is severed from that dynamism we call it dead. The only difference is, that in the world of the mind we do not commonly employ the term "death"; we prefer to say conventional, dogmatic, static. Mr. Eliot's position is that of a man who has withdrawn from growth—in our meaning, withdrawn from life. *He* is static, his soul's transfiguration is past, whatever progress he conceives must be a mere consolidation of himself into forms already uttered. His intellectual, spiritual and poetic "life" is a rationalization of this death deep within him.

We hold now, I believe, the key to T. S. Eliot. He is a man who has abdicated; but since he has been deeply sensitized to life, the articulation of his experience remains an exquisite, lingering echo. Such abdicated men have always existed, and have never been vital: even in periods of cultural stability (like that of Dante, for example), the cultural whole had constantly to be re-created by dynamic men. But in our age, where stability has foundered into chaos, and where the need for spiritual growth has become absolutely identified with the bare struggle for survival, the discrepancy between a man like Mr. Eliot and adequate leadership becomes enormous.

What we have really defined in our portrait of T. S. Eliot is a type of minor poet. He is in the tradition, neither of our major poets—Poe, Whitman, Melville—nor of the great Victorians. He is close to a cultivated and popular figure like Thomas Gray; and his "Waste Land" is a poem as good, and of the same nature, as the "Elegy." Gray also was a technical innovator with an immense appeal because he foreshadowed, unconsciously, what was to become the dominant appetite of Europe: closeness to nature. From the energy of this appetite, Titans were to evolve the method for absorbing and controlling nature. But in Gray, the motion took a reactionary form: a sentimental harking back to the values of Puritanism (and to the language of Milton). The analogy with "The Waste Land" is complete. Here, too, is technical innovation together with a vague foreshadowing of what is *now* the dominant need of the world: the need of an organic, a livable Whole in which all men and all man may function. This foreshadowed need gives to the poem its pathos, its unity and its importance. But, as in Gray, it is negatively stated by an evocation of a sentimental memory and by the use of old materials—in Mr. Eliot's case, more diffused and catholic, since no strong Milton stands immediately behind him.

The questions remain: why has Mr. Eliot been a leader and what does his leadership reveal about our literary generation? The questions are swiftly answered. Even in an age of confused standards, there is recognition of literary merit. Mr. Eliot's clarity, it is true, is achieved not by integrating the chaos that has bewildered us, but by withdrawal. Yet to the men whom the cultural dissolution has frightened and weakened (the majority of men), these limitations make him only more acceptable. A long time ago, I wrote of what I called "the comfort of the limit," and explained its appeal to many types of mind lost in our modern chaos. Only athletic souls can face a world that has become, perhaps more than any other era, an overwhelmingly open and darkened future. The temptation to limit this world, either by rationalistically charting its future (a disguised reactionism) or by merely advocating its reform in an image of the past, is great and manifold.

All the dogmatisms of our day are really such "limits"—such simplifications of the real. There is the dogmatism of science (the comfort of limiting reality and its mastery to problems of mechanics and addition); there is the dogmatism of cynical despair (the comfort of giving up hope and therefore struggle); there is the dogmatism of a pseudo-Marxian dialectic (the comfort of explaining the human tragedy in terms solely of a simple, solvable class struggle). And, for the weakly poetic, there is the haven of an elegiac past, like Mr. Eliot's, in which great poets still sing and sure priests thunder.

The one way of life that has no limit and affords no comfort is the way ahead—into the bitter and dark and bloody dawn of a new world, wherein mankind shall integrate without loss the stormy elements that make the chaos of our day, and its promise.

1932

FOUR: SOME PRACTICAL CONCLU-
SIONS FOR THE SURVIVAL OF MAN

1. SOLIDARITY IS NOT ENOUGH

(Notes written in the Great Textile Strike of 1934)

a.

At dawn, they are all outside the mills: men, girls, mothers with children. The huge structure, submerged in mist, leaps suddenly with lights; the gates swing open; nobody goes in. The men talk in lively groups, the mothers smile, the girls have put on their glad rags and there is song in their throats. At the doors stand a few guards, glumly. In half an hour, they swing the gates shut and the lights snap out. The crowd of strikers, sure of its strength, strolls up the long flank of the mill, stretches in the morning sun; idles down to the next mill where stands another crowd before shut doors.

The strike has begun gaily. Men and women have joy of themselves in their common purpose, like a young animal discovering the health of its body.

Over on the North Side, before the open gates of a mill stands the crowd of strikers. Half a dozen girls pass forward, their heads low, their shoulders hunched. They are going to work. As the guards let them in, women call after them: "Ain't you ashamed!"; men mutter angry and then ugly words. The thousand strikers understand the six disloyal girls; a sharp doubt stirs in them all, particularly the women. "We need the money too . . . maybe they're right. Maybe we'll lose and only the girls will win. . . . Rent . . . milk . . . coal . . . winter coats for the children." The strikers are murmuring against their own fears . . . the faithful presence of poverty and cold . . . which they see personified in the six girls. The girls are at work now. The mill has become the form of their betrayal, and of the fear of the strikers. Already the holiday mood is gone.

b.

Fall River molders in the ruins of an industrial era. Small mills, built like castles with Colonial windows and with ivy on the brick, have been abandoned to the sweatshop rats. And the wood houses of the workers have died into festering shanties, the streets rank as rotten teeth. A man climbs the outside stair of one of these dead houses and enters a room at dawn. A mother stands at the stove; three men bend over a mimeograph machine in the far corner; and from two cots four children eagerly look up at the comrade.

He takes a leaflet, reads it, and nods. "Here's another we need at once." The children hear the words: ". . . the independent unions . . . because they hate the U.T.W. they won't come out. We got to show 'em that they must come out. We got to make 'em see, even if the A.F.L. did doublecross 'em, we must stick together. . . ."

The men huddle again over the mimeograph machine. One of them is Portuguese, the first shaft of sun lights his fine hard mouth; another is a French Canadian, lumberly, musical, a Northern spruce walking the world. The man who has come in with the text of the new leaflet is a Yankee with the lantern jaw and gangling limbs of his Puritan forefathers.

"Here, you drink coffee first," sings the mother.

"No time——"

"You drink coffee first," she insists.

c.

Back in the South Side of New Bedford, five thousand strikers gather round the bandstand in a park to hear their leaders. Near by the harbor waters dance in the morning sun, dance up to the silent shadow of the mills. But a little along there is a line of mills athrob with labor: the great tire-fabric plants called the Fisk and the Devon, which recognize no union and worked clear through the six months' strike of 1928.

William Batty, chairman of the strike committee of the U.T.W., gets to his feet. He is a burly fellow with a sharp nose and piercing eyes in his red face. He praises the strikers, he praises the President, he hurls his contempt and hate at the "Reds who are trying to make trouble." One gets the impression, as he talks, that the strike belongs to him and to the other leaders: the workers are accessories and servants. "Leave it all to us," is the burden of his message. "Washington"—sacrosanct word; "Strike headquarters in the Carpenters Building"—a Temple which only U.T.W. leaders are good enough to enter. The man has power, and has shrewdness. No doubt of that. Look at the heavy shoulders, the thin-lipped mouth. But where does he belong? He is standing on the bandstand a bit above the workers, he is talking a good deal down to them: one hears, in the rumble of his hatred for communists and shop committees, the echo of other voices, more shrewd, more potent: voices of politics and Money.

After Batty comes Ferdinand Sylvia, U.T.W. organizer and local favorite, who is running for State Representative on the Democratic ticket. A little, passionate Portuguese he is, and clever; the hard black eyes are nobody's fool. How he praises the workers! "I'm proud of you. You're making history today. We got a great friend in the White House who will help us against the bosses. . . . All you got to do is stick together. We'll go back to Washington and do the rest." There is no personal enthusiasm in the crowd for these leaders. But there is devotion to the cause which these men lead; and above all, there is the will, tense and a little wistful, to believe that they are truly leaders.

Sylvia speaks of the tire-fabric mills that are still working and holding New Bedford from a 100 per cent tie-up. "Go down and picket," he cries. "Get 'em all out!" The mass, five thousand strong, moves quiet down the harbor.

d.

A youth with the high forehead of a poet, the Socialist Minister Glen Trimble, starts the picket line before the Fisk and Devon plants. Batty waves the crowd on the opposite side of the street to join; a couple of hundred men, women, girls, are soon patrolling. They are having a good time. They sing "Who's Afraid of the Big, Bad Wolf" and, in lesser number, the old I.W.W. "Solidarity" song. Down from the windows peer the workers who refuse to strike. In the eyes of some is a defensive disdain: "If I can despise the strikers, I'll not feel the need to join them." Others are torn in conflict. Some of the boys and girls look down in veritable terror: not terror at the pickets, but at something in themselves that holds them back . . . that makes them fear to join their sisters and their brothers. *Fear of their own fear*—the beginning of wisdom.

I slip into the office and ask for the manager. He says he'll talk to me, provided I do not disclose his name for publication (I do not blame him). The same stale line about his "happy family of workers," and the conscientious refusal to let "outside and alien organizers interfere in our affairs." "We figure," he says, "we can run our plant best with our own men. We give better minimum wages than NRA has asked for."

"But," I ask, "aside from the issue of wages, don't you recognize a democratic, an American, a human issue? Labor is struggling to organize, like the bosses and business. Aren't you working against the American spirit by discouraging your men from getting together? You admit conditions are bad in other mills. Why don't you encourage these workers to help their brothers by joining the same union?"

The managerial eye grows cold and blank; the hands twitch. Then, obliquely: "I don't get you. What good would it do if these men struck with the others? If one is starving, is it better that two starve?"

I realize the hopelessness of making a class-bound man hear the theme of loyalty and dignity in another class—in the class which he must exploit and degrade in order to survive. I expected no better. But as I return to the town center (while the pickets march) for a bite to eat, I find that the waitress is on the side of the strikers; the barkeep across from the best hotel, mixing me an excellent Tom Collins, says: "Sure, the tire-fabric mills should strike!" and the garage mechanic who fills my tank is warmly and openly with the strikers. This was not the case four years ago at the last great strike. Even a cop on the corner confidentially leans to me and says: "I guess the boys've got it!"

Up in the Labor Temple sits a little Scot, Abraham Binns, and runs the works. Dispatches pickets to hesitant outlying mills; phones Washington, puffs his pipe, and wonders, if Federal Relief backs down, where the funds will come from to feed the strikers. A sincere old-timer, he is, with a good eye for the detail of the battle and no vaguest notion of what, *really*, the battle is about. A thirty-hour week, a minimum wage? Sure! But that a world is breaking and has to be replaced by another lest the heart of mankind perish? . . .

I ask him about the National Textile Workers Union.

"They're communists," he burrs, as if to say: "They've got the smallpox."

The workers think they can force the bosses to abolish the stretch-out. Binns sees that, and he'll fight for it, too. But he does not guess that what the workers really want is to live, and *that they must create a new world to live in.* What chance has such a leader against Capital, the shrewdly conscious foe that knows, indeed, it is fighting *to live* and for its world to live in?

e.

Yonder in Hazelwood Park, a young woman is talking: she knows what Binns and Batty have never dreamed of.

It is dusk of the first day. Seventeen thousand of the twenty thousand textile workers of New Bedford have come out; the exceptions being the tire-fabric mills. The talker is Ann Burlak, organizer of the N.T.W., herself a weaver and the child of Ukrainian workers of Northern Pennsylvania. The Boston and local papers have put the spotlight on Ann. She is the "red flame"; she is reputed to be "in hiding in the tenements of the South Side," and the police announce they will run her in "on the slightest provocation."

Ann is a tall blond girl in her early twenties. Her body bespeaks tenderness and grace; you feel that, were it not for a stronger love, she'd spend a lot of her time dancing. The firm jaw, the clear eye, the intelligent brow, make you understand why there's so little time for dancing. On the bandstand, all around her, is a bunch of kids. They frolic about, none too silent, in the way of children; and I wonder how she manages to keep her mind, and her hearers' minds, on her subject. The local N.T.W. organizer, Walter Burke, has the same concern; and he tries to shoo away the kids. But he is far too gentle about it; the kids refuse to go; and when Burke observes that they are not troubling Ann he gives up. Then it comes to me, that far from disturbing this reputed "fire-eater," the gathered children give Ann Burlak the appropriate setting. Truly, she is speaking for them; of the gay young world they can inherit, if their parent-workers know what they want, and fight for it, and know how to fight.

How different her tone from the U.T.W. leaders who harangued their crowd from the same stand! Ann Burlak appears to have faith in the workers and to be pleading with them to take hold of their own battle. She has to go easy. If she tells them straight what their leaders are up to, dickering with politicians and capitalists, they will scare. If she tells them straight what her motherly heart is full of: that the bosses cannot lose under capitalism, that the workers under capitalism cannot win, they will turn pale, and glance about them and cease to listen. It is a subtle task, this leading of the ignorant American workers to the realization of their own needs, of their own powers, of their own nature. And Ann Burlak does it well. Gradually, unobtrusively, she draws her hearers to the facts about "arbitration," to the shortcomings of the U.T.W., to the single devotedness of the slandered "Reds." The men and women listen. They have come, many of them, to have a look at the "red flame"; a good show for nothing. "They say she's hot stuff," explain the boys in the bench before me. Curiosity and frivolity fade, as the tall young woman gives her sensible heart and her motherly mind to her hearers. Mothers find themselves face to face with the truth: the bare cupboards of their homes, the bare bodies, the bare futures, of their children. Men see with their eyes what for long their hearts, despite the palaver of journal and politics, have known: that they, the workers, live in an enemy country! Latin, Slav or Yankee, they live in a land possessed and ruled by foes who are sworn to exploit and to degrade them.

At the close of her pleading to the workers to know themselves, to respect themselves, to be themselves, Ann Burlak tries to lead them in song. The men and women pitifully follow. And I am minded of the singing at a camp meeting which I recently attended. How the words rang for Christ's second coming! Surely, had Christ been in his heaven, he must have answered these splendid ringing voices. And the thought came: When the workers of America learn to sing the coming of their world on earth as their fathers, the Christians, sang for their world in heaven, the Revolution will not tarry.

f.

It is midnight, after the first day. Around the Fisk and Devon mills, gravid with lights and labor, stand battalions of police: the comparatively kindly town constables with clubs and the sinister khaki-clad motor-cops with guns in their holsters and tear gas in reserve. On the park side are massed the strikers, a good ten thousand. Glen Trimble harangues them.

"They won't let us picket? We'll see about that. All of you here at the crack of dawn. And when the workers file in to work, we'll have a picket line for them to pass through."

A Negro in the crowd, in a quiet penetrant voice, says: "Why wait till tomorrow? Why not picket now?"

The crowd turns toward the mill; Trimble accepts the challenge. The police clubs stop them. The picket line halts, wavers, turns. And its repressed energy gathers in hands behind. Stones fly from the park side, and smash the mill windows. The police press forward.

Seven hours later, huge shut vans roll up to the red buildings and disgorge officers. Far off, beyond an empty lot, fully a fifth of a mile from the mills, stands the crowd and boos as the tire-fabric workers pass through to their jobs. Near the gates, they form hesitant knots. A man stays behind, while his wife enters. A girl looks up at a bevy of her sisters beckoning from a top mill window, grasps her bag and joins them. The police, guns swinging, slide across the empty lot, and the workers fade in the grey background of the harbor.

"There'll be no picket line," shouts the police chief at

Batty and Sylvia. "We had enough last night. Look at them windows. Just you let your men come up, and we'll take care of 'em."

But while the clubs and the guns mass at the Devon side of the huge block, and the crowds die before them, another corps of workers comes to birth on the farther slope of the mills; a line forms . . . marches.

The sun rises, the mill throbs. The clusters of hesitant workers have vanished, either inside to the machines or away. Suddenly, a gate swings open. The crowd rises in voice: "THEY'RE COMING OUT": and forward, four abreast, march the Fisk workers to join their brothers and sisters.

Sylvia crows like a cock. "I'm proud of you!" And to Mary Vorse and me: "Tell 'em in Washington and New York, New Bedford has the world's best workers." Even the cops smile. The walk-out is 100 per cent. Now what? . . .

I think of the heroic tiny groups of revolutionary organizers throughout the nation: individuals, isolate, threatened, resourceless save for their own luminous spirit. Pleading with the workers, against the workers, to know themselves, to be themselves, to fight the good fight; while the official leaders and the pack of papers and the towns and the churches vomit their fear of the new world in the form of insults and lies. Workers, like everyone else, get the leaders they deserve. The workers are pitifully ignorant. Ignorance is the mother of misleaders.

I think of the great show of strength that the Textile Strike—like San Francisco yesterday—has summoned. And, while Ignorance is in the saddle, of the inevitable betrayal.

When the American workers *know* what they are, there'll be a different story.

That is the task of all young men and women: let thousands, each in his own way, go among the people, and humbly, quietly explain the cause of Life, which is the cause of Revolution.

Solidarity is not enough.[1]

2. WITH MARX, SPINOZA . . .

a.

This essay would not have been written at this hour had it not been for the dark hour of the German Jews. But their catastrophe is the deepening, within the crisis of the world, of a threat that for two centuries has gathered against Jewry. Judaism has never solved the challenge of the modern world; and this challenge is now a crisis—one of those historic crises from which Jewry must be reborn, if at all, through the threshold of death.

I do not stop to swell the lamentations that the fate of half a million highly cultured Jews has aroused in all sane people. My object is more stern. It is to analyze the response of the Jews in the United States to Hitler: to expose and study from the response certain traits of modern Jewry. There has been, in all the tears and rage, one constant refrain. "Why are we persecuted?" cry the leaders. "We are not different from you Gentiles—not in any point of thought, conduct or allegiance, that *counts*. In Germany, we are good Germans; in America, we are good Americans. There is no reason for this persecution." Now, Jews have often suffered persecution; although I suspect never by such ruthlessly efficient methods as the German. But Jews have always known why they were maltreated. It was because they were different; in thought, in conduct, in allegiance, in all that counted, a peculiar people. It was because they were Jews.

[1] A short time after this article was written and published, the five hundred thousand textile strikers were sold out by their "leaders" in Washington.

This might cause great sacrifice. But since Jewishness was the treasure of their lives, source of their beauty and joy, they deemed even the price of persecution not too great to pay for being Jewish. They took the persecution for granted, meeting it as shrewdly as they could. The stress of their energy and will was focused, not on avoiding or denying reasons for persecution, but on being Jews. Here, then, is an enormous difference. For the first time in a history of three thousand years, the leaders of Jewry do not know why they are persecuted: for the first time they disclaim any reason for persecution.

This sheds new light on the German Jewish disaster. Are these half million victims to be considered undifferentially as suffering human beings? Then they deserve no more pity and help—no more and, of course, no less—than the millions of other sufferers of our dark age: than the Negroes of our South, for instance; than the countless families broken by unemployment; than the communists whom Hitler and the Balkan sadists are torturing and maiming. But such pooled pity does not satisfy the Jewish leaders. In their appeals and reports they are careful to separate their cause from others. They imply that German Jewry calls for more than its quantitative share of the concern of a world riven with anguish; they assume, indeed, that a great people, whose value to mankind is high, is being menaced. Now this claim, on the evidence of the past, can be denied by no intelligent man. The Jews have through the centuries made contributions to the Western world that are inestimable, and organic. But are not the contemporary leaders confused in time? Should the Jews be saved today for what they were in the past? Such a plea runs counter to all natural law. What is there *alive* in contemporary Jewry to distinguish it from any other quantitative group of human beings?

The answer, alas! is, there is nothing. There are still, it is true, traditional Jewish communes in Eastern Europe and North Africa. But we do not hear from them; they provide no Jewish leaders. Indeed, the modern world no longer gives them nurture or function, and they are doomed by their own archaic form. The Jewry that protests against Hitlerism and is menaced by it the world over, and that assumes its past worth as argument for its present survival, is a "progressive" Jewry, freed from that past. It is the Jewry that cries: Why are we persecuted? Let us examine it, then, for Jewishness—and in its most prosperous member, the Jews of the United States.

First, I must define the Jew; and this, fortunately, can be done without raising the old problems of race and nation. To be a Jew has always meant *to live a certain way of life:* a way which, evolving with the ages and with the cultural-economic conditions of the lands, was yet an organic growth from a single tradition. This tradition was one; and the Jewish groups made it organic with their lives. Other nations had prophets, the Jews enacted theirs. Other nations had arts, the Jews lived theirs. Other peoples had high standards for personal, communal and cosmic relations: the Jews, by the minutiae of their 613 commandments, made flesh and bone of their vision of the divine and the eternal. The defining Jewish trait is *unification* of values, personal and communal, into an organic body of behavior. The defining Jewish term is *action*.

The Jewish principle—unity of value and deed, harmony of person and group—has always had a dual form. That the values of the person shall be fulfilled in the community, there must be *social justice*. And that within the cosmos there shall be preserved and furthered the values of men and of Man, there must be *God*. Social justice, of course, was an aspiration limited by the economy of the particular land and era—limited, that is, by *possibility*. What did God mean to the

Jew? At first by miracle and confusedly, then rationally, God meant the dynamic immanence, in the world of matter and of man, of what the person most deeply recognized as his own truth and worth. God meant the principle of order, the will to unity, in an otherwise chaotic multiverse. God meant *value in Being*. The Jews, as a people, were the first to understand that this Value-in-Being could not be abstract, not diffuse, not impersonal, although it transcended individuals; but was myriadly focused and fleshed in human lives. This means that for the Jew every man and woman holds a purposive and creative place in life's dynamic process.

Now, bearing this definition in mind, where—outside the vanishing Old World ghettoes of our East Side—are the Jews? Where in New York, in Cincinnati, in Chicago, in San Francisco? The American Jew is as divided in his ideals and his behavior as any Gentile. His amusements and his arts, his family life and his business methods, his loyalties to class, state and God, are the same tissue of contradictions. Like any Gentile, he scrambles for the dollar, lives for his belly, shares in the stampede for cheap delights. As businessman, he also exploits his brother; as citizen, he votes for the same liars, crude or gilded. He shouts the same chauvinistic phrases and is ready, with the rest, in time of war, to rush with the courage of Gadarene swine to his destruction. He enjoys (and writes) the same inane novels, movies. In a society whose crucial trait is the abyss between ideal and deed, he—the Jew —is indistinguishable from his neighbor. Is the "Jewishness" of these modern Jews a dynamic pattern of action? or is it a mere moldering heap of sentiment, vanity and habit?

I am speaking of the prosperous American Jew; not yet of the rank and file, the humble clerks and clothing workers, artisans and mechanics. These, as Jews, are passive. And in so far as they have Jewish leaders to make them act (as contradistinguished from labor leaders, for example), they choose the very type who have grown great by shrewd collaboration with a world that is the antithesis, in every value, to what is Jewish. This is a cardinal point in the lethal condition of American Jewry. Its leaders and spokesmen, in their loyalty to the exploiting class, have dangerously identified the Jew with a bourgeoisie that is degenerate and doomed. In the Middle Ages, the Jew was allied functionally with the rising burgher class whose destiny it was to break the feudal system. This alliance was one reason for the Jew's survival. But burgherdom, in medieval Europe, played a different moral part from the grande bourgeoisie of today. In the realm of practicable action, the burgherdom stood for social justice and intellectual freedom, as against the exploiting landowning gentry and the landowning church. Technically, the profit system always meant exploitation of labor. But socially, this early bourgeois exploitation was in the direction of justice, since it was a departure from slavery and spread the margin of leisure whereby man's culture could alone advance. Until the invention of the machine, some exploitation of men was needed in order that a privileged portion of mankind could think—and at last, by perfecting the machine, and spreading possible leisure to all humanity, abolish the need of human exploitation altogether. The alliance of medieval Jewry with burgherdom was therefore within the rhythm of advancing social justice, and hence harmonious with Jewishness. But today, the dominant bourgeoisie is the power of stratified social injustice: it is the power of war, of spiritual death and intellectual ruin.

The intensity of American Jewish allegiance to the exploiting class can be measured by the lives of the prominent Jewish leaders.

Almost without exception they are lawyers, judges, merchants, bankers, proprietors of newspapers and other vast affairs; men who have grown great in the American game of grab, men indistinguishable in spirit, mind and action from thousands of other divided men who (with like shamelessness) call themselves Christian. In a few instances, they are writers and rabbis—apologists, rank or subtle, of the exploiting classes.

Since their deeds are contradictions of their ideals, are such leaders Jews? Is a folk that such men lead, a Jewish folk? From the Jewish premise that value and vision must become action, a trait of Jewry has ever been to create true Jewish leaders.

But it may be said, there are other Jews, greater than these: not necessarily American, yet the real leaders of Jewry. There are Albert Einstein, Sigmund Freud, Alfred Stieglitz, Henri Bergson, Leon Trotsky . . . others. These men are great, and are leaders, and are Jews. But they are not leaders of Jews. They are leaders of scientists, philosophers, artists, revolutionists. They and other great Jewish men of our times are products of Jewish life; but modern Jewry cannot claim them. They are the offspring of the old communal Jewry which still existed in their formative years. And the fact that they have been forced to function quite outside modern Jewry is another proof of its present dissolution. The Jewish world no longer holds its men of genius; the highest products of its spirit, of its intellectual discipline and of its sense of life, leave the parent body. And the world of Jews, in deadly division from the Jewish spirit, chooses leaders who hasten its death.

Consider now the pitiful, the ironical condition of the Jew. To suffer for a cause that our soul loves is bearable: is, indeed—since we must suffer—man's most enviable destiny. But to suffer for nothing! To be hated and ruined as a Jew, when one's life is not Jewish! The Jews of Germany, taken as a whole, exist *inertially* because their past way was

Jewish and because it takes more than a generation to destroy a way of life so strong and so vital. If two hundred years ago, they had ceased living as Jews, Hitler and the Nazis, who are ignorant men, would probably not have heard of them. Hitler persecutes them now because in a confused way he has inherited what was a real reason, then, for a German in revolt against Western civilization to dislike real Jews who had so much to do with its creating.

But that is only half the picture. The Jews are allied with an agonizing and desperate middle class. When that class flourished, the Jews, functioning in it, were tolerated by it. Now that it droops and its spoils dwindle, it turns—like a man in a panic—against its weaker neighbor. It is the principle of "every man for himself"—the basic law of bourgeois life. Oh, the ironical confusion in the fate of the modern Jew! He is persecuted by barbarous and desperate men because of ideals that he no longer lives: and he is persecuted by a class to which, in the main, he is loyal, because he is a rival of its barbarous way of life—a way that contradicts his own ideals!

This is Germany today: who doubts that with variations it may be America tomorrow? that it may be any capitalistic country where the Jew, *in his present*, is a minority factor in a desperate middle class and *in his past* a reminder of the liberal culture of the Western world, against which that desperate class is in revolt?

b.

Now for the final questions: How can the Jew survive in the modern world, *and why should he survive?* To answer clearly, I must first state some of the reasons why he survived in the past. And since the kaleidoscope of Jewish generations is so great, I take the latest period of undisputed Jewish health: the Middle Ages (which lasted for the Jews until the eighteenth century), when the Jews lived, harmonious and whole, within a Europe of violent divisions, and often savagely hostile.

1. Jewry's strict unity of ideal and conduct made the community, although small and surrounded, an efficient body. All its energy was conserved for itself and applied functionally for survival; whereas in a greater community where value and deed are divided, there is conflict, loss of energy, disease.

2. In Judaism, both ideally and actively, there was no separation between man and group. Although infiltrations from Alexandrian and Platonized Egypt corrupted the ancient Hebrew knowledge that there is no personal immortality, this superstition of a surviving individual soul (the deepest cause of the failure of European cultures) was never strong against the healthy Jewish unification of individual and commune. Therefore, medieval Jewry had no destructive egoism—no "great men"—to mislead it for discordant personal ends. (The egoistic leader battens on the accumulated egoisms of his rabble.) In Jewry, the leaders were as organic to the commune as an eye or a brain to the body. Moreover, these leaders were not soldiers, not megalomaniacs of fame and money: they were the seers and the thinkers. Here, then, was a social body whose eyes and brain literally led it—in contrast to our modern world in which the eye and the brain often appear to be discards or decorations.

3. Jewry had, despite theological and cultural differences, a deep community of values with Christian cultural leaders. These recognized the worth of the Jewish ethic; the beauty of the Jews' concept of Godhead as immanent in human action. The best in Christian Europe at all times respected, and often learned from, the "hated" Jews. And during the ages when the church was strong, it had enough influence to defend the Jews against extremities of persecution.

4. Through these times, *Jewry had an economic function.* Its activities in international commerce, banking, exchange, and in the practical sciences of communication and of navigation, did a necessary work in feudal Europe. And this allied Jewry with the struggling middle class—the burghers who were to inherit and transform feudal Europe. Without this function and the alliance with a rising economic class, Jewry's inner harmony of action could not have saved it. For there would have been lacking a

harmony of function within the larger body of the Gentile world.

To return, now, to our time; the Jew obviously can survive, if the immutable essence of the Jewish social organism can somehow be transformed to function in the modern world. And obviously, the Jew should survive, if this essential Jewish nature still has a part to play before mankind. These questions are the subject for a book—which I shall write, if I live long enough. Here, I can but sketch my answer.

The Jewish principle of value-in-Being, of God and social justice, of the *enactment* of value by individual and group, did not exist *in vacuo*. It existed within a matrix. And this matrix was the agrarian economic-cultural world—a world so basally static that the eighteenth-century Galician Jew shared it, fundamentally unchanged, with Amos and Isaiah. So long as the matrix held, the Jew could follow the commandments of his prophets *as interpreted by twenty centuries of fathers.*

We may now see why the Jewish organism broke in the impact with the modern world. Modern industrialism destroyed the simple, paternalistic economy under which the Jewish commune *approximated* social justice. And modern thought and science corroded the theologic-ethic form under which the Jew knew God. To survive, the Jewish principle must be transfigured into modern terms. Judaism must embrace an again workable program approximating social justice: and that means the unequivocal destruction of the unjust anarchy called industrial capitalism. And Judaism must redefine what it has always meant—or meant to mean—by God.

Now, let the reader answer: Is the principle of social justice needed today? And that *Man* may live, must there be, not an anthill system, but a living social form that nurtures the inward need of every human being to create and to share his inward vision and value? If your answer is Yes, then there is need in the world of what has been, for nearly thirty hundred years, the Jewish principle. And as if history urged that this cardinal dual need of the world may yet be the peculiar business of the Jewish people (there have always been, in all nations, saintly and isolated men who lived and died for it, as greatly as any Jew), the need stands most forcibly answered in the work of two Jews—Jews of a "new remnant," Marx and Spinoza.

I place Marx first, because in the perspective of function he comes first—although Spinoza lived two centuries before him and profoundly influenced his thinking. Marx, from the Jewish premise of history as an organism evolving toward "good," has given to the industrial world a realistic logic and a technique of social justice. Time, of course, has amended or refuted many details of his plan; yet it is nonetheless categorical that every man who wants to *enact* social justice in the modern world must be a Marxist in spirit although he may reject certain Marxist dogmas. The modern Jew, if he is to exist, must interpret Marx as a prophet as surely as his forebears interpreted Moses and Isaiah. Marx (despite chronology) comes before Spinoza, because the social discord is a disease immediately threatening the survival of civilized mankind; and because collective consciousness comes before mature self-consciousness. Marx without Spinoza is an imperative, immediate, primitive first step in action. Spinoza, without Marx, remains an abstract philosophy, removed from possible action.

But as Marx is the man who most surely projected the prophetic aspiration of social justice into a workable modern program, Spinoza is the prophet who has completed the purifying of the knowledge of God into the God of inwardness, of substance and of action. If Marx carries on Moses and Ezra, Spinoza carries on Isaiah and Jesus. It is he who has best established the organic being of God *in* matter and in human thought; who has made rational the ancient mystic intuition that the cosmic dwells within the man in so far as the man grows self-conscious. By giving value to matter in a form acceptable to the age of science, Spinoza will crown the work of Marx, who gives reality to a program of social justice in the age of machines.

Now, it may be that Spinoza and Marx are the swan song of Jewry: the final message of a great people before its ultimate death. It may be that the work of unifying and enacting their contributions shall fall to other peoples. There is a Soviet Union in the world, and China, and the two Americas; from such virgin soil may come the fulfillment of the prophets. I do not know. But I do know that, if the Jew is to survive as an organic group, he must enact his modern prophets as his fathers (after rejecting them, also) enacted the prophets of Scripture. And I conclude by broadly sketching what the modern Jewish way of living must be.

To begin with (for, I repeat—in the field of action, Marx comes before Spinoza), the Jew must renounce loyalty to the exploiting class. Without that, all his "service" is a "vain oblation." Today, as twenty-six centuries ago, the word of the prophet is true:

> Bring no more vain oblations;
> It is an offering of abomination unto Me;
> New moon and sabbath, the holding of convocations—
> I cannot endure iniquity along with solemn assembly. . . .
> Cease to do evil;
> Learn to do well;
> Seek justice. . . .

"*Learn* to do well!" In our industrial world, this means active allegiance to the class whose historic function it is to abolish economic exploitation—the base of social injustice and of war—by doing away with economic classes altogether. This new allegiance will not be easy; since the Jews for centuries have been forced to earn their bread within the middle class, it will have the value, by itself, of a religious conversion. But this new loyalty as a group does not mean that the Jew will be submerged in the working class or in any proletarian body like the communists. He must fight for the workers (and the farmer and the intellectual, too, are workers), help them with his brain and body; but he may be detached from them, at least at present, because of his particular stewardship of values—"the realm of God," in each man, with which the harried and hungry worker has not had time to grow familiar.

The revolutionary proletariat cannot trouble about God. There are good functional reasons for the atheism of most Marxists. The word "God" has been monopolized so long by the apologists of the class of exploitation: theologians, philosophers, poets! To detach (as Spinoza did) the reality in God from all the accumulated lies is a problem that calls for subtlety beyond the present anguished state of the masses; for energy that the masses and their immediate leaders *cannot spare* from the day's struggle. It is unhistorical to expect the active revolutionist of our time to do more than reject the false "God" of the churches and the synagogues. Yet the true experience of God must not die even in the heat of revolutionary battle. The first Marxist ends cannot be won and man be raised from animal penury and fear into the human stage of security and leisure unless the individual finds life good: and this can be only through the Spinozistic sense of God. The experience of the divine in mortal life must be preserved. Wherefore, there is need today of a people, scattered through the nations, that know and nurture the experience of God. By the tradition of ages, by their ancient prophets and their modern thinkers, the Jews have inherited the challenge and the *right* to be such a people.

This Jewish "remnant"—and only the remnant, through the ages, has preserved the Jew—will be loyal to the class of social revolution; but through its consciousness of God it will be still separate, and must remain so. It will understand the functional "atheism" of many simple-minded revolutionists, and not demand that it be understood in return. The God in man will be the still secret treasure it must lovingly preserve against the day when men, free of fear and hunger, learn to look within themselves where God is. Thus, the Jews will still be a peculiar people. And they will be subject to the dislike and distrust of the zealot for whom the word "God" is anathema; although it was in the name of God that his values of social justice and individual dignity were preserved and prepared, through the barbaric ages.

Now, a majority cannot rise to so high a challenge of rebirth. Bankers, merchants, lawyers, professional men and politicians, even artisans and mechanics among the Jews, will not yield their old allegiance to the middle class, although that class turns (as it is turning!) against them. And these will disappear in the general human welter, as Jews have disappeared in Assyria, Babylon, Alexandria and Rome. But what a magnificent remnant there may be! The teacher, the doctor, the engineer, the clear-eyed man of commerce who knows and hates the rottenness of capitalist commerce, the Jewish worker and the student—above all, the Jewish student! Already, these are on the side of the productive class that alone holds the energy to remake the world. Already, they accept Marx. Let them fulfill this knowledge with devotion to the inward value—the God whom Spinoza has explored in man and in matter—and there will be again, in the world, a Jewish remnant!

Persecution? It is already here, even in America; and as the capitalistic era shrinks, darkens and despairs, it will grow worse. The lesson of Hitler, in offering the Jew as the traditional scapegoat for the accumulated rage of a bewildered people, is bound to be learned; already we have our little Hitlers, profiteers of suffering stupidity and blindness. The Jewish people are going to suffer. And for those who are individually and innocently hurt, and who know not why, there can be no soothing words. Before their anguish, we can only bow our heads, humbly, as they enact the world-old mystery of pain. But at least, for the conscious Jew, the real Jew, there will again be reason for Jewishness, reason to bear his persecution; and comrades to help him bear it. And if individual Jews die, their death will be in the cause of humane life; no man can ask a higher guerdon. And the history of the Jews will hearten them with knowledge, that when a people is ready to be persecuted and to die for a good cause, the cause lives—and the people.

Postscript:

This article, which appeared in "The New Republic" in 1933 and was reprinted in many journals, is itself an abbreviated form of an essay published in French by "Europe," of Paris, and in Spanish by "Sur," of Buenos Aires. I have used it here, rather than the longer version, because both are a project or programmatic abstract of the essay I must someday write, in which all the terms of my argument will be more fully and fundamentally defined. Recent attacks on socialism and communism by prominent Jews—rich men, shallow, slavish, scared, of the kind I have described, or by truckling labor leaders, make the writing of this essay an imperative duty.

I trust it is clear in my conclusion about the possible leadership of a Jewish "remnant" in our recreative task, that I have not mentioned the like necessary rôle of a Christian "remnant," only because this paper deals specifically with the Jews. That the prophetic-revolutionary strain is not dead in the American Protestant churches is proved by the labors of such men as Reinhold Niebuhr—one of the truly creative minds of America.

3. FROM MANY MESSAGES TO MANY PEOPLE

i. War Is with Us Now

To the First United States Congress Against War,
Held in New York, 1933

Two thousand delegates from every part of the country, and of every shade of progressive opinion, are meeting in New York in a Congress Against War. A most laudable enterprise; and a most needed. For war threatens the world; and with war, civilization, still staggering from the blows of the last conflict, may definitely founder. The crisis is immediate and tragic. But no congress of good men can avert it. All that this congress can do is to bring men's consciousness to focus upon the present danger; and to raise men's consciousness to the pitch of intensity where it becomes action.

Before everything else, we must become aware that *war is already here!* The political and economic setup of the modern nations IS war. Battles on land and sea, millions of lives destroyed, cities and fields laid waste, are but a concentrated form of the jungle anarchy that is called "government" in the metropolis, that is called "diplomacy" in the embassies, that is called "business" in factories, mills, mines and markets.

So long as we have nations playing the lone game of power and aggression, or banding together like packs of wolves in "alliance" against other nations, we have war—*war in peace.* And all the congresses of the world will not prevail against the inevitable, periodic outbreak of this constant war into pitched battles.

So long as we have a social system within each nation that divides the citizens into classes whose economic basis is exploiter and exploited; a social system in which success means power gained at the expense of others and enjoyed to the exclusion of others, we have war—*civil war* in peace, within each nation. The small ruling class is brutalized by its success in enslaving others; the large classes are brutalized by their slavery—brutalized the more if they are not conscious of enslavement. In such a social system (and all the "planned economics" of capitalism can only make it more dangerous by disguising it), it is inevitable that the state and the nation will reflect, on a large scale, the jungle spirit of individual men. It is inevitable that the jungle greed of such a state and nation will come into conflict with the greed of other nations where the same system prevails. It is inevitable that this *normal* state of conflict shall break out, from time to time, in formal warfare.

But our present condition of war is even deeper! So long as war prevails in the internal economic structure of each nation, it will prevail as well in the internal psychic structure of the men and women who constitute the nation. A society that is a rationalized jungle of greed and violence, encourages the lust for individual power in all men and women and atrophies the social instinct in all men and women. The members of such a society war upon each other in their individual lives: and each individual soul is itself the seat of warfare. Of course, such divided men band together in gangs, classes, nations, to make war upon other gangs, classes, nations.

War has been the constant condition of what we call civilization. War between individuals, war between classes, war between peoples—each seeking profit and power at the expense of others. But there is a new factor in the situation of today.

Modern science has made war deadlier than it has ever been: so that war now threatens—not only persons and individual nations, but all mankind. And this new factor of science, by its potentiality of large-scale production and co-operation, has also made the old systems of exploitation and rivalry no longer needed.

This is the crucial state of the world—its mortal danger and its hope. War, as never before, is a menace to human survival. And war (military, economic, social war) has been made unnecessary, as never before, by our modern mastery of means of production, distribution, communication, whereby it is feasible today *for all men* to live in plenty and with leisure, without enslaving or exploiting others.

The United States Congress Against War represents a good impulse. But men's protest against war is not a new event in the so-called Christian world. It has been futile, throughout the ages, *because war was organic in men's way of living.* Similarly, this congress will not pass the limits of "good intentions" unless it writes down formally in its record that the abolition of war means revolution. Fundamental revolution. Revolution in the social structure of the nations, and revolution in the souls of men and women.

ii. *To the Students of Cuba*

(*April, 1931*)

I am following with deep emotion your struggle to renovate—indeed to re-create—the life of Cuba. I am poignantly aware of the terrible dilemma that confronts you. Your government is the slave of irresponsible financial interests of the United States, and of the State Department at Washington which with cynical hypocrisy is launched on a deliberate campaign to imperialize the entire Caribbean. If your prostitute government remains in office, Cuba will continue to

be a "factory" for American investments, a "factory" protected by no laws such as limit exploitation on American
soil; since you Cubans are not citizens of the United States
and your political "independence" more and more is coming
to mean the privilege of our exploiters to work in your
country with a ruthless irresponsibility which they would not
dare to display in their own. Yet, if you overthrow this
government, it may mean the landing of American marines
in Havana and the swift setting up of a new rule which will
be the replica of Machado's—the other horn of the dilemma!

What can you do? What can a citizen of the United
States urge you to do? In a way I am ashamed to speak to
you, ashamed to mention my own sorrow and my shame,
as a native of the oppressor country, who is helpless to help
you. Men like myself in the United States are powerless.
There is no enlightened public opinion here with any *punch*
to it. Most of our good will is Platonic, in the bad sense
of the word. And who, here, is interested in a *students'*
revolutionary movement? Our intellectuals, as a body, have
lost contact with the spiritual, the *human* source of art; our
student groups are too pampered and too infantile to get
excited over anything but football.[1] You are alone in your
fight, alone with the student bodies and the workers of other
Hispano-American countries who, for the most part, are as
dispossessed as you. You are alone with the truth!

Yet I can say to you: Go on! If for no other reason,
go on because only then will you be happy. Do not let
so-called practical affairs and worldly wisdom compromise
your ideal. Look at the men who have made these "necessary
compromises": the successful men, the rulers of the world.
See what ugly, misshapen, miserable men they are. Look well
at the "practical" men, and do not go the hideous way which

[1] Since this was written, a strong revolutionary students' movement has
sprung up in the United States.

they have gone, and of which the ignoble shambles of the modern world is the result. Even if you are imprisoned, even if you are shot down (as some of you have been), you must have the satisfaction of knowing that you are living the sole way that makes life tolerable. The enemies who have sold themselves for dollars are not happy; the indifferent ones, in Cuba, in the United States, who follow opportunism—for success, for pleasure, for power—are not happy. They must drug themselves with ever more success, more pleasure, more power, lest they awake to the intolerableness of their way of living. And that is why they hate you: because you are the constant revealers to themselves of their own nullity. They must deny their nullity; and by a common psychologic mechanism they do so by denying *you* who make them cognizant of it.

I cannot promise you success in your present endeavor to free Cuba and to bring Cuba to real independence. It would be false to promise it. *You* may not succeed in actually overthrowing the hideous anarchy of which men like Machado are mere minor servants. So to do requires more than your good will; it requires method, technique and long hard work. But this triumphant method can come only from such will as yours. Before you achieve it, perhaps you individually will be crushed, since the ordered anarchy and greed of the modern world *has* method. But even if this is so—this worst which must be bravely envisaged, it makes no difference in what you must do, not merely from a sense of duty, but in order to be happy! You must go on struggling to free and to reorganize your country; knowing that that labor is its own reward; that the man who gives his life for freedom, by that fact is alive and is free.

You know that your problem as Cubans struggling for independence is not apart from that of most of the other nations of America Hispana. Yet you are divided from your allies, not alone by mountains and deserts and seas, but by proud persistent nationalisms, by differences of race and culture—the differences of Indian, Negro, mestizo, criollo. You are all rich in plunder, and the imperialist power feeds on it the better by exciting the disunities between you. But you are profoundly gifted peoples; your resources of the spirit are as great as the resources of your lands—greater, surely, than the difficulties inherited from your historic pasts. You will help yourselves and one another, synchronously, by deeper self-understanding. For brothers who fulfill themselves achieve thereby not homogeneity, but harmony. Without harmony, both your lands and your cultures would be taken from you. But you are already far on the way to achieving this organic unity among you, in cultural terms and in terms of political aspiration.

The imperialist power exploits you and incites you to fratricidal war, because it has allies within your borders: your own capitalists and their servants, the politicians. If you effectively fight the domestic enemy, the foreign enemy will at last be helpless against you, even as he was helpless against revolutionary Russia. I know that your task is more complex than was Russia's, because you are not politically united. But, essentially, it is one problem.

And it is our problem, too. We in the United States fight the same foe as you. This, when we attain a conscious intelligentsia and a conscious working class, will serve to unite us.

Only from the platform of War Against Capitalism can you effectively meet your national problem. For your foe is only superficially an alien government; more deeply it is the capitalist power with its twin heads: the Machados at home, the armed Dollar abroad. Most deeply, it is the ignorance of all the people—in Cuba, in America Hispana, in the United States.

Students of Cuba, you have come out into the clear air of action; you have created leaders for yourselves, and a program. You are blessed in this. I find myself almost envying you, rather than pitying you despite your anguish and your struggles. My heart and my mind are with you. If I could feel that my word warmed you in the slightest degree, heartened your perseverance, it would be for me an inexpressible joy, who am alone here in this great country—alone, and unable to act for and with men like you who stand for everything I cherish.

NOTE: *This is one of many messages by the author clandestinely introduced, printed in pamphlet form, and distributed, in Latin-American countries under brutal dictatorships. It has been re-Englished from the Spanish text.*

iii. The Touchstone

on the anniversary of the October Revolution, 1935

More than ever, in this day of spiritual and social confusion, the attitude of men toward Soviet Russia is a touchstone of the quality of their good will. By this criterion three large groups stand forth.

There are, first, the enemies of the Soviet Union: and these are the souls whose true love, despite all their fine words of God and Man and Freedom, is for their pocketbooks. Their real nature is manifest in their leaders, archetypes of human ugliness and degeneration—the Hearsts, the Hitlers, the Hoovers. A second group consists of the "liberals," the "socialists," the idealistic "revolutionaries" who are so busy deploring the mistakes and injustices committed in the Soviet Union that they have no time to understand or to defend it. These are men (when they are sincere) so infatuated with their own private notion of what truth and justice should look like that the spectacle of a great nation, heroically serving truth and justice with the humble tools of humble human nature, leaves them cold. Essentially, these are men devoted to their own egos: men whose professional love for mankind masks a childish and shallow and ill-tempered self-adoration.

The third group consists of those who know that in the Soviet Union a people is dedicated to the task for which in all ages the inspired few—the prophets and the poets— have given their lives: the task of founding upon earth, at last, a culture not of slaves but of men, a society of universal justice, in which human truths shall be sought and expressed by the common and communal life of all men and women. They know that this people consists not of gods, but of humans. They know that this people must meet and overcome, in their great undertaking, the obstacles of a hostile world and, no less, the obstacles of their own enslaved past and of their faulty natures as human beings. They know that the labor of the Soviet Union is the more precious because it is the work of humble men and women, subject to trial and error; and that those who reject this labor because of its failures and imperfections are at heart cowards. They know that if the dark years, in which we have lived since the Great War, shall appear in the perspective of history as the time of a great Dawning, the reason is the light that has come since 1917 from Russia.

These sincere men and women, today more than ever, while the clouds of aggressive ignorance and ill will gather upon the world, must declare their devotion to the Cause of the Soviet Union.

iv. To Romain Rolland on His Seventieth Birthday

Your seventieth birthday comes at a time when France holds in her hands the immediate destiny of the Western world. The result of the struggle for power in France between the elements of reaction typified by the Croix de Feu, which are the forces of death, and the elements of re-creation typified by the Front Uni, which are the forces of life, may well determine the result, at least as it affects those still living, of the same struggle throughout the Occident. If France fails, Great Britain fails; the sinister forces in the United States, emboldened by a century of capitalist anarchy, may sweep America into the same disaster. If France fails, Western man may fail: a period of overwhelming darkness may intervene for us all, before that future time when our progeny once again takes up the Torch, held aloft meanwhile—who knows for how long?—by the Soviet Union and perhaps by certain parts of China, India, America Hispana that prove inaccessible to fascist armies.

In this crucial scene of mankind, as so often in the past, France plays a leading role. And we, who celebrate your seventieth birthday, Romain Rolland, perforce look upon you as the symbol of our hope in your great country. You are a great man, a great *person*, Romain Rolland, because you are a symbol; because a world spirit speaks *through* you. At this hour of crisis and of celebration, for many in my country, you incarnate the genius which for eight centuries has sustained French culture.

This genius is a kind of "common sense," rare alas!—both individually and collectively rare. It is "common" only as essence, as the universal, is common. It is compounded of a ruthless clarity in meeting the Real and in relating its parts

together; of an invincible courage in following whither the
Real leads at whatever sacrifice of individual peace and comfort; and of a creative vision in so mastering the facts that
they may ever more closely conform with man's intuition
of his dignity and destiny.

As I look about me at the world in which I have now lived
for over forty years, meeting men of all qualities of mind and
temperament and talent, I am appalled at the rarity of this
"common sense"; and I am no longer amazed at the cruel and
dolorous pass to which the world has come. Men of genius in
the usual sense of the word are not rare; nor men of physical
courage, nor men of imagination. But terribly rare is the
man who, capable of knowing the truth, continues to serve the
truth beyond the point at which such service begins to make
him suffer; terribly rare is the man of imagination who, finding that he can sell his gifts at high price unto the prostitutes
and exploiters who rule the world, elects still to give his gifts
into the hands of his humble brothers; terribly rare is the
man who, possessing courage, does not get drunk with it and
lose his control of reality, finding it easier to move armies or
mobs than to master his own ego.

Men of this rare "common sense" will, perhaps, someday
be more common; this, then, will be a different world. But
until that time of maturity arrives, these men are historic.
You are one of them, Romain Rolland. In you, there is no
break between conviction and action; between recognition
of the truth and every word and deed within your power
to fulfill it; between the responsibility you feel for your
dignity as an heir of Man and the responsibility you feel for
your dignity as a servant of men. Ten years ago, I called
you a *whole man*, Romain Rolland. I cannot improve this
term, today. The whole man is he who possesses this common
sense I speak of.

I pray that France may duly celebrate the seventieth birthday of her great son and heir to those intellectual and ethical qualities which have made France great. If she does so, it will have to be by her actions. France knows where the truth lies: will she have the common sense to serve it? She knows that truth lies first of all in fearless realization of the collective economic freedom which can alone make *true* those principles of *Egalité, Fraternité, Liberté*, which now for a hundred years she has flaunted on all her public buildings. To this end, the people of France must grimly sever from their loyalty to *La Patrie* those greeds and inertias and self-indulgences of class which are the germs of fascism and of death. The hour has come when France must accomplish the promise of her great tradition to herself and to the world. She must mature into realization. It will hurt, it will be heroic. But if France fails now, she goes down; she commits that suicide of the spirit which ever precedes decomposition of the body.

Great nations mirror their powers and their vision in the lives of their great mem. Let France, today, look to herself by looking to you, Romain Rolland. Let her study the clear progress of your thought from the humanitarian idealism of your bourgeois youth, through the trial of war which schooled you to find the truth in *facts*, and to the strong revolutionary realism which is your deed, today. What France sees, in studying you, let her understand to be the symbol of her own ineluctable course, if she would continue to be France.

. . . This prayer to France, this challenge to France, this confidence in France, is my way, Romain Rolland, of celebrating your seventieth birthday.

January, 1936

NOTE: *This letter, before publication, was read at the great mass meeting held in the Paris Trocadéro, on Romain Rolland's birthday.*

v. To the Premier of France

Dear Léon Blum: I presume to address you in this personal form because you are more than the head of a French government, you are more than leader of the People's Front of the French nation: historic circumstance has made you arbiter of the present destiny of Europe, perhaps of us all. To fulfill your role, only a true man can suffice. And it is to the man that I am speaking.

All the world knows just what is happening in Spain. The Spanish people last February by a great majority chose a government of their own—somewhat similar to the one you are now leading. Having created a government of their own, they proceeded by means moderate and legal to create a Spain of their own. And as their program began to take effect, the enemies of the people of Spain, they who hate the people because they exploit them and because their privilege depends on the continued degradation of the people, took arms against the nation. Alone, these reactionaries would have failed, for they had almost a whole nation against them. Even with the trained mercenaries of the army, with the resources of vested property and vested superstition, they would have failed. But there were allies at hand—groups of the same kind, some in power and in possession of their respective countries, dealers in falsehood and blood, manipulators of ignorance and confusion. With the military and economic aid of these enemies of the Spanish people, and of their own peoples, Spain is being invaded, Spain's democracy is being crushed, the world is being forced to stand by day after day while the machines manned by mercenaries and by the lusters after power destroy the naked body of a nation.

Léon Blum, this is no civil war of Spain; this is the conquest of the Spanish people by an armed international class to whom the destruction of life in the defense of property is an everyday routine. This class knows no frontiers. Its henchmen, called Hitler, Mussolini, Franco, the Tories of Great Britain and America, may mouth national slogans, but they are of one brotherhood, they adore one Baal and one Mammon. Was the conquest of Ethiopia a civil war? Plenty of African troops fought with Mussolini against the Negus who to them was a local exploiter less desirable perhaps than the Italian. But who fights against the loyalists in Spain? A military caste traditionally removed from sympathy with the people, a clerical caste trained to submission to the powers that be, all the dupes and victims of these castes—in other words, the forces, whether in Spain, in Italy, in France or in Britain, who are the sworn enemies of you, your party and your allies.

This is not a civil war in Spain; this is the civil war of Europe. This is a war of attempted conquest, Léon Blum, waged by all the elements you have devoted your life to combat against all the values you hold dear. It is your war, Léon Blum; it is our war.

The fascists of Italy and Germany know this. They know that the fascists of Spain are fighting *their* battle of conquest. Therefore they are giving aid to their own kind. And the reactionaries of Japan, the United States, of every nation where money or privilege is in power, by the force of credits and propaganda are helping the men of their own stamp in Spain in order that their machines may prevail against a defense of mere human flesh and blood.

This, Léon Blum, is the war in which you have declared that France must remain neutral.

In all Europe there are three governments that can claim with validity to represent the interests of the entire people. They are Spain, which is fighting for life; your government, and the Soviet Union. The U.S.S.R., far removed from the immediate scene of battle and menaced by the two most aggressive militarist states of the world, Germany and Japan, cannot act alone; cannot act at all without regard to the decision of its sole ally, the French Republic. If the Soviet Union made legal its overwhelming sympathy for the Spanish nation as against your neutrality pact, you, Léon Blum, would fall; the People's Front of France would fall; there would be chaos in France to match Spain's, and perhaps a similar fascist uprising.

What does this mean, Léon Blum? It means that yours is the decision. In all Europe, France alone can act; France by the unified nature of its government and by the immediate threat to it both east and south, must act.

The world knows where your heart lies in this struggle. We know that if you could purchase victory for Spain with your life, you would gladly give your life. We know that what holds you back is the refusal of the British government to join you, is the criminal leadership of English Labor, is— in a word—your fear of war waged against the lives of your people by the united fascists. Yes, that is the superiority of the fascists over men and women of the democracies. The fascists, despising life, readily risk it; despising the lives of others, readily mislead and destroy them; whereas at the Left are they who hesitate because they think, because they feel, because they are more wholly human.

But, Léon Blum, it is a true saying: He who hesitates is lost. There is another old saying: He who loses his life shall find it. The words originally had a supernatural meaning. We can give to them a modern, psychological, rational form. We can say: "He who through fear of losing what he values dares not run risks is sure to lose what he values." You fear war if you aid the Spanish people; you fear to alienate Britain; you fear to provoke the enemy who are giving aid to their factions by every means in their power. And your fear is helping the enemy; your fear is making more hopeless the cause of the people not only in Spain but in Germany and Italy, who need encouragement to rise against their executioners. Your fear is making more assured the position of the fascists when at last, made mad by their successes, they choose to unleash their war against you. Your fear—if need be—to risk war now is making war inevitable; and meantime your hesitancy and caution are throwing to the fascists the first battles.

Léon Blum, we who in everything human know ourselves superior to the fascists must equal them in daring and in resolution. Otherwise, our hatred of war and love of humanity will defeat us and deliver the world to the war makers. There are times when the best strategy is to get one's eye on the goal and to move toward it. This is the strategy of the fascists, and it has been victorious in Ethiopia, on the Rhine and elsewhere. It is a strategy not every nation is able to pursue. Britain is too divided to pursue it. France has the power, the perspective, the government—and the incentive!— to pursue it.

Already the aid of the fascists to their kind in Spain, while France rigidly and solitarily remains neutral, is demoralizing the masses of all countries. They say to themselves, in England, in France, in Brazil, in the United States: "The fascists help their gangs; we leave our people to be massacred and their cities to be bombed." The masses do not understand that the U.S.S.R. must act with France, must uphold *your* hand, Léon Blum. None of us understands what holds you back. Your "neutrality" is breaking the heart and spirit of the peoples, everywhere, who soon or late must fight *your* battle.

If I have presumed to address this letter to you, Léon Blum, it is because I know that my anguish is that of millions before the tragedy of Spain; and that my expectation of your leadership is that of millions everywhere—not excluding those in Italy and Germany—who cannot act alone, but who are waiting to follow. We implore you: Recognize the facts in Spain. Recognize that *there is no neutrality* in this irrepressible conflict between the two possible futures of mankind—the way forward to human dignity, the way backward to slavery. Open the frontiers of France for aid to the legitimate government of Spain before it is too late! Help them with food, guns, planes, credit, and above all with the moral force that will be theirs when they know that the French are their comrades. If you do this, at once, you will be doing merely what one legitimate government should do for another; you will be doing merely what the fascists, the world over, are doing for their conspirators in Spain.

If you do less than this, Léon Blum, you are betraying what your country represents, what your People's Front gave you the mandate to perform. You will be betraying mankind.

October, 1936

vi. Values of the Revolutionary Writer

(This address was read at the first session of the American Writers Congress held in New York in April, 1935.)

1. Definitions

The world stands at the crossways. It goes forward into the socialist order, or human culture, not as we know it but as we aspire to create it, will perish. I do not say the way forward is certain. The life of man is at issue; and with man the alternatives are present, at all times, of life or of death. They are present now. But this is certain. To agonize within the present system, to refuse to get clear by the social revolution of the working classes, means the plunge of Western man into a darkness to which his productive and his intellectual forces, if they continue uncontrolled, must doom him: a darkness from which even the intimations of light that have made our present, will have vanished. This makes clear that the cause of the socialist society is not, finally, a political-economic problem: it is a cultural problem: it is *the* human problem.

I propose to show the specific value, in this crisis, of the literary work of art—not as a chorus of revolutionary politics, not as an echo to action: but as *an autonomous kind of action*. I propose to show that above all in America today, owing to our peculiar cultural conditions, the revolutionary writer must not be a "fellow traveler": that his art must be co-ordinate with, not subordinate to, the political-economic aspects of the re-creation of mankind.

This requires some definition of history and of literary art (for we are engaged in making history). Fortunately, I may point to the historic sense of mankind, implicit in Marx, as of a body which, like all organic life, evolves by reason of inward assimilations of an objective world from which it wins sustenance and on which it reacts—all according to a pattern which is the nature of the organism: a pattern which in man is capable of great variations chiefly through the process of what, vaguely, we call consciousness.

The part of consciousness, or if you prefer, of *experience*, in historic evolution is important for us because it leads straight to the social function of art. The work of art is a means (among other things) for extending, deepening, our experience of relationship with life as this organic whole. The feeling of intimate kinship with any part of the objective world is what we mean by beauty. As this relationship expands to an inclusive social form, it is what we mean by culture. The basic social function of art is *so to condition men that they will, as a social body, be the medium for the actions of growth and change required by their needs.* These social actions, to be healthy, must be performed within the true experience of *the whole of life involved*—and the conveying, the naturalizing, of this experience is the especial function of art.

I will make this plain. Suppose a man needs to hammer nails for his new house. He must hit the nails square on the head. But in order to do this, the man must be in good general condition. If his eyes are poor, if his brain is dizzy, all his technical skill of wrist-action won't save him from hammering nails badly. No man, it is obvious, is in shape for even an act so simple as hitting a nail on the head unless his body and mind are a fit *medium* for the job. No society of men or class of men is in shape for any needed action, save in so far as it has been conditioned to become the *effective medium* for that action.

In simple societies, the prime conditioning arts are lyrical: they are music, the song, the dance. By means of the experience absorbed and sustained through them, the folk becomes the effective medium for the kind of action its emotional and economic needs, and the needs of its rulers, call for. In our world where a chaos of forces is breaking down the life of man before our eyes, the chief conditioning art— although all arts have their place—must be one to synthesize our complex pasts and present, and to direct them. This is the art of words, by which man captures the worlds and selves that have borne him, and renders them alive with his own vision.

We know now, roughly, the kind of social action to demand of our literary art. It is in general to condition men for the multitude of direct actions of which their life consists: it is, with us, the crucial task of conditioning our readers—who we hope will be the workers, the farmers, and their allies, to become the effective medium of revolution.

This subtle process of *conditioning* is not to be confused with the work of direct *preparation* for daily struggle: work which falls primarily to the teachers, the theorists, the organizers of party and of union, who are largely conditioned by the accumulated work of writers. And it must be clear that this work of conditioning the social body, however invisible it seems, is the direct action of the writers. Words, of course, are also instruments for "preparation": reportage, pamphlets, slogans, manifestoes (this paper is a kind of manifesto), have their legitimate uses in political work. But only in so far as the need of the revolutionary *medium* is understood; and as the main function of literary art, *which is to create this medium*, prevails. The writer who forgets this, in order to bend his art to some seemingly more immediate task, weakens the organic health and progress of mankind by betraying his integral part in it. And in a world full of hunger, of hideous injustice, of threatening war, only a clarity rare, hard and heroic, will hold the literary artist to his own often thankless, often obscured, yet fundamental, action.

2. *The American Writer Under Capitalism*

I apply at once these definitions to the special problems of the American revolutionary writer. To this end, we must first glance at the general state of readers and writers in our country.

We have never lacked literary talents. But the economic soil in which they rooted was washed away ere the roots could hold. We have had great writers. They have been influential abroad, where an organic cultural life possessing what we still lack—memory and consciousness—could employ them. Here, a Poe, a Whitman, a Thoreau, a Melville, could win only sentimental disciples because the discontinuity of ethnic and industrial conditions made their message obsolete more quickly than a generation could mature to hear them. We Americans are weak—infinitely weaker than the peasants of China, America Hispana, or old Russia—in that intuitive connection with soil and self and human past, which makes of a folk an effective medium for creative action. In this, our common state of cultural malnutrition, the need of sound literary art cries aloud. But our writers have been attainted by the disease they must help to cure. A sense of impotence, derived from their unconnectedness with the vital classes of the American world, has delivered them up to a succession of European fads and dogmas; and their reflections of foreign literary styles, like the shallow glints of a kaleidoscope, have added up to nothing. When they have turned to our world, our writers have been unable to resist the overpowering pulls of the capitalist system. They have been entertainers, purveyors of candy and cocktails. When at the end of the War, they began to rebel in numbers, their revolt was hollow: an exhibitionistic beating of drums or a snarl and a sneer.

Now the deepest cause of their subjection as writers, and of their impotence, is the hidden ideology of the American system, which—liberal and conservative alike—most of our writers have absorbed. *And this is painfully to the point,* because—whether they know it or not—the same ideology prevails among our revolutionary writers. Far too many of us have taken over the philosophy of the American capitalist culture that we are sworn to overthrow.

3. *The American Revolutionary Writer*

This American ideology, which has ruled from the beginning—from the time of those prophets of bourgeois business: Benjamin Franklin and Alexander Hamilton, the true masters of our way of life—is a shallow, static rationalism derived from the thinnest, not the deepest, eighteenth-century minds of France and Britain: an empirical rationalism based on fact-worship, on a fetishism (both unscientific and un-poetic) of the finished cut-and-dried report of the five senses, which is not remotely related to the organic rationalism explicit in Spinoza and implicit in the historical dialectic of Marx. Had this vulgar rationalism ruled in seventeenth-century England and France, there would be no modern science. It is, since it ignores the organic and evolving nature of man, by definition the foe of all creative work: the foe, therefore, however hidden, of art and revolution.

Briefly, I will disclose symptoms and attitudes in our revolutionary writers, which reveal (although the writers know it not) this sterile philosophy. . . .

(1) Disbelief in the autonomy of the writer's art; in its integral place *as art* in the organic growth of man and specifically in the revolutionary movement. This self-distrust makes the writer capitulate *as artist:* leads him to take orders, *as artist,* from political leaders—much to the dismay of the more intelligent of said political leaders. It moves the American writer to misapply in his art borrowed foreign definitions of values which have cogence in their place and time of origin; but are meaningless here. This is a carry-over of the faddism of middle-class American writing.

(2) From the same inorganic view of life and hence of art, comes the servile or passive concept of revolutionary literature as primarily "informational," "reflective," "propaganda." This is, of course, borrowed from the mid-Victorian, middle-class idea of utilitarian or moralistic art. There is no reason why good literature should not be of high documentary importance, and have a strong political appeal. Indeed, in a

dynamic age like ours, a profound literary art, insofar as it must reveal the deepest evolving forces of man at the time, must be "propaganda" for these forces and for the goal of these forces. But this kind of propaganda derives from the work's effectiveness as literary art and is dependent on it.

(3) What murders the effectiveness of so much of our revolutionary writing? The clue is the word "murder." We all know that murder is a conspicuous American trait: there are more murders, we are told, in the United States in a day than in some European countries in a month. Now murder is a sort of short cut: it is an oversimplified solution of a problem—say, a nagging wife or husband—by simply getting rid of them. It eliminates the *life* of which the problem is a factor. What murder is to the art of life, this dead philosophy is to knowledge; and translated into literary terms it becomes "oversimplification." Call it, if you prefer, a kind of misplaced or *forced* direct action. Here are some of its results:

(a) Novels, aiming to reveal the revolutionary portent and substance of our world, which are stuffed with stereotypes . . . or imitate the spiced journalese of newspaper reports of surface events . . . or echo the bravado (hiding weakness) of the Hemingway-Dashiell Hammett school . . . or borrow the drab pedestrian effects of Victorian realism— as if these were adequate to convey the body—tragic, farcical, explosive, corybantic, tender, deep as hell and high as heaven, of American life!

(b) Proletarian tales and poems which portray the workers as half-dead people devoid of the imagination, soaring wills and laughter, which are the springs of creation—and of revolution.

(c) Laborious essays in criticism and literary history in which the organic bodies of the works of poets and prosemen are mangled and flattened to become mere wallpapering for the structure of a political argument.[1]

(4) In these refusals, often by men of genuine literary gift, to recognize the material for a deep revolutionary art, lies the one ideological taint. Its final evil is to turn Marxism itself into a dogmatically, mechanically *shut* philosophy. And the effect of this, were it to prevail on our eager, unschooled and sensitive youth (workers as well as writers), would be to repel them: indeed, to drive many of them (and not the worst because the worst bewildered) to seek a home in reactionary schools of thought which do lip service to old forms of man's organic intuitions.

If the youth of America are drawn by the decayed loyalties of nationalism and church into the ranks of fascism, it will be *in part* because our revolutionary writers have been thwarted, by this dead rationalism implicit in the dying capitalist culture, from making clear that life today—in the depths that call for sacrifice, loyalty and love—is on the side of revolution.

The American revolutionary writer . . . to act his part, which is to create the cultural medium for revolution . . . must see life whole. He will have a political creed; if he is a generous man, it will be hard for him to forgo some share of the daily political-industrial struggle. But his political orientation must be within, must arise from, his orientation to life as an artist. Any course of action, any creed, lives within the dynamic substance of life itself: *and this substance, in all its attributes, is the business of the artist.* Therefore it is proper to state that the artist's vision of life IS the material of his art.

[1] I have read only three volumes of Marxist literary criticism in the English language: "The Liberation of American Literature," by V. F. Calverton; "The Great Tradition," by Granville Hicks; and a short book by John Strachey. All three are of this category.

There is much confusion among us as to "material" and "subject." The subject of a book is a mere label or container; it may mislead or be empty. Our revolutionary poet or prose-man, by his loyalty to the working class (whether born in it or not) and by his natural selection of strong, expressive subjects, will write more and more of the struggles of farmer and worker. But if his vision be sound, it will make—*whatever his subject*—the material for revolutionary art. The term "pro-letarian" applied to art should refer to the key and vision in which the work is conceived, rather than to subject. It should be a qualitative, not a quantitative, term. A story of middle-class or intellectual life, or even of mythological fig-ures, if it is alight with revolutionary vision, is more effective proletarian art—and more effective art for proletarians—than a shelf full of dull novels about stereotyped workers.

I wish to characterize two of our specific problems.

We writers have two highways for reaching mastery of our material. We must go into life . . . in persons and in self. These two ways are really one; and the writer must follow them together, else he will make headway in neither. If we look upon persons or classes, save with the eye of self-knowl-edge, we will not see them; and if we look inward upon self, save with an eye disciplined by objective understanding, we will see only the mists of egoism which are the true self's denial. Even more complex is this double way we must take, and never cease from taking. If we look upon persons of one class we will not know them unless we see the class opposing. If we look upon the present of any scene, we will not know it unless we see within it the past . . . and its dynamic direction: its future. *This is the dialectic of the artist.*

Because classes are in mortal conflict, *and because we have taken sides,* does not mean they have nothing in common: it means they have life in common. The class struggle, for us, is a focus of light, a modern form, by which timeless ingredients of human nature common to every person are revealed. It is not a substitute for understanding, but a kind of *spectrum* wherein hunger, passion, love, pity, envy, worship, dream, fear, despair and ecstasy receive a dynamic modern order.

The other branch of our simultaneous highway is the self. Self is the integer of value and of social action, the norm and form of life as man may know it. The revolutionary writer must understand the *person*, or his portraits of social struggle will be flat and ephemeral as the poster on a billboard. As early as Shakespeare, Cervantes and Racine, the artists were creating the image of the "lonely Soul," the "atomic will" —an image which served to make the *medium* in which the Protestant-bourgeois, individualist economy could flourish. We must have poets to sing the image of the new and truer person: the person who knows his integration with group and cosmos; the person through whom the Whole speaks.

Only by bringing home the timeless human values in the class struggle to every member of the exploited classes and to the sensitive of all classes (for under capitalism all decent men and women are oppressed) can the writer stimulate the will to revolutionary action. Only by deepening his comprehension of cultural historic forms, such as religion, in which, however faultily and impurely, man's profoundest intuitions of his organic nature were embodied, can the writer touch the *spirit* of the American worker and farmer and middle class, to release their spirit from obsolete forms into new creative channels. And only thus can we save them from the decayed devotions which are the treacherous bait of the fascists.

Thus, for the American revolutionary writer to give less than the whole picture is poor philosophy, poor art—and poor strategy.

We are aware there is war; we have declared this war to be ours; and we know that in war strategy is important. But this is a war whose battleground is the world—the world of extension and, no less, the world of inward depth. In this battle are countless separate struggles. Many, engaged on their particular fronts, are forced by the crisis of their position to ignore its relativity in the whole; or to misprize and forget values which do not appear to apply to their one urgent need. Therefore we writers must know the breadth and depth of the whole struggle: know its background and its foreground: know its ultimate values within its immediate aims: in order that, by the common experience of our work, the balance and unity be kept; that in the fever of struggle no human heritage of truth and freedom languish; and that the great war for Man move, without error or blindness, to its issue.

Our special work is the universal. In our field there can be no strategy but the whole truth.

If a writer doubts this, I doubt he is an artist.

If we believe that communism is the organic next step of the world to be released by freeing the world's forces of health, we must believe in the art revealing man's depths which bear this destiny. We will embody in our work the substance of life: the blood, the bone, the eye, the conscious embrace of necessity whose child is freedom—knowing that in so far as we create this truth, we are moving, and moving those who hear us, toward the Revolution.

vii. The Writer's Part in Social Revolution

(An address to the International Congress of Writers for the Defence of Culture, held at Paris, June 21-25, 1935.)

We are all here, not as Frenchmen, Germans, Americans, but as men of letters who conceive their art as an articulation of the human spirit. Each of us bespeaks his class and his country only in so far as he voices deeply his self, and thereby voices mankind. This is the irreducible character of the artist. Whether he knows it or not (and in our day, most do not know it, whence the fragmentary and corrupted nature of their works and of themselves as men), the artist is one who acts on the premise that the universal lives in the particular; that cosmos lives in the person. This is the meaning of the mysterious words "beauty" and "truth" applied to art. As we share the universal in a particular form—a painting of a tree, a story of a beggar—we call it the experience of beauty. We feel the unity between self and some other object, a unity which (far from destroying) heightens and *makes true* the particularity of both the self and the object. And whether we know it or not, we value this experience of truth and beauty; we love it as somehow good. This is another irreducible trait, beneath our differences, of us all. The conflicts of our actual existence may so weary and confuse us that we believe we long for death; may fill us with distrust and despair: it is love of life, none the less because wounded and twisted, that writes the darkest of our pages. In so far as a man seeks beauty, he knows that life *is* value; for the recognition of beauty is nothing but the joyous acceptance of our part and our participation in the body of living.

In periods of normal cultural rhythm, when the social body moves moderately well in all its organs, this act of conscious participation in life as a whole, the essential act of the artist, can remain implicit in the quiet body of his story or song or picture. Such times see no Congress of Writers such as this one. But today the forms and modes of human existence, unevenly evolved, have broken the equilibrium which is life itself. Today, the active and aggressive faith in life, the revelation of its intricate harmony, which is the sole science of the artist, is so at variance with the actual world that we feel the need of a direct action, transcending the solid, quiet, slow certainty of art, to reinforce our love and our vision in the experience of the people.

All this may seem to you irrelevant esthetics. But you must pardon me, for the application I wish to draw from it (my brief message to this Congress) is relevant.

The revolutionary hour in which we live is but the present phase of the process, centuries old and destined to outlast almost the memory of economic conflict, whereby man (not a privileged, exploiting class, but man as a whole) will emerge into a conscious culture; even as the child at a certain physiologic stage must become adult or go down into degeneration. The key of the present phase of the long process is economic; therefore the importance of the class struggle and the imperative of entering it on the side of the workers. But the process itself, now as ever, is organic. By which I mean that *the whole of man*, heart and mind, subtlest sense and deepest intuition, as well as belly and loin, must partake of it—or it miscarries.

The orthodox revolutionary creeds, which are the technique of the transition of this crucial hour, do not comprehend the whole man. They stress, rightly, the aspects of mass social-economic action. They slight other parts of man: the intuitive, the intimate, the personal which leads to the cosmic—phases which are the concern of the creative writer. But since the process of man's growth must at all times be complete, these phases too must enter the revolutionary movement. Since they lag, blame not the political leaders but the writers. Since in consequence even the immediate economic aspect of the whole process lags, and threatens to miscarry, again blame (at least in part) the writers.

Excluding the hordes of parasites and peddlers who dare call themselves "writers" only in a world where illiteracy thinks it can "read," we might divide our writers into two groups. The first stress the sensuous, the personal; strive perhaps after the mystic; ignore utterly the masses of men, and that vast region of each man's life involved in economic forces. The other group, often recruited or converted from the first, in the enthusiasm perhaps of their discovery of the social-economic factor limit themselves to it or at least permit their awareness of the intimate, infinite dimensions of human life to become dulled. Their work, like the first group's, is inorganic. And what is worse, the great Cause—man's rebirth —to which they are devoted continues, because of them, deprived of elements needed to make it whole and to make it live.

Of course, the values of the creative writer, as I have named them, are of the very stuff of the Revolution which, indeed, is the expression in terms of urgent human need of just these values. At the heart of socialism and communism, bequeathed to it direct by romantics like Rousseau who saved it from the contradictory theological impedimenta of the church, lies a view of men and of man which the degenerate humanisms of the eighteenth century and the sectarian Protestant creeds had abandoned. It is the view of human history as one organic body, growing by tragic effort toward consciousness and justice; it is the view of the individual (in so far as he is *real*) as an integer of this body, so that the health of the whole and the health of every part are one; it is the view that universal meaning is inherent in material behavior, and therefore, that society becomes by its actions the immanent presence of timeless value. This view, which I call the *organic* view, is implicit in every major artist, however dissident may be his intellectual convictions. It runs with infallible continuity from the Egyptian sculptors and the Hebrew prophets through the patrists, through the builders of the Gothic, through the great sixteenth- and seventeenth-century founders of modern science, through the systems of Spinoza and Hegel—ineluctably leading to the historical-prophetic vision of Karl Marx.

But in the eighteenth century there had grown strong a countercurrent in the thought of Europe. So successful was the conquest of facts about material bodies, the capture of their movements in the laws of mechanics, that certain men, hungry like all men for simplifications, cut down the organic humanisms of Erasmus and Rabelais, the organic rationalisms of Spinoza and Newton, to a dogmatic empiricism of the five senses. Theirs was a "universe" containing everything that moved by mechanical law—everything, that is, except life. And the victories of applied science were so great that these shallow empiricists swelled in prestige; while the organic view grew enfeebled, being confined to artists with no "scientific" magic to win them credence, to mystics overburdened with theologies that contradicted their intuitions, and to simple men and simple women with no intellectual weapons.

The nineteenth century, of course, brought giants who, in philosophy, literature and the sciences, revived the organic view. In Marx, who belongs to his century's great tradition, the organic view of man is fundamental, and is complete as in perhaps no other modern thinker except Spinoza and Goethe. But this shallow empiricism was in the air. Marx, overanxious to attack theological creeds and theological metaphysics, at times fell into the use of easy terms borrowed from the vulgar materialists whom he despised as much as he hated the idealists against whom he aimed them. There are contradictions in Marx—great prophet, great historical philosopher, great economist, but too harried a man to be a complete logician. Often on the same page with an unsurpassed word about man's primal unity, in thought and deed, with the dynamic principle of all life, one will find uncritical outcroppings of sensationalism, phrases from the eighteenth-century materialists whom he rejected, implicit denials of the validity and primacy of man's intuitive organic sense—all of which betray the premise of the Marxist dialectic. These flaws in his work have been stressed as virtues in our Western world by sterile men to whom a dogmatic reduction of life to the report of the five senses offers comfort; and it has been a blight upon our revolutionary growth.

I have no time, nor need, to expatiate upon the symptoms of this blight. The course of socialism in nineteenth- and twentieth-century Germany, France, England, America, is full of them. Witness the degradation, one might almost say the disappearance, of the *true person* from revolutionary letters as the individual is shrunk from an organic integer of cosmos to a mere quantitative factor of the collective mass, possessing no inwardness—in consequence of which the human mass likewise becomes denatured. Witness the simplification of the human being to a passive product of environment—a fallacy which any man who has ever planted a carrot seed next to a pea in a garden knows enough to laugh at. And the failure, in judging the course, both hideous and heroic, of contemporary events, to allow, in some adequate modern term, for what our fathers fancifully called the demonic and the angelic aspects of human nature. Witness the degradation of literature from being an integral part of life's creative process to a mere reflection of events falsely conceived as "objective" or to a mere instrument for some surface action. Witness, in such poor thought as this, the decay of logic and the decay of metaphysics. Witness, above all, the dangerous failure to distinguish between the true essence of religion—its creative role in human culture—its major role, indeed, in the genesis of socialism, and religion's outworn theological and class superstructures.

All such systems indicate the contempt for human life and destiny which comes when man is cut off from his primitive participation in the cosmos without finding a conscious synthesis (the task of the writers!) to replace it: all, regnant in the vulgar revolutionary thought of Western Europe and America, strike at the very heart of revolutionary meaning. In agricultural lands, such as Russia, China, great sections of America Hispana, the folk have not lost that immediate integration with life, through soil and self, which is the organic sense in its first phase. The revolutionary doctrines of the West, even with their present limitations, tend to free these peoples from the imposed dualism of their priestcraft, to discipline them for technical advance against the cloudy helplessness in which their misery has mired them, and to release their instinctive monism so that it should flow with ease into the organic view and form of a communist order. This procedure is particularly plain in the Soviet Union where, despite an orthodox terminology which frequently sounds mechanistic or traditionally dogmatic, the true foundations of organic Marxism are understood and are being passionately enacted by the people.

In our industrialized countries, the case is different. Science, prostituted and misapplied, has for a hundred years plowed down the primitive monistic intuitions of the masses: the same vulgar empiricism which attaints our literature flouts its obscene excesses in every penny paper, every school, every church. The stress on the "environmental," the "behavioristic," the "economic" man, the failure to appeal, in revolutionary terms, to *the whole man,* stimulates the mechanolatry to which we are already enslaved; dims further our enfeebled sense of wholeness from which alone fertility and power issue; and threatens our whole birth-period with disaster.

I do not deny the economic-political causes of fascism. But only psychological and cultural factors in all the people can explain its spread. Among these factors, pre-eminently in Germany, was the failure of both great revolutionary parties to lead forward into fresh forms of loyalty and action those primordial intuitive energies of man which, balked of their future, flow back into the rotted channels of church, state, race, devotion to a Fuehrer mouthing decayed loyalties —there, of course, to be exploited by the sinister high priests of Money.

I do not mean that the revolutionary cause in its present form fails to enlist the heroic loyalties of numbers of men and women. The concentration camps of Hitler give the lie to such a statement, as does every industrial struggle of the world from the Saar to California, where you will find them: the young crusaders for Man, the geniuses of social vision, clear-eyed, quiet of soul. These are the gifted vanguard who, of their own lyric health, absorb and express what is deeply organic in the revolutionary movement. But the world cause cannot rely exclusively on heroes or on the natural poets of action. Its Word must be such as to fire also the more cautious, the more conservatively rooted. And the more subjectively sensitive must also be entrained, those hosts of men and women (teachers, poets, mothers, subtle and humble craftsmen) whose religious and esthetic instincts are balked by the antireligious and antiesthetic conventions of most Marxists. For each youth who is driven into the fascist ranks because he finds it easy to adore his own petty ego magnified in a Fuehrer or a Duce, there are a score of men and women too decent and intelligent to be tempted by these obscene gestures, who yet remain unmoved while the world cries for them, because the appeal of Revolution *seems* to deny those very depths of man, secret and mysterious, whence the creative will and energy must issue.

The New World of which the old world is in travail is like an embryon. Until it be whole, it cannot be born. What intimate *knowing* moves the embryon, long after its organs and muscles are complete? This knowing of completeness is the final phase of completion. When it is there, and not before, the being issues forth; a new life breathes. . . . I sometimes feel that all the organs, the limbs, the brain and nervous system, of the New World exist. They are the laws of science, the methods of production and communication, the treasures of literature, art, religious wisdom; and, embodying these, the mass of workers possessed of the will and the power, together with their indispensable leaders, drawn from all classes, the intellectuals, the teachers, and technicians. Why, in this hour of travail, when death threatens the generations of man, does not the new life issue? The final integrality is lacking . . . the final completeness which is organic consciousness, the *knowing* harmony of all the parts, making them move to life, making them breathe together. This, within the ready social body, is the function of the writer.

4. TERRE HAUTE HOTEL

Outside the nine cells [1] of our ward runs a corridor which is left open part of the day, and through its barred windows I can see the country. Right under my eye is the mellow muddy river that Theodore Dreiser's brother sang, long ago. On the banks of the Wabash I see a huge pile of discarded cars, rust-rotted fragments of machines, shanties paintless and broken-roofed, the homes of human discards among the industrial refuse. This view outside the jail makes me feel at home in the jail. The bars shut me into, rather than out of, a familiar world.

The men in the ward enhance my feeling of having come more close to the America that put me here. There are details,

[1] The author accompanied Earl Browder, communist candidate for President of the United States, on a tour of Midwest industrial cities as a newspaper correspondent and was jailed with him in Terre Haute.

of course, inanimate or crawling, to which I am not used; but like the iron-barred windows, the grated doors, these separating elements are superficial; they do not avail against the growing knowledge that to be in this jail, among these men, and with the police and the chamber of commerce outside, is to be at the heart of a common experience and (given the society we live in) to be in the right place.

The men of our ward have set up a "kangaroo court" to deal with their day-by-day needs, problems primarily of supplementing the vile, scant prison food, of bringing in tobacco, of keeping the ward comparatively clean. The chief of the court is a big fellow whom I'll call Jack, a natural leader. Jack's boyhood was rooted in the shanties along the banks of the Wabash; joy for him, from the earliest days, meant escape from everything familiar—and the best means to it, whisky. Jack found a good job in a local gymnasium. One night of payday, he left a bootleg dive and was attacked by a gang who knew that he had dollars in his pocket. There was a fight; a policeman butted in, and a chance blow of Jack's great fist sent him to the pavement, fracturing his skull. The cop died, and when Jack got out of jail, the police hounded him and no more jobs were open. Jack had to eat, he had to drink, he had to have a girl; so he became a bootlegger. From then on, he has spent half his time in jail. When he's out, he falls inevitably back into the one way he can think of to make a living: a way of disorder, of course.

But here in jail (where he has more essential freedom than outside), Jack is an orderly man. His cell is clean, his clothes, his toilet articles, his library of magazines, are arranged in shipshape fashion. With a Flit can, he holds the bugs in abeyance. And with his authority as chief of the kangaroo court, he keeps order in the ward, teaching the newcomers and the vags who are let in for the night their duties and their places. Jack is a great reader, and if what he reads is trash, the reason is that trash is all he knows—a point in common with the vigilantes. He is the kind of taciturn man who, when he talks, talks well. I note, in his description of his friendship with the little children of his brother, the tenderness that is in him, the kind of tenderness that I have often felt in pre-adolescent boys for very little children. Utterly wanting in Jack is a critical sense of the society he lives in, is a concept for understanding and bettering his place. Mentally, spiritually, he is a child, because he has been stopped from growing; but in his fixedness of immaturity certain virtues of the boy remain untarnished. I observe this, when he comes into my cell, of his own accord, and shows me the trick of driving the bedbugs to cover. And I shall not forget his bringing out to me, as a spread for my bread, his jar of peach preserve, a homemade gift from his mother; and his sensitive lie, when he feels my hesitation (I know already what good food means in jail): "Go ahead, eat all you want—I don't eat that stuff much."

Jack's right-hand man is Pop, who supervises the ward's housework, cooking, cleaning, laundry; an old man of sixty doing time for perjury. Pop's grey face has a beauty difficult to decipher, until one catches its two main elements: a child-like, animal gaiety impervious to experience and an old man's pain, the two transfused into a mask, sly, ironic, covering them both. Pop also is a child; he'd play treacherous tricks on you if he chose; that is clear. But it is also clear that if you touch his emotions decently, he may not choose. He's a child brought up among hostile and undiscerning masters. He does not question their authority, nor does he conform. He escapes by remaining in the limbo of his boyhood, a psychological place beyond good and evil but saturated with feeling and humor.

Tony is the kind of chap who affects white buck shoes, and even in stir tries to keep them polished if not clean. He wears a saffron necktie and his blond hair is pushed up from his vague blue eyes in a pompadour. Tony is being held for manslaughter—killing a truckman while driving his car in a state of intoxication. He used to be an iron molder; but molding jobs have run thin in the mills since the production of capital machines has dwindled; and bad times have reduced him to the status of a common laborer. He likes the boys in jail; he's having a good time doing nothing.

In this, he is like the farm boy from the Kentucky border —Willie—who denies the grand larceny charge that has put him here, but visibly enjoys his moratorium from cribbing corn and milking. Willie, with brand-new blue overalls, curled-up amber hair, baby blue eyes, could take the part of the farmer's son in the melodrama, the youth smelling of clover who comes to the big city to reclaim his girl lured by the wicked traveling salesman. Willie is handsome, nonchalant, illiterate, with many a childish virtue. Back on the farm he has a wife and two kids. He is glad to be free of them for a while, and time for him does not go beyond the vague measure of a season.

When night falls, the lock on the door frequently grinds and the homeless men are turned in for a night's lodging. Not to dull my story (which has a point, if you'll be patient), I'll describe but two of these night-guests. One is an old man, dweller in the filthiest shanties of the Wabash, an aged human body clad in squalor. Sam has been south, picking cotton, and he tells us it doesn't pay. That's why he's back home. He hails the tin dish of malodorous slop called supper with delight; although he has no teeth, the pork chop gets gnawed to the bone.

Beside Sam is a riveter, a young South Indianan who has helped build bridges from Bayonne to St. Louis. He's broke, but he expects a job tomorrow. Meantime, he shows us where a molten rivet missed his pail and caught him in the belly;

his clothes ablaze, he jumped to the elevator, dropped to a tank of water and then spent three months in a hospital bed. But he's all right now: to prove it he takes hold of a steel butt on the ceiling with the forward half of his fingers and chins himself six times. Old Sam jumps up, and chins himself twice, giggling with pride. Sam's body is still gamy and beneath his dirty unshaved beard is the bland face of a boy, a face essentially sweet. . . .

Do not judge that I am sentimentalizing this common, typical group of failures. There are, of course, vicious men in jails, just as there are vicious men out of jail. They are the exception in both categories, and I'm sure I do not know in which one will find relatively more. Perhaps the vicious among convicts are as rare as the Mellons, Rockefellers, du-Ponts, among businessmen; as the Hearsts among journalists; as the Hitlers and Huey Longs and Coughlins among politicians. Every broad social group has certain basic traits; in the criminal group not viciousness is such a trait, but *childishness*. Without a doubt, the percentage of rotten men among criminals is so small it is no wonder that every single man in my ward of the jail happens to be a decent person.

That they were all childish was not accidental. It may help to explain why I liked these men. I have always felt at ease among children. And perhaps this means that I am something of a child myself. And this draws me closer to the point of my story.

Two inmates of our ward, mugged and fingerprinted like the rest of us, I have not yet named. They are the communist organizers, Andrew Remes and Charles Stadtfelt. Stadtfelt is a young man with a playboy's smile and a body pitifully invaded by tuberculosis. So slight is Stadtfelt's resistance that every hour or so he must dive into his lousy bunk, under mine, for a rest. When he emerges, there is a cigarette in his mouth, a laugh in his eyes and a jest on his tongue. Stadtfelt's way of curing his consumption is to forget it, and devote his life to bringing on the Revolution. There is no feverish strain in his good humor; it comes from a harmony of the whole man which tubercular bacilli have not yet broken. The second communist, Remes, is studious and unsmiling. Brought in later than I, the first thing he does is to ask me for an explanation of why the Soviet Union does not officially help the Spaniards. Back and forth in the corridor we walked, while he put his questions. But the sobriety of Comrade Remes is not objectionable to the camaraderie of the others. His intellectual preoccupations trouble them no more than his working out the crossword puzzles in the old papers (while they hunt tales of daring gunmen and passionate lovers). Instinctively, they are aware that Remes looks at the bosses with eyes parallel to theirs.

These bosses are the symbolic "fathers" who keep the boys behind bars. They have tools. Lowest are the turnkeys, for the most part men brutalized by long practice of mechanical repression without understanding; men dehumanized to the bare repressive function. A little less low are the police, dull incarnations of conformity to the rules the criminals break; professional opponents, players of the same game as the lawless but on the other side of the line and held in contempt by the crooks, who instinctively sense that to obey the rules of our society means less fantasy, less generosity, less feeling, than to break them. The true fathers are rarely seen by their unfortunate children: they are the respectable citizens, the taxpayers, the makers of the rules, the builders of the courts and jails, the dealers of prison terms. Implicitly, men like Jack, Pop, old Sam and Tony regard them as children regard grownups.

These pillars of society are less childlike than the jailbirds. But they are not the mature men fathers should be. If they were mature (and the crooks instinctively know this), there would be less filth in jail, there would be no need of jail at all, there would be less misery, corruption, injustice, in the chaotic outer world which the jail's false order impotently strives to correct. The lawbreakers are children; the sustainers of the legalized anarchy called the capitalist system are neither children nor grown men. Call them men in a transition between infancy and adulthood: that will explain their natural selection for eminence by a society that is itself an epoch of transition. Capitalism is a transition age between the naïve childhood of the race and that mastering maturity in which alone the dreams, values, inventions of childhood, transfigured, may flower.

This explains why the "children" are in jail; why the men who have not grown up build the jail and place the "children" in it: it explains also why the communists, who are creating a form for maturity, are in jail with the "children." The two communists in our ward (not to mention the leading communist in a ward belowstairs) legitimately stand for a will, a discipline, a method, whereby men may outgrow the irrational chaos of capitalism, may mature to a society for both grown men and children. By this truth, symbolically, the communists belong in jail. For the values which they strive, through changing the laws, to bring to normal life are kin to the values which the criminals, by breaking the laws, impotently struggle to retain. The mature man rounds the cycle, giving organic form to the lyric impulses of childhood—the need for joy, for play, for freedom, which man outgrows at his peril.

But this natural conjunction of child and mature man in a jail, as against the halfmen who put them in jail, may be still further broadened. After we had been released, Chief of Police Yates came up to us. Yates is a jaunty young man, smooth and hard-eyed, half a machine, a type too common in this world, without whom fascism could not function. He is simply the shallow young man, wanting to get along in a hurry, who sells out to the forces in immediate power—the owners of the Machine; and who wants for his reward, not so much a fat pay envelope as freedom to give play to his desires, less destroyed than repressed into sadism by the dull business world of which he also is a victim.

Yates saunters up to us, and tells us with pride of the congratulatory cable he has received from Berlin. Capitalist society has already driven back into infantilism the weakest members of the working class; and you will find some of them in jail. Fascism is a method for finishing the process! Fascism would *infantilize* all the workers; not in order to put them into jail if they are good boys, but to put them into a brown, black or silver shirt, and stick a slogan in their mouths and call them the fatherland's army. Fascism is the program for the forced regimented infantilization of the people; implicit or explicit, it must be the program of all rulers under capitalism, since these rulers, by the nature of their transitional order, are themselves caught in a transition before maturity, are not men enough to lead men or to work with men, and are compelled, before the threatening maturity of the masses, to drive them all—through force, falsehood, ill nurture—down to a morbid, regressive, infantile level.

Either down to infantilism or forward to the revolutionary beginning of a human order in which normal men may normally mature: that was the choice, palpable as human bodies, within our ward's barred windows. In the Terre Haute jail I had our world with me: the atavistic, careless and abnormal; the future, striving to be; the dolorous, dangerous present. I felt at home there. . . .

1936

INDEX